ISBN 978-1-333-25758-3
PIBN 10479427

1 MONTH OF
FREE
READING

at
www.ForgottenBooks.com

By purchasing this book you are eligible for one month membership to ForgottenBooks.com, giving you unlimited access to our entire collection of over 700,000 titles via our web site and mobile apps.

To claim your free month visit:
www.forgottenbooks.com/free479427

English
Français
Deutsche
Italiano
Español
Português

www.forgottenbooks.com

Mythology Photography **Fiction**
Fishing Christianity **Art** Cooking
Essays Buddhism Freemasonry
Medicine **Biology** Music **Ancient
Egypt** Evolution Carpentry Physics
Dance Geology **Mathematics** Fitness
Shakespeare **Folklore** Yoga Marketing
Confidence Immortality Biographies
Poetry **Psychology** Witchcraft
Electronics Chemistry History **Law**
Accounting **Philosophy** Anthropology
Alchemy Drama Quantum Mechanics
Atheism Sexual Health **Ancient History**
Entrepreneurship Languages Sport
Paleontology Needlework Islam
Metaphysics Investment Archaeology
Parenting Statistics Criminology
Motivational

THE SEA-FISHING INDUSTRY

OF

ENGLAND AND WALES

PRINTED BY
SPOTTISWOODE AND CO. LTD., NEW-STREET SQUARE
LONDON

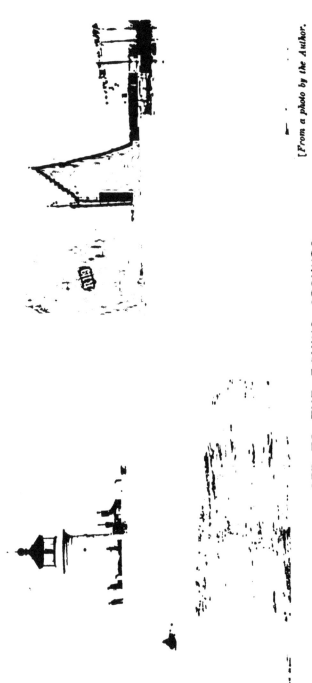

OFF TO THE FISHING GROUNDS.

RAMSGATE HARBOUR.

[From a photo by the Author.

EA-FISHING INDUSTR

OF

ENGLAND AND WALES

A POPULAR ACCOUNT OF
THE SEA FISHERIES AND FISHING PORTS
OF THOSE COUNTRIES

BY

F. G. AFLALO, F.R.G.S., F.Z.S.

WITH A SEA FISHERIES MAP
AND
NUMEROUS PHOTOGRAPHS BY THE AUTHOR
AND OTHERS

LONDON: EDWARD STANFORD

12, 13, & 14, LONG ACRE, W.C.

1904

TO THE WARDENS AND MEMBERS

OF THE

WORSHIPFUL COMPANY OF FISHMONGERS

THIS BOOK IS DEDICATED BY THE AUTHOR

IN APPRECIATION OF THE GENEROUS SERVICES

WHICH THAT CORPORATION HAS RENDERED

TO THE FISHING INDUSTRY

PREFACE

THE reference to the sea fisheries in a recent Speech from the Throne, following so closely on the first appointment of a responsible Minister of Fisheries, may be taken as a happy augury that this great industry is at last to receive a measure of the attention which it has always deserved in vain. The attitude of His Majesty's advisers towards the fish trade would seem to have undergone a wholesome change since the day when, only five years ago, a noble lord stated in the Upper House that the problems affecting our sea fisheries required ' far less study ' than that involved in the salmon-fishing question.

The existing popular work on our sea fisheries was written by Mr. Holdsworth, under the title of ' Deep Sea Fishing and Fishing Boats,' thirty years ago. It is a most interesting book and invaluable to the student of history ; but, apart from the fact that it has long been out of print, it belongs to the era which immediately preceded the introduction of steam trawling. The fishing industry as we know it to-day had no existence. Coal and ice have of late years enabled our trawlers to fish every ground between Iceland and Portugal, so

that grounds a thousand miles distant now feed the
quays at Hull or Plymouth as readily as did the Dogger
Bank and Silver Pit in Holdsworth's time. Old ports,
then in the height of their prosperity, are fallen into
decay ; new centres, like Milford, then unknown, are
now in the front rank.

The recent attention devoted to the proper study
of marine biology at Plymouth, in Lancashire, and
in international collaboration, over a large area of the
North Sea and neighbouring waters, is another condition of which Holdsworth had no conception. As the
seas gradually become fished out, the need of scientific
investigation is certain to press its claims more insist-
ently, and we are only peering dimly across the threshold
of marine biological research. An eminent professor at
the Naples laboratory once assured me that it would take
years and years to work with any degree of satisfaction
the fauna of Naples Bay alone, so that the material
presented by the North Sea may safely occupy all the
science of Northern Europe for a century to come. The
literature of the subject remains somewhat scanty so far
as the general reading public is concerned. Important
semi-popular works on the natural history of our sea-
fish, like those of Professor McIntosh and Mr. J. T.
Cunningham, have doubtless reached a large number,
but so much can scarcely be said for the very admirable publications of the Scotch Fishery Board, the
Marine Biological Association, or the Permanent International Council for the Exploration of the Sea.

The present work sets itself necessarily on a far lower
plane than these authoritative publications. It attempts

no more than to set before the people of England and Wales something of the historical development and present grandeur of the fishing industry. The sea fisheries of Scotland, which have long been controlled by a separate body and which are prosecuted along different lines, would require a volume to themselves; and those of Ireland, save where there was need of incidental mention of the mackerel-fisheries, have likewise been excluded from the scope of the book, the basis of which was, moreover, an extended tour of the fishery ports between Berwick and the Solway, by way of the Land's End.

Even so imperfect a sketch could never have been attempted, much less carried through, but for the ungrudging help given to the author by the Railway Companies, by the Clerks and Inspectors of the Sea Fisheries Districts, by the Harbour Masters, Officers of Coastguard, and Clerks to Urban District Councils. A number of gentlemen interested in the fishing industry at Hull, Grimsby, Boston, Yarmouth, Ramsgate, Hastings, Brighton, Brixham, Plymouth, Newlyn, Milford, and Fleetwood will perhaps prefer similar collective acknowledgment of their kind assistance. One exception, however, with or without his approval, must be made in the case of Mr. Charles Hellyer. The evidence which, from time to time, he has given before Parliamentary Committees shows that he possesses as intimate an acquaintance with the commercial details, and as broad a grasp of the greater issues, of the subject as any man living. Yet he took infinite pains to explain technical points to my not over responsive understanding,

and he made time out of an exceedingly busy life
to read almost the whole of the proof. And it is
impossible to be content with less than personal and
individual mention in the case of Mr. J. Wrench Towse,
Clerk to the Fishmongers' Company ; Mr. C. E. Fryer,
of the Board of Agriculture and Fisheries; Messrs.
E. J. Allen and W. Garstang, of the Marine Biological
Association; Professor Herdman and the late Mr.
Dawson, of the Lancashire and Western District ; Professor McIntosh, of St. Andrews; Dr. T. Wemyss
Fulton, of the Fishery Board for Scotland and Council
of International Exploration ; and Mr. Alexander Meek,
of the Northumberland District.

The results of a tour of the ports, some of which
were subsequently revisited more than once for further
information, have been freely supplemented by reference
to the Journals of the Marine Biological Association, to
a number of Reports and other publications of the
various Sea Fisheries Districts, to the 'Publications de
Circonstance,' issued in connection with the North Sea
Scheme, and to the always interesting columns of the
'Fish Trades Gazette.' Where not otherwise specified,
the photographs are by myself. To Messrs. Reinhold
Thiele, A. S. Rudland, and W. Brown, who have taken
a dozen photographs to supplement the collection
taken by my own N. and G. reflex, a capital instrument
for this class of work, thanks are also due, as, lastly,
to many who have lent a hand in revising the proofs.

F. G. A.

TEIGNMOUTH : *September* 1904.

CONTENTS

CHAPTER I

LIFE IN THE SEA

Distinction between Economic and Biological Problems—Facts of
Practical Interest—Definition of a ' Food Fish '—Fish Culture
The Egg, the Larval, and the Post-larval Stages of a Fish—Round
and Flat Fish—Migratory and Stationary kinds—Rock-dwellers
and Sand-dwellers—Mapping the North Sea—Plankton Investi-
gations—Fisheries ruined by the Migrations of the Fish—Spawn-
ing Grounds and their Protection—Eggs that sink and Eggs that
float—Habit of Shoaling in Fish—Migrations of Mackerel—The
Herring—A Cold-water Fish—Comparison with the Pilchard—
Curious alternation of the two at St. Ives—The Sprat—Habit
of Spawning near the Land—' Whitebait ': its Composition in
Summer and in Winter—Flat Fish—The Plaice—The Sole—Its
Spawning in the Aquarium—Introduced into Scotch Waters—
The Cod Family—Periodicity of Hake—Disagreement as to
Spawning Grounds of the Cod—Recent abundance of Young
Haddocks—Comparison between the Fish landed at Scarborough
and Plymouth—Food of the Grey Mullet—Removal of Seaweed
on the Cornish Coast—Rivals of the Fishermen—Fish that Hunt
by Sight, by Scent, by Touch—Technical Instruction for Fishermen—Artificial Fertilising of Spawn at Sea—Plan suggested by
Mr. Fryer and Mr. Garstang—Reliable Information available
from Fishermen—Dr. Wemyss Fulton's latest Method of Collecting Statistics .   .   .   .

CHAPTER II

PRODUCTION

Difference between Production of Fish and of other Foodstuffs—
Fisheries contrasted with Agriculture and compared with Mining
—Hard Life of the Fishermen—Adam Smith on Wages and Em-
ployments—Two Principles on which Fish are caught in Nets—

PAGE

Trawling—Statistics of Men and Boys Employed—Origin of
Trawling in England—Smacks at Lowestoft, Ramsgate, and
Brixham—Holdsworth on the Otter-trawl—The Trawl and its
Beam—Steam-trawling—The Otter-trawl—Its Catching Power—
Other Advantages—Curious Form of Trawl used in Lincolnshire
—Mr. Kyle's new pattern of Trawl for Scientific Work—Hull and
Brixham—Wages and Profit-sharing—Steam-ports and Smack-
ports—Dogger Bank—Scarborough—Discovery of the Silver Pit
—Hull—Grimsby—Ice—Fleets sent to Iceland—Brixham Smacks
in the Bristol Channel—Trawling by Day and Night—The
Trawler disliked by other Classes of Fishermen—Future of
Trawling—The Drift-net—Principle on which it works—Neglect
of British Anchovies—Vast Numbers of Herrings landed at
Yarmouth—Steam-drifters—Manner of Using the Drift-net—
Bait used by French Sardine-fishermen—Privileges accorded to
Drifters—The Seine or Sean—Ground-seines in Estuaries—Con-
struction and Use of the Seine—The Tucking-seine—Inde-
pendence of Steam—Fish Caught in the Ground-seine—The
Trammel—Other kinds of Nets—Capture of Fish by Hook and
Line—Cost of Bait for Long-lines—Difficulty of getting Bait at
Plymouth and Milford—North Sea Cod-fishery—Floating Cod-
chests—Hand-lining for Mackerel—Long-lining—Line-fishing for
Soles—Complaints against Trawlers—Different patterns of Crab-
and Lobster-pots—Baits and Method of Use—Two kinds of
Shrimp—The Shrimp-trawl—Maryport—Shrimping with Horse
and Cart—Oysters—Whelks—Cockles—Mussels—Boiling Lob-
sters and Crabs—Tainted Living Lobsters—Smoked and Cured
Fish   30

CHAPTER III

DISTRIBUTION

Billingsgate—Harbours owned by Railway Companies—Exports and
Imports—Transport by Land and Sea—Hull Carriers at Billingsgate—'Single Boating' and 'Fleeting'—Billingsgate and Shadwell—Harbours—Fishing Centres without a Harbour—Qualifications of a Fishing Harbour—War Office at Plymouth and
elsewhere—Ice—Salt—Coal—Home Grounds—Natural Harbours—Drift-net Ports—Centres of Crab, Lobster, and Prawn
Fisheries—Work done by the Railways—Strain on the Companies' Resources—How Steam has aggravated the Difficulty—
Owner's Risk Note—Returned Empties—A Possible Remedy—
Billingsgate—Inspection by Fish Meters—Condemned Fish—The
Fishmongers' Company—The National Sea Fisheries Protection
Association—Charter relating to the Inspection of Fish .   .   81

CHAPTER IV

LEGISLATION

PAGE

Fishery Laws—Private Ownership—Territorial Limits—Act of 1868 —Act of 1877—Act of 1883—International Convention—'Sea Fisheries Regulation Act, 1888 '—Creation of Sea Fisheries Districts—Ports outside such Jurisdiction—Endeavour to include Yarmouth and Lowestoft—How a District is Created—Acts of 1891 and 1894—Limits and Bye-laws of the Sea Fisheries Districts of England and Wales—Other Laws—Foreign Fisheries Legislation—Portmarks—Proposed Protection of Spawning Grounds—Close Time for Herring and Mackerel—Objections to these Proposals—Laws to Check the Trawler—Closure of Selected Areas—Extension of the Three-mile Limit—Increase in the Mesh of the Trawl—Prohibition of Landing and Sale of Undersized Flat Fish—Lord Onslow's Bill—Opposition and Amendment—Fishery Board for Scotland—Good work done by it—Fisheries Administration in Ireland—Report of the Committee on Ichthyological Research 123

CHAPTER V

SCIENTIFIC INVESTIGATION

Greater Demand for Fish—Two Remedies for the Decreased Supply and Higher Price—Artificial fish-culture—Legislation—Need for Greater Knowledge—The Marine Laboratory—Dr. Dohrn's Station at Naples—The Marine Biological Association—Its Laboratory—Other Laboratories—Work done by Professor Herdman and his Assistants—The Liverpool Laboratory Reports—Mr. Meek's Laboratory at Cullercoats—Conferences with Fishermen—The North Sea Investigations—The Stockholm Conference—Biological and Hydrographical Investigations distinguished — The Christiania Conference — The Copenhagen Meeting—The 'Huxley'—Mr. Garstang's First Report—Marked Plaice—System of Rewards examined—Deductions from Results—Information Obtained from the Fishermen—The 'Huxley's' North Sea Work—Plankton Investigations in other British Seas—Criticisms of the Christiania Programme—Views of Professors McIntosh, Herdman, and Ray Lankester—Broader Reasons for this Country's Co-operation—Policy—Economic Gain . 185

CHAPTER VI

THE FISHERY PORTS: THE TWEED TO THE THAMES

PAGE

Paramount Importance of the East Coast—North Sea Fisheries
Migration of Trawling from Devon—Recent Development of the
West Coast—Four Sea-fisheries Districts on the East Side—
Coastline under no District—Berwick-on-Tweed—Wolf-fish—
Other Stations in Northumberland—Evidence of Mr. Dent as
to Depletion on that Coast—Mussel Bait—' Brat-nets '—Line-
fishing—Typical Craft at Cullercoats—Crab-pots—Proposed
New Marine Laboratory—Work of Mr. Alexander Meek—North
Shields: Its Qualifications as a Fishing Port—Local Associa-
tions and their Objects—Superiority of Hull and Grimsby—
Sunderland and Hartlepool — The Yorkshire Coast — Tidal
Harbours—Disabilities of Whitby Harbour—Scarborough: the
Trade and the Corporation—Scarborough as a Herring and
Trawling Station—Brixham Men on the Yorkshire Coast—
Scarborough Market—Meaning of ' Offal '—Hull Fleets—Water
Carriage to Billingsgate—Details of Catches—Railway Rates—
Grimsby and the Great Central Railway—The Great Strike of
1901 — Cod Chests — Boston — Trawling and Shell-fisheries—
Yarmouth Deserted by Trawlers—Sale of the 'Short Blue'
Fleet — The Shrimp-trawler — Steam-drifters — Lowestoft and
the Great Eastern Railway Company—The Thames Estuary—
Dr. Murie's Report—Leigh—Pollution and Shell-fish—Berried
Lobsters at Harwich—Stow-nets for Whitebait—Sprat Fisher-
men and the Conservancy—Medical Evidence and Southend
Oysters 209

CHAPTER VII

THE FISHERY PORTS: THE THAMES TO PLYMOUTH

General Review of the Ports—Whitstable and Emsworth Oysters
Unimportance of Hampshire and Dorset—The Solent—Bourne-
mouth—Isle of Wight—The South Side of the Thames Estuary—
Ramsgate—Share of Profits Taken by Steam Gear—Fishing
Grounds — Profit Sharing — The Harbour — French Visitors—
Decline of the Herring-fishery—Dover and Folkestone—The
Dungeness Fisheries—Kettle-nets—The Sussex District—Denge-
marsh and Galloway—Hastings—Rye Bay and other Grounds—
A Harbour for Hastings—Brighton—Former Trade with France—
Selsey—Cost of Bait—Undersized Lobsters—Decline of Poole
Fishing—Swanage and Lulworth—Dorset and East Devon—A
Plea for Inshore Trawling—Decline of Exmouth Herrings—
' Sprats ' and ' London Sprats ' at Teignmouth—Fixed Nets at
Babbicombe—Landings at Torquay—Importance of Brixham—

PAG

Pioneering Work by Brixham Fishermen—Stocker Bait—Mumble-
bees—Plymouth Barbican—The Bait Difficulty—Plymouth and
Government Yards—Careless Gun Practice 267

CHAPTER VIII

THE FISHERY PORTS : CORNWALL AND THE WEST COAST

Varied Fisheries of Cornwall—Importance of Migratory Fishes in
its Returns—Trawling and Drift-net Ports—Mackerel-seining at
Looe—Mevagissey—Seasons for the Drift-nets—'Jowders'—The
Harbour—Analysis of Fish Landed—A Self-contained Port
The Sardine Factory—Other Products—Falmouth to Mount's
Bay—Penzance Harbour—Preference of the Buyers for Newlyn
The Newlyn Riots of 1896—Mousehole—Breton Crabbers at
Scilly—A Visit to one of their Vessels—Mullet-seining at Sennen
Cove—The Seaweed Grievance — Pilchards and Herrings at
St. Ives—Privileges of the Seine-boats—Record Catches at
St. Ives—Enterprise of the L. & S. W. Railway Co. at Padstow—
Natural Disabilities of the Port—Unimportance of the North
Coast of Devon — Cardiff — Swansea — Improvements in the
Harbour—Advantages of Railway Monopoly to a Fishing Port—
Stake-nets at the Mumbles—Decline of Fishing at Tenby—
Development of Milford by the Great Western Railway Com-
pany—Natural Advantages and Disadvantages of the Port—
Its Progress—Trawling-fleet—Steam-liners—Mackerel Trade—
Greater Development of the North Side of the Bristol Channel—
Pwllheli — Scientific Work of the Lancashire and Western
Authorities — Fleetwood — Falling-off of Morecambe Bay
Fisheries—Shrimp-trawlers and the 'Shank' Trawl—Completion
of the Tour at Maryport—Solway Fisheries—Cumberland Dis-
trict—Résumé of the Tour 305

CHAPTER IX

THE FUTURE

Difficulties of Prophecy—Rapid Developments—More Southern
Grounds—The Canaries and Morocco Coast—Hopeful View
Taken by Professor McIntosh—Importation of Colonial Fish—Ex-
tension of the List of 'Edible' Fishes—Colonial Fishing Indus-
tries—Mr. Chamberlain's Fiscal Programme—Cape Fisheries—
Canada and Australia—Fisheries in Former Times—The Present—
Summary of Results of Preceding Chapters—Probable De-
velopment of Legislation—Optimism of Professor McIntosh—
'The Resources of the Sea' — His Arguments Examined—
Fish Culture—Promise of the Future—Science and Peace . 356

INDEX 377

a

LIST OF ILLUSTRATIONS

[Where not otherwise stated, the photographs are by the Author]

	PAGE
SEA FISHERIES MAP OF ENGLAND AND WALES . . . *facing*	1
OFF TO THE FISHING GROUNDS (RAMSGATE HARBOUR)	*Frontispiece*

	PAGE
COD AND HERRINGS	2
Photo, Reinhold Thiele.	
GARFISH AND MACKEREL	14
Photo, Reinhold Thiele.	
PLAICE, TURBOT, AND SOLE	21
Photo, Reinhold Thiele.	
BEAM-TRAWL	37
From a Plate lent by Mr. W. Hearder.	
A TYPICAL SMACK	41
OTTER-TRAWL	42
From a Plate lent by Mr. W. Hearder.	
THE OTTER-TRAWL, AS IMPROVED BY MR. SCOTT, OF GRANTON	43
Reproduced by permission of the Marine Biological Association.	
STEAM-TRAWLERS	44
A STEAM-DRIFTER, GREAT YARMOUTH	62
THE SAND-EEL SEINE, TEIGNMOUTH	65
TRAMMEL	69
From a Plate lent by Mr. W. Hearder.	
A CULLERCOATS CRAB-POT	76
THE SHRIMPER	77
PRAWN NETS AND CORKS	80
BILLINGSGATE MARKET	82
Photo, A. S. Rudland.	
WAITING TO UNLOAD	83
THE DUTCH EEL-BOATS, BILLINGSGATE	87
Photo, A. S. Rudland.	
HULL CARRIERS AT BILLINGSGATE	91
Photo, A. S. Rudland.	

	PAGE
THE EARLY MARKET	92
BRIXHAM TRAWLERS IN PORT	95
ICE FOR THE SMACKS	98
A TRAWLING PORT	101
HOW THE FISH COMES TO BILLINGSGATE	102
RETURNED EMPTIES	112
THE PROCESSION OF PORTERS, BILLINGSGATE	116
Photo, A. S. Rudland.	
THE 'CONDEMNED' BARGE, BILLINGSGATE	117
Photo, A. S. Rudland.	
THE FISHMONGERS' HALL	124
Photo, A. S. Rudland.	
THE MARINE LABORATORY, PLYMOUTH	190
THE 'HUXLEY'	202
DECK OF THE 'HUXLEY' (SHOWING THE BEAM-TRAWL)	204
A MAY MORNING, SCARBOROUGH	210
HAULING THE SALMON-NETS, BERWICK	214
TYPE OF BOATS USED AT CULLERCOATS	217
THE FISH-MARKET, NORTH SHIELDS	219
SCOTCH HERRING-BOATS AT HARTLEPOOL	223
LOW TIDE, WHITBY	224
Photo, W. Brown.	
VARIOUS FISHING CRAFT, WHITBY	227
Photo, W. Brown.	
LOW TIDE AT SCARBOROUGH	232
HULL TRAWLERS	237
GRIMSBY DOCK	241
THE QUAYS, GRIMSBY	242
By permission of the Great Central Railway Company.	
BUSY TIMES, GRIMSBY	248
By permission of the Great Central Railway Company.	
ON THE SHORES OF THE WASH	251
Photo lent by Mr. H. Donnison.	
A SHRIMP-TRAWLER, YARMOUTH	255
COMING ALONGSIDE	256
THE TRAWL-MARKET, LOWESTOFT	258
THE EBB TIDE, LEIGH	263
DREDGERS AT WORK	265

PAGE

TRAWLERS IN RAMSGATE HARBOUR 270

WHISTLING FOR THE WIND. 272

FOLKESTONE HARBOUR 275

A FISH AUCTION ON HASTINGS BEACH 277

SMACKS OFF HASTINGS 279

ON BRIGHTON BEACH 281

SELSEY BEACH 283

WAITING FOR THE BREEZE, BRIXHAM 289

A SLACK TIME AT BRIXHAM 292

THE BARBICAN, PLYMOUTH 297

THE FISH-MARKET AT PLYMOUTH 300

DRYING THE TRAWL-NETS 303

LOOE MACKEREL-BOATS 309

MEVAGISSEY: THE POOL 312

MEVAGISSEY: THE INNER HARBOUR. 313

NEWLYN HARBOUR 321

MOUSEHOLE 328

BRETON CRABBERS OFF ST. MARY'S, SCILLY 330

ST. IVES 333

EARLY MORNING AT SWANSEA 337

MILFORD 343

A MAIDEN VOYAGE (FLEETWOOD) 348

SHRIMP-TRAWLERS RACING FOR THE OPEN SEA (FLEETWOOD). . 350

MARYPORT 353

TRAWLERS IN THE POOL 359

LOW TIDE IN A KENTISH HARBOUR 366

AS THE TIDE COMES IN 367

THE DAY'S WORK OVER 375

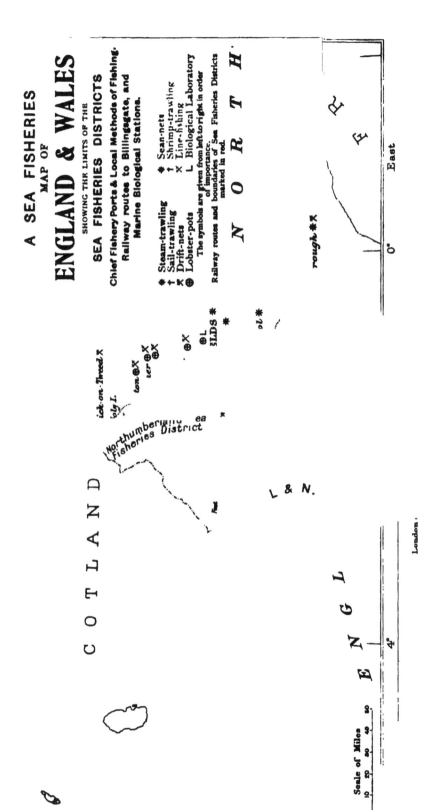

A SEA FISHERIES
MAP OF
ENGLAND & WALES

SHOWING THE LIMITS OF THE
SEA FISHERIES DISTRICTS

Chief Fishery Ports & Local Methods of Fishing.
Railway routes to Billingsgate, and
Marine Biological Stations.

* Steam-trawling   * Sean-nets
† Sail-trawling   † Shrimp-trawling
⚓ Drift-nets   ✕ Line-fishing
⊕ Lobster-pots   L Biological Laboratory

The symbols are given from left to right in order
of importance.
Railway routes and boundaries of Sea Fisheries Districts
marked in red.

NORTH

FR

East

rough *✕

0°

SCOTLAND

ENGL

L & N.

Northumberland
Fisheries District

ick-on-Tweed ✕

bly I.

ton ⊕✕

ver ⊕✕
⊕✕

✕

⊕ L
ELDS *

*

70 *

4°

London.

Scale of Miles
10 0 10 20 30 40 50

SEA-FISHING INDUSTRY
ENGLAND AND WALES

CHAPTER I

LIFE IN THE SEA

Distinction between Economic and Biological Problems—Facts of Practical Interest—Definition of a 'Food Fish'—Fish Culture—The Egg, the Larval and the Post-larval Stages of a Fish—Round and Flat Fish—Migratory and Stationary Kinds—Rock-dwellers and Sand-dwellers—Mapping the North Sea—Plankton Investigations—Fisheries ruined by the Migrations of the Fish—Spawning Grounds and their Protection—Eggs that sink and Eggs that float—Habit of Shoaling in Fish—Migrations of Mackerel—The Herring—A Cold-water Fish—Comparison with the Pilchard—Curious alternation of the two at St. Ives—The Sprat—Habit of Spawning near the Land—'Whitebait': its Composition in Summer and in Winter—Flat Fish—The Plaice—The Sole—Its Spawning in the Aquarium—Introduced into Scotch Waters—The Cod Family —Periodicity of Hake—Disagreement as to Spawning-grounds of the Cod—Recent abundance of Young Haddocks—Comparison between the Fish landed at Scarborough and Plymouth—Food of the Grey Mullet —Removal of Seaweed on the Cornish Coast—Rivals of the Fishermen —Fish that Hunt by Sight, by Scent, by Touch—Technical Instruction for Fishermen—Artificial Fertilising of Spawn at Sea—Plan suggested by Mr. Fryer and Mr. Garstang—Reliable Information available from Fishermen—Dr. Wemyss Fulton's latest Method of Collecting Statistics.

BEFORE coming to the subject of this volume, the manner in which fish are taken from the sea and brought to our tables, it will perhaps help us to a

B

better understanding of the prosecution and protection of our fisheries if we glance superficially at a few of the conditions of life in the sea before man interferes with the balance. It is because the solution of the economic problems is so closely bound up with a knowledge of the biological conditions that some of those in charge of marine laboratories show reluc-

[Photo: *Reinhold Thiele.*

COD AND HERRINGS.

tance to distinguish between the two branches of investigation. For this uncompromising view of the breadth of marine biological research there is much to be said, but it also has its dangers. It requires little effort to demonstrate that the rate of growth of our food fishes, the nature of their food, the dangers they run from natural enemies, the extent, direction, and season of their migrations, the time and place of their spawning, the temperature of the water and the character of the ground most suited to their well-being, are all germane to a proper grasp of the problems of either more efficient fishing or more restrictive legislation. Some heads of biological departments are, however, inclined to strain their prerogative and to include in their programme of ' practical ' research such academic matters as the structure and functions of the head kidney in teleosteans, the renal organs in crustacea, the accessory visual organ in flat fish, and similar microscopic exercises. So long as any institution is not subsidised by the trade or by Government for strictly economic work, these biological studies are very proper to the laboratory. Where, however, such financial aid is considerable, particularly in the case of marine laboratories maintained by sea-fisheries districts, the labours of those engaged ought rather to be confined to inquiries into the migrations of the pilchard and mackerel, the establishment of a ratio between size and sexual maturity in flat fishes, the promise of a British fishery for the hitherto neglected anchovy, experiments in the production of artificial baits, essays in the artificial culture of food fishes, and the solution of similar practical problems, all of which have at one time or another exercised the workers at Plymouth and elsewhere.

Even in order to understand the method of catching fish in nets or on the hook, some little knowledge of the habits of these creatures is a great help, though the anatomical and pathological aspects of the subject may in great measure be excluded for this particular purpose. The chief facts in the life story of the more important fishes, as well as an admirable bibliography of the subject, including material in several languages,

will be found in the third 'Publication de Circonstance'
of the North Sea Council. It is entitled, in its English
version, 'The Literature of the Ten Principal Food
Fishes of the North Sea'; and the ten fishes in question are the mackerel, cod, haddock, whiting, turbot,
plaice, dab, sole, herring, and anchovy. Whether, in
view of the unaccountable neglect of the anchovy
everywhere between the Mediterranean and the Zuyder
Zee, that fish can, strictly speaking, be regarded as a
more important food fish in those parts than the skate,
wolf-fish, or coal-fish, is a matter of opinion; but if
the selection is open to criticism, the treatment is
unexceptionable.

In the present introductory chapter the merest
outline must suffice. In the first place, taking at once
the commercial rather than the biological standpoint
of interest, it is desirable to define a 'food fish.' The
line between a food fish and another that cannot come
under that category is by no means hard and fast.
Whether a fish is good to eat or not is largely a question of taste. The epicure would include the salmon,
trout, red mullet, cod, sole, whitebait, and turbot,
with perhaps the roe of the herring; and there his list
would close. The poor man eats ray and even dog-fish.
He enjoys large sprats, but the gourmet will not eat
sprats unless they are quite small, and then only when
they are called 'whitebait.' Are we, then, when we
speak of 'food fishes' to include only those fishes which
are commonly seen at the fishmonger's, or are we to
include every fish that can be eaten for lack of choice?
Professor McIntosh and Mr. Masterman, in their 'Life
History of the British Marine Food Fishes,' all but
ignore the skates and rays. In this I personally agree
with them; but, however unpalatable to the sensitive

taste, the skate is very widely appreciated by the masses, by whom it is, when in season, regarded as a great delicacy. It is inexpensive, and it possesses certain qualities which recommend it. On the other hand, their sins of commission are less easily condoned. It would be ill requiting many acts of kindness if I were to invite Professor McIntosh to dine on boiled gobies! If he ever saw one of that group in a fishmonger's shop, it must surely have been in the land of Lilliput. Nor, I imagine, has Mr. Cunningham, who has the same contempt for the skate, ever encountered either a sucker or a rockling on the tables of the polite. At most, these small kinds are deserving of study because they constitute the food of our food fishes. In the same way, the practical marine biologist must acquaint himself with the life history of all manner of micro-scopic floating organisms, on which the more important fishes feed, as well as with that of such predatorv creatures as sharks, porpoises, seals, and sea-birds, which feed on them according to that unpleasant law by which Nature makes common cause with rapine. But to describe them as ' food fishes ' is a course which challenges criticism The herring, cod, plaice, mackerel gurnards, bream, garfish, dory, red and grey mullet, and skate, with such of their relatives as are commonly offered for sale, are the true food fishes.

So far, however, as a comprehensive study of the subject is concerned, the line is drawn only with the reservation that the intelligent inquirer will wander very far on either side of it. As regards the more practical facts in the natural history of each fish, or group of fishes, which will help him to grapple with the problems of the fishing industry, these must clearly include every condition tending to regulate their distribution [1] and migrations, their food, their sensibility to changes in the weather or temperature, the size at which they first become mature,[2] and the extreme limits of their growth.

The economic study of our sea-fish must begin at the egg. If anything serious is to be attempted on a remunerative scale in the way of sowing, as well as reaping, the harvest of the sea, the seed will be the eggs of fishes, though in all probability it will be found necessary to rear the young fish until it is capable of feeding and defending itself. For this reason, not only the egg, but also the larval and post-larval stages—fishes, it must be remembered, undergo metamorphoses, like frogs or insects—must be very carefully studied. Until we know the precise moment at which the little fish is first able to seek nourishment and to escape from its many natural enemies, fish-culture can be nothing more than a scientific pastime. Turning out thousands of fishes in the critical, helpless stage of extreme youth only means feeding the rest, though one eminent advocate of such operations has argued that even this has its advantages, since the artificially hatched fishes will be slower to escape, and a corresponding portion of Nature's supply will thus be left immune. This seems to me to presuppose that the predatory fishes have an absolutely constant feeding capacity, whereas the least experience in the aquarium is sufficient to show that their appetites are in the majority of cases indefinitely elastic.

A walk through the fish-market during business hours reveals two distinct types of fish. There are

---

[1] The word 'distribution' is here used in its biological sense of geographical range, not commercially, as in Chapter III.

[2] *I.e.* capable of depositing eggs, or (in the male) of fertilising them.

round fishes, like the cod and mackerel; and there are flat fishes, like the sole and turbot. The skate is also a flattened fish, but not a 'flat fish' in the same sense as the sole or plaice, since it belongs to a very different group. For the fisherman, however, the two, though morphologically distinct, have the same interest. Both live in the sand; both are caught in the trawl. The fisherman therefore groups his fishes somewhat differently from the biologist. The trawler associates the skate, plaice, sole, cod, hake, ling, and gurnard, which to the biologist are representative of four different families. The drift-netsman associates the mackerel, herring, and pilchard, whereas the man of science separates the first from the other two. In the ground-seine, which, like the other nets, will be fully described in the next chapter, we find bass, grey mullet, and sand-eel, three very distinct types of fishes. The hook and line catch all these at times, with the possible exception of the pilchard, but the only regular line-fisheries in English waters are for cod, skate, mackerel, .whiting, and sole, the herring being in addition taken for bait on the coast of Scotland on a tackle known as a 'dandy-line.'

The migration of fishes is obviously of first importance to those who have to find them before they can be caught. In our own species, the love of travel is absent or present in the individual; in the fish world all the members of a species practically act alike in this respect. It would be impossible, of course, not to admit that, as in the case of migratory kinds of birds, a few may stay behind, but such units are of no practical importance, and we may therefore say that all herrings, all mackerel, all cod are migratory. The herring, then, may be taken as the type of a migratory fish. If there is an absolutely sedentary fish, it is perhaps the conger eel. The plaice would come between the two. There is, on the one hand, some evidence of regular movements among plaice in the English Channel at the spawning season; on the other hand, the circumstance of recapture of marked plaice liberated under the auspices of the international scheme of scientific investigations (see Chapter V.) proves that the fish is by no means absolutely sedentary in the North Sea. It is open to doubt, indeed, whether any sea-fish can be so described. In addition to the wanderings of the more restless fishes, we have also to study the areas of distribution of those which are less given to moving about.

It is difficult to apply hard and fast rules to the manner in which our food fishes pass their lives. With certain reservations, it is true, we can distinguish between those kinds which reside on the sand and others more commonly occurring on rocky ground. As a general rule, the flat fishes are examples of the former, the conger and bream and pollack of the latter group. By way of exception to either, however, we have the case of large plaice being commonly hooked on rough ground, and of the group of flat fishes known as top-knots evincing an invariable preference for a rocky bottom; while the conger eel is taken in great numbers in the trawl, a net not adapted in the ordinary way to fishing the more rocky grounds. The 'shell-fish,' which is the collective trade name for the two important groups of crustaceans and molluscs, are capable of similar division; the crab, lobster, prawn, oyster, and mussel live among the rocks, while the shrimp, whelk, cockle, and scallop are found on soft ground. There are two kinds of shrimp, the pink and the brown. The former has affinities with the prawn family, and in many localities indeed it goes by the name of 'prawn.' The only fishes which seem to be absolutely indifferent to the nature of the sea-bed, and for excellent reasons, are migratory kinds like the mackerel, pilchard, and herring, which pass much of their time near the surface of the water. Another case of characteristic situation is the preference of bass and grey mullet for estuaries. (The salmon, the smelt, and the shad, which spawn in our rivers, are regarded as freshwater fishes, and are therefore excluded from the present work.) Not only do the regular fishermen of the North Sea know that they will find a preponderance of plaice or haddock, for instance, on certain 'banks' or fishing-grounds, but in many cases long experience has acquainted them with the grounds frequented by only small fish. Mr. Alward, one of the leading members of the industry at Great Grimsby, was the first to attempt a fishery map of the North Sea, though the example has since had many imitators. Such a map is invaluable, not so much that it may help newcomers to find the fish—too many know where to find them as it is—but rather as an aid to legislators in discussing the proposals, which are from time to time made, to close certain areas to trawlers in order that they may serve as nurseries for the little unsaleable flat fish.

The truly migratory fishes, like the herring and mackerel, run no risk of exhaustion under present conditions. In their case, therefore, the investigations of scientific men may rather be directed towards so thoroughly understanding their migrations as to be able to assist the fishermen to intercept them with their nets. Temperature, drifts, and the food of these species are the natural clues to such knowledge; and the last-named is chiefly studied in the form of 'plankton,' that mass of microscopic organisms with which every bucket of sea-water teems. The fine-meshed collecting nets used by scientific expeditions over vast areas of the sea and at various depths have gradually extended our knowledge of this wonderful plankton, which has been the subject of long monographs in several languages. The Germans have paid special attention to its investigation. How important is a more intimate knowledge of the movements of these capricious fishes may be illustrated by the tragic failure of the French sardine fishery ; while a near relation of the sardine, to wit the herring, failed as completely at Exmouth some years ago, suddenly determining a once valuable fishery and compelling the unfortunate fishermen to sell their nets at a loss. It has been said that the sardine itself, which we call a pilchard, and which has been scarce on the East Coast of Scotland ever since the first third of the nineteenth century, was previous to that period abundant in those seas, but I have been unable to collect any evidence of this. The anchovy, another member of the same family, also appears subject to similar sudden desertion of localities long inhabited by it; but we have hitherto neglected the anchovy in our seas, so that its travels need not here detain us. Fishes may migrate either in a direction parallel to the coast or in a direction almost at right angles with it ; in other words, changing from the deeper offshore to the shallower inshore water. The tendency of later investigations of the subject of migration appears to have been to substitute this movement between the deep and shallow water for many cases formerly regarded as extensive voyages between the temperate and the arctic seas. We have

our winter and summer fishes just as we have our
winter and summer birds ; and the mackerel and grey
mullet appear along our south coast with the swallow
and the martin, just as the cod and whiting come later
with the wild duck and the woodcock.

The spawning grounds and seasons of our important
food fishes must be the subject of unremitting study
until we have arrived at something very near exact
knowledge of them. Not until then can it be worth
while even discussing proposals for closing certain areas,
save perhaps experimentally, as has been done by the
Scotch Fishery Board. It must be borne in mind that
protection of the spawning fish alone is possible ; protection of the spawn itself, save possibly in one case, is
out of the question. The herring, alone among our
important fishes, deposits an egg heavy enough to sink
to the bottom in sea-water. The eggs of the plaice,
cod, or mackerel, even those of such near relatives of
the herring as the pilchard and sprat, float in the water,
and are consequently borne hither and thither, at the
mercy of tides and storms, and beyond the pale of protection. The spawn of the herring sinks to the ground
and attaches itself to weeds and stones, and in such
situations it might perhaps, were there any necessity
to encourage so prolific a fish, be found practicable
to protect it. The other consideration suggested by a
knowledge of this peculiar character of the herring's
egg, as distinguished from that of other fishes, is that it
alone, lying as it does on the ground, might suffer from
the operations of the trawl net. If, for instance, we
consider the case of Bigbury Bay, a famous spawning
ground for winter herring just east of Plymouth, we
shall find the whole of the Mevagissey drifting-fleet
busy there soon after Christmas, catching these herrings,

bursting with roe, for the Plymouth market. A little later, on some of the deeper water spawning grounds in the North Sea, though not so close in land as the one here named, we shall find the trawler himself on the spawning grounds, not indeed in search of herrings, but in pursuit of the haddocks which gather there to feast on the herring's spawn. Here, then, is a nice exercise for experts to argue to a conclusion : whether the trawler does the herring more harm, by disturbing its spawning grounds, than it does good by catching one of the herring's greatest natural enemies, the haddock.

The season of spawning is, from the strictly economic standpoint, of less consequence than the place, for no measure for establishing a close season for sea-fish would be compatible with the proper supply of the markets. If, as is declared by the fishermen, the mackerel and some other fishes decline a bait before spawning, a measure of protection might be achieved by allowing line-fishing even in the protected spawning areas, thereby catching those individuals not in the critical condition which calls for special encouragement.

Something has already been said in the present chapter, and more will be said in the next, on the different methods by which sea-fish are caught for the market. It is important to distinguish broadly between a fish like the herring, with a hundred natural enemies in addition to man, and one like the plaice, of which man is the chief foe. The distinction is twofold. The different methods by which the fishes are caught, depending in turn on the manner in which they pass their lives, are the most important. The herring has nothing to fear from the trawl and very little from the hook. It dies in thousands, it is true, in the drift-net, but for every fish taken in this way at least a thousand in all probability escape. When, on this assumption, and on the basis of the five or six hundred million herrings landed at Yarmouth alone in the winter of 1902, we attempt to calculate the herring population in our seas, we reach figures that might appal even an astronomer. With the plaice, so far as man is concerned, it is another matter. Even in the larval and post-larval stages, and more particularly in the very small adult stage, it is destroyed in incredible numbers in the shrimp-nets. The sweeping trawl gathers up every plaice that lies in its path. Considered, on the other hand, in respect of their natural enemies, excluding man, the two change places. Here, it is the plaice with few troubles. A passing skate may dig it from its sandy burrow; a watchful cormorant may choke over it, should it get stranded at low tide; but its form and habits are equally conducive to safety where a hundred others perish. The very habit of shoaling in the herring makes it the victim of dashing hake, tumbling porpoises, and pouncing sea-fowl; and, as if to make matters worse for itself, it must needs swim in serried crowds close to the surface, laying itself open to simultaneous attack from above and below. When, therefore, the advocates of restrictive legislation are met with the optimistic assurance that man is only one of a hundred enemies, they should accept the argument in respect of the herring (for which protection is never suggested), but they should most strongly reject it on behalf of the flat fishes, the legitimate objects of protection by such laws.

One or two facts in the life history of the more important fishes may now be considered in their bearing on the fishery problems.

The mackerel, one of the chief fishes in our markets, particularly during the summer months, is caught by

one of three methods : the drift-net is the chief of these ;
next comes the seine ; lastly, hook and line.   A few,
comparatively speaking, are taken in the trawl, but
these do not form a regular source of supply.   The
habit of the mackerel to swim in shoals is of the
greatest benefit to the fisherman ; indeed, but for this,
the fish would have to be taken in the trawl, like others
of less gregarious habit.   The trawl, sweeping up every
fish in its path, can catch numbers even where these

[*Photo: Reinhold Thiele.*
GARFISH AND MACKEREL.

are not all of a species ; the drift-net depends on shoals
and catches only one kind of fish at a time, for a different mesh is used for mackerel, pilchard, or sprat.   Of
this, however, more will be said in the next chapter.
All that is here intended is to show how important to
the fisherman is this habit of swimming in shoals and
so near the top of the water as to be plainly seen by
watchers posted on the cliffs for that purpose.   Why
the mackerel should, to its own detriment, swim in

shoals in this way, it is not easy to say. It may be regarded by the fish as a measure of protection, but if ever there was a case in which union does not make force, it is that of a shoal of fish. If only the mackerel and the herring could learn the strategic value of advancing in open order, it would be a bad day for the nets. What is more probably the true explanation is that just the right conditions of food and temperature attract all the fish of a species to one area of water, and as soon as these conditions cease to be favourable they all, with one impulse, move in search of pastures new. The habits of the mackerel undergo certain changes with the seasons. Our knowledge of these movements is far from complete, but, thanks to the records published by the Marine Biological Association, we are less ignorant on the subject than we were five years ago. For the first six months of the year the shoals appear to hug the surface, working eastward and northward from more remote areas off the west coast of France and the south-west of Ireland, gradually appear- ing on the coast of every county on the south coast of England. About the end of July, a little earlier or later according to the weather and temperature in different years, the shoals break up; the Cornish mackerel season is over, and the drift-nets turn their attention to the pilchard fishing; the mackerel are now taken on surface-lines. Later still, with the autumn break-up of the weather, the mackerel go to the bottom and are then caught on ground-lines. In early spring, when spawning, the female mackerel refuses a bait, a habit attributed by the fishermen to blindness, by biologists to the sickening of the fish during a critical period. The two migrations of the mackerel, in spring and in autumn, which may be compared with those of, for instance, the quail, are regarded by some as dictated by two distinct motives. Food is thought to be the object of the first; spawning of the second, a conclusion which rests on the fact of the spring fish being practically empty, while those taken inshore in autumn are crammed full of fry and other food. In spring, the mackerel are thought to feed chiefly on copepods and medusæ, and the greater ease and rapidity with which such light fare is assimilated may in part be responsible for the description of these spring fish as 'empty.' Biologists on either shore of the Atlantic have agreed that a temperature of 45° F. is the lowest favourable to this fish, but this statement is apparently criticised in some quarters. The garfish, which some people refuse to eat on account of its green bones, is really a most excellent table-fish. It is not specially fished for, but is taken in company with the mackerel both in the nets and on lines.

The herring is a migratory fish of even greater importance than the mackerel. While this is true even of Great Britain, the relative importance of the herring is considerably increased if we consider all the maritime countries of northern Europe. The part played by the herring in, for example, the past history of the Netherlands, would furnish material for one of the most striking romances of commerce. In Scotland, too, it was upon the great herring-fisheries that the Scotch Fishery Board, a model for all later institutions of the kind, at once scientific and administrative, was founded. With the exception of the bare-hooked 'dandy-line,' on which herring are taken for bait in Scotch waters, the fish is taken almost entirely in the drift-nets. Unlike the mackerel, it is a cold-water fish. It comes to us from the Arctic circle, and there, in fact, it reaches its greatest development. Even the herrings from the colder regions of the North Sea grow to a larger size than in the neighbourhood of Plymouth, where the average temperature throughout the year is considerably higher. Whether or not the herring is ever met with in that comparatively warm sea, the Mediterranean, I am not certain. The sardine, or pilchard, its near relative, is, of course, abundant there; but I never saw a herring in any of the fishmarkets, and I have visited those of half a dozen Mediterranean countries at different times of the year. In fact, I believe that all the best authorities regard the herring as a northern fish, outside the Mediterranean region, its European range being determined to the south by a line drawn through the middle of the Bay of Biscay.

That so important a food fish as the herring should have been the subject of much investigation is only what would be expected. The old notions—they hardly deserve the name of theories—of long migrations to and from the Arctic Seas, together with many wonderful legends about hibernating with their heads buried in the mud, have long since been exploded. Indeed, just a century has elapsed since it was first made known that the egg of the herring sinks to the bottom of the sea. For a considerable time, indeed, a similar property was by false analogy attributed to the eggs of other food fishes. The trawler was in consequence long blamed for destroying their spawn.

In what is known as the larval stage, that is to say, immediately after escaping from the egg, the young herring lives at the bottom of the sea. As it increases in size, it gradually makes its way to the surface. The larval pilchard, on the other hand, passes its whole life, even from the hatching out of its egg, near the

C

surface. It is therefore exposed to the influence of storms and to depredations by surface-feeding fishes, even in the larval stage, a period at which the herring is immune. It is curious that two fishes so closely allied as the herring and pilchard should be caught at different seasons; but this is such an enormous convenience to the fishermen, who are thereby enabled to put away their pilchard nets in the West Country before the herring shoals enter their bays, that there is some excuse for the anthropocentric view of those who hold that all these matters are providentially arranged for the sole advantage of man. What is perhaps even more remarkable, though less appreciated by some of the fishermen, is that a good year for pilchards is generally followed by a bad year for herrings. This alternation of seasons has long been recognised at St. Ives, though no scientific explanation has as yet been given.

The sprat, which, if we exclude the anadromous shads and the neglected anchovy, is the only other member of the herring family in our seas, spawns somewhat further up inlets than the rest; and this choice of shallower, less saline, water is regarded as aiming at the safety of the egg, which would sink in such a medium, and develop undisturbed on the bottom. Such a theory is purely hypothetical, but it furnishes an interesting contrast with the case of the freshwater eel, which descends to the sea to breed, perhaps in order that its small egg may float free in the denser water instead of sinking into the suffocating mud.

The whitebait of City dinners is not, as some folks imagine, and as even scientific men held half a century ago, a distinct species, but a mixture of young herrings and young sprats. The proportions in which both species occur vary according to the season of the year. In summer the herring may number more than 80 per cent. In winter the discrepancy may be even greater, the sprats being then in the majority, and composing in many baskets over 90 per cent. of the whole. The whitebait-fishermen have been regarded in some quarters as great destroyers of immature flat fish, and it is probable that in some estuaries they do considerable damage in that direction. As regards the whitebait fisheries of the Thames estuary, however, one of the most important centres on our coast, Dr. Murie expressly repudiates this charge in Part I. of his recently published Report. He demonstrates, from analysis of a number of boxes, that the extraneous material, which also includes jellyfish and shrimps, forms at any time only a very small proportion of the whole.

The life-history of the flat fish—by these are meant the plaice and its kindred, and not the skates and rays —is more interesting to the biologist, who studies their metamorphoses and colour changes, than to the practical fisherman. The information which we need is not in order to assist the latter towards a greater efficiency, but rather to put such reasonable check on his activity as, while not depriving him of the means of earning a livelihood throughout the year, shall also give these valuable food fishes a chance of reproducing their species, instead of being destroyed and wasted before they have spawned even once. Some of the measures which have been suggested in order to gain this end are discussed in Chapter IV., while in Chapter V. will be found an outline of the scientific work carried out for the better information of the legislator. It will here suffice to enumerate, in respect of the plaice, six important facts, for a knowledge of which we are indebted to the marine biologists working under the Scotch Fishery Board and under the auspices of the Marine Biological Association and the Lancashire and Western Sea Fisheries District :—

1. The plaice spends its whole life, once its metamorphoses are completed, on soft ground permanently within reach of the trawl.

2. Its maximum recorded length of 28 inches in Scotch waters is greater than that reported from the Irish Sea (26 inches), or from the Plymouth district (24 inches).

3. It reaches maturity (*i.e.* the stage at which it is first capable of depositing its spawn) at a smaller size in the English Channel (15 inches) than in the North Sea (17 inches). Like the herring, therefore, the plaice seems to reach its highest development in colder seas.

4. It spawns in the English Channel some time between January and March, and in the Irish Sea from February to April, whereas in the North Sea it is found to spawn as late as the month of May.

5. Few plaice are trawled in water of a greater depth than 100 fathoms.

6. Though not commonly reckoned among migratory fishes, the plaice has a tendency to seek the deeper water in the colder season of the year.

The precise value to the legislator of these results of the labours of Messrs. F. J. Cole, J. Johnstone, J. T. Cunningham, E. W. L. Holt, and others will be more apparent when, in a later chapter, we discuss their bearing on the measures of protection hitherto considered. It is here sufficient to draw the reader's attention to an important distinction (*vide* 2 & 3 *supra*) between ' undersized ' and ' immature.' Commercially speaking, a plaice may be immature, though it is no longer undersized—that is to say, a plaice may be marketable in size, although not yet able to deposit its spawn. The importance of being able to distinguish between mature and immature plaice, even at those seasons of the year at which the fish is not full of tell-tale spawn, is obvious. Dr. Petersen has made some very interesting investigations in this subject, a preliminary communication on

[*Photo: Reinhold Thiele.*

PLAICE, TURBOT, AND SOLE.

the results of which forms the first of the 'Publications de Circonstance' of the International Council. The two symptoms of maturity there discussed are the spinulation of scales on the operculum of the male and, in both sexes, the presence of pale rings round the orange spots on both body and fins. An admirable coloured plate, showing the female plaice with and without the rings, accompanies the text.

The other flat fish which calls for protection is the sole. To this valuable and interesting fish Mr. Cunningham has devoted a careful monograph, but the facts at our command are less ample. Biologists fix the spawning time of this fish between February and June, and its minimum length, when mature, is said to range between ten and eleven inches. Further, the female may deposit a hundred thousand eggs. The sole has often spawned in captivity, and Professor McIntosh is said to have succeeded in introducing soles from the English coast to the waters on the eastern seaboard of Scotland, though what evidence there is of the fish being more plentiful there since he made this interesting experiment I have no notion. The matter lies outside the geographical scope of these pages and is referred to only in passing.

The cod family is interesting chiefly in respect of its spawning and migrations. The irregular years of abundance of hake are attributed by biologists to what is called 'periodicity.' This is a condition of irregular, as distinguished from regular, migration. On the movements of cod during the period immediately preceding the spawning time, there is some difference of opinion. Professor McIntosh is of opinion that it seeks the deeper water for that purpose, whereas Mr. Cunningham thinks that it migrates inshore. The spawning time of codfish is usually associated with the spring of the year; but Dr. Wemyss Fulton has shown (see 'Publications de Circonstance' of the International Council, No. 8) that in the North Sea cod spawn in the autumn.

The haddock, in some respects the most important member of the family, was formerly thought to hide among the rocks, thereby escaping, during its early years, the operations of the trawl. Facts, however, modify views; and the immense catches of very young haddocks, known in the trade as 'chats,' which North Sea trawlers have been making of late years, show the need of some other explanation of the prolonged scarcity of these young fish. It may be that both the haddock and the herring have benefited by the trawler destroying such quantities of dogfish and other formidable natural enemies. Twenty years ago these young haddocks were plentiful off the coast of Scotland, but they were caught on hand-lines and not in the trawl. Tons of 'chats' are sold as manure; others are skinned and sold under the attractive name of 'Scarborough whitings.'

Even the distribution of certain familiar fishes in our seas is most difficult to understand. Seeing that there is no land barrier between the North Sea and English Channel, and seeing that the difference in temperature is during some seasons of the year very small, one would think that fishes abundant off Scarborough would find their way round to Plymouth. This, however, is by no means the case. The trawlers of Scarborough work, it is true, a great distance from the Yorkshire coast, while fish is brought to Plymouth Barbican from as far away as the Portuguese coast. Yet, even allowing for such a wide range of activity, it is evident that red mullet, megrims, hake, and large soles abound in the Plymouth market, whereas Scarborough salesmen have chiefly to dispose of coal-fish and wolf-fish, species which are rarely seen at Plymouth.

The food of fishes is another matter of great importance. The case of the grey mullet, even though it is not a food fish of first rank, is most interesting, though, as it is caught wholly in the seine-net, a knowledge of the nature of its food is of use rather to anglers. A grievance, however, which recently came up before the Cornish Sea Fisheries Committee, illustrates the need of accurate information on these matters. It appears that the mullet-fishermen of Sennen [1] found the fishery falling off, and this result they attributed, rightly or otherwise, to the removal of large quantities of a peculiar seaweed on which that fish is said to feed. The practice of removing this particular weed for food, and many coarser kinds for farm manure, is very common in the West country, and the position becomes complicated by the fact that much of the work is done by the wives and daughters of the fishermen themselves. Whether the grey mullet eats the weed, as alleged, or not, these submarine coverts must form very valuable protection for young fishes of different species. When, however, the subject was brought before the Cornish district authorities, specimens of mullet with the weed adhering to the gill-covers were put in as evidence. The gills of the haddock have also been found so overgrown with mussels as to suffocate the fish, but whether in either case there is sufficient evidence of the fish having fed on the plant or mollusc is open to question.

The practical application of a wider knowledge of biological principles is involved in the consideration of such proposals as have from time to time been made for the fishermen to wage war on their natural rivals, the seal, cormorant, shag, dogfish, octopus, and porpoise.[2]

---

[1] In their Seventeenth Annual Report the Fisheries Inspectors corrected an earlier error to the effect that the Sennen mullet were caught in the trammel, instead of, as is the case, with the seine.

[2] Foreign governments recognise the need of such measures. The Finnish Fishery Society spends nearly £200 a year in paying fees for the destruction of seals, otters, skuas, and other destructive fowl, and the

The cormorant and shag doubtless lend a certain pictu-resque interest to the shore, but they are none the less formidable competitors of the fisherman. The quantity of fish that a full-grown cormorant can consume in the course of a day is very large.

It is more particularly in estuaries, where sea and salmon-fisheries thrive side by side, that feeling has been strongest against the cormorants and divers; and the old municipal register of Newcastle contains the record of a price having been put on their heads in the Tyne district as far back as the year 1561. Proposals have more recently been laid before the Northumberland Board with a view to reviving some such bounty system. Even the confiding seagull is not wholly above suspicion in some localities, but its ser-vices as a scavenger and by way of warning fog-bound mariners off the rocks by its raucous cries go some way towards exculpating it. It has its critics, however, and as recently as April of the present year, a Fellow of the Royal Society endeavoured to convince a meeting of the Belfast Natural History and Philosophical Society that, during the herring season alone, the 2,000,000 gulls (*sic*) of the United Kingdom cost the nation no less a sum than £24,000,000. The assumption and in-ference by which he reached these extraordinary figures were so full of obvious fallacy as to require no discussion, in addition to which he took no account of the services rendered by the birds. One of the most determined enemies of the netsmen in the Plymouth district of late

Government contributes another £100 to the same work. The fishery laws of Prussia allow owners of inland fisheries to destroy by any means in their power otters, kingfishers, herons, ospreys, grebes, and cormorants. The French authorities in like manner pay a premium equivalent to 8*s.* of our money for the destruction of every white-nosed dolphin killed on the north-west coast of that country.

years has been the octopus. The authorities have very wisely circulated among the fishermen consular reports from Southern Italy, in which it is demonstrated that acetylene gas has been ingeniously adapted to the capture of that fatally curious mollusc in the Mediterranean, on the shores of' which sea it is a favourite article of food among the poorer class.

Something was said above of the importance of studying the food of fishes. Almost as useful is a knowledge of the manner in which each fish seeks its food, whether guided by sight or scent. The proper understanding of this habit finds a practical application in the experiments carried out with the object of devising an efficient and inexpensive artificial bait to take the place of the natural in time of scarcity. The want of bait at certain seasons is a pressing trouble with the Devon hookers; and even on the north-east coast, where the mussel is exceedingly abundant in inlets like the Wash, bait is sometimes so scarce that line fishing is at a standstill. The invention, therefore, of an artificial substitute would confer lasting benefit on the industry; and in the case of fishes caught on the hook at night, it becomes important to distinguish between those which hunt by sight and those which find the bait by the aid of their sense of smell. The conger eel is generally regarded as a fish which finds its food by scent. The chief evidence in support of this view is that the conger declines a bait which is in the least degree tainted. Predatory surface-swimming fishes, on the other hand, like the mackerel, which hunt an escaping prey in the most brilliantly lighted strata of the sea, are in all probability guided by their eyesight. Whether a third sense, akin to our sense of touch, is used to aid the red mullet, cod, and other fishes provided with sensitive 'barbels' is another question, and one that does not materially affect the search for an artificial bait.

There has during the past five years been considerable agitation for more systematic technical education for our fishermen. The movement commands less sympathy on the part of the men themselves than could be wished. When, some time ago, the Lancashire County Council offered a sum of £100 for fishermen's studentships, the scheme was not enthusiastically received, and there was but one applicant for the two £60 scholarships offered by the same body in connection with marine biology. In his report on the subject, however, Professor Herdman attributed this apathy to insufficient notification of the proffered advantages. In the management of technical education it is even more important than in the marine laboratory to give almost exclusive preference to practical matters. Lectures such as those given under County Council authority by Mr. Cunningham on new methods of curing nets are admirable; but natural history lectures, save to the very young, are apt to be received with suspicion wherever modern science clashes with ancient superstition. In the 1903 Report of the Lancashire Sea Fisheries Laboratory, Mr. Scott and Mr. Johnstone give a summary of the classes for fishermen at Piel, and the subjects dealt with are of a practical nature and admirably presented to those who attended. I understand that these classes are so successful that more fishermen have of late applied for admission than can be given places.

Another excellent subject for instruction is the artificial fertilising of spawn out on the fishing grounds, as suggested by Mr. C. E. Fryer, of the Fisheries Department, and formulated by Mr. W. Garstang, of the Marine Biological Association. Fish which, when removed from the trawl, are seen to be running with spawn, are laid on their back in a shady corner of the trawler's deck. The spawn of the male fish is what we call ' soft roe '; that of the female is ' hard roe '; and the method of utilising what would otherwise be wasted is to squeeze a ripe male into a bucket of clean sea water and then several ripe fémales of the same species into the same bucket. The soft and hard roe is then stirred for a few minutes gently with the hand; the whole is left for nearly a quarter of an hour and then thrown overboard. It is not pretended either that all the fishermen on board our trawlers could be induced to perform this useful work, or that, even if they did so, all the spawn thus treated would eventually hatch out. Still, even if success attended comparatively few efforts, something would be done in the direction of restocking the sea.

Besides, however, imparting information to the fishermen, much may be done with judgment in the nature of learning from them. Scientific men are rather too apt to underrate the value of such information, and it is satisfactory to note that the latest method of collecting statistics, as advocated by Dr. Wemyss Fulton, is to enlist the co-operation of intelligent and reliable masters of trawlers.[1] When I had the honour of giving evidence before the Committee on Ichthyological Research, I stated that the masters and men on our fishing-fleets were often to be depended on in these matters, but at the time my belief in their usefulness was not enthusiastically shared. Now and then, it is not to be denied, the fishermen, with a repugnance

[1] See *Twentieth Annual Report of the Fishery Board for Scotland*, Part III., p. 74

for the interviewer which they share with some in higher
stations of life, find a pleasure in wilfully misleading
official inquisitors, but, as one who mixes with them
as much, perhaps, as most unofficial landsmen, I do
not hesitate to describe them as generally obliging
and accurate when information is sought in the right
way.

CHAPTER II

PRODUCTION

Difference between Production of Fish and of other Foodstuffs—Fisheries contrasted with Agriculture and compared with Mining—Hard Life of the Fisherman—Adam Smith on Wages and Employments—Two Principles on which Fish are caught in Nets—Trawling—Statistics of Men and Boys Employed—Origin of Trawling in England—Smacks at Lowestoft, Ramsgate, and Brixham—Holdsworth on the Otter-trawl— The Trawl and its Beam—Steam-trawling—The Otter-trawl—Its Catching Power—Other Advantages—Curious Form of Trawl used in Lincolnshire—Mr. Kyle's new pattern of Trawl for Scientific Work—Hull and Brixham—Wages and Profit-sharing—Steam-ports and Smack-ports—Dogger Bank—Scarborough—Discovery of the Silver Pit—Hull —Grimsby—Ice—Fleets sent to Iceland—Brixham Smacks in the Bristol Channel—Trawling by Day and Night—The Trawler disliked by other Classes of Fishermen—Future of Trawling—The Drift-net — Principle on which it works—Neglect of British Anchovies—Vast Numbers of Herrings landed at Yarmouth—Steam-drifters—Manner of Using the Drift-net—Bait used by French Sardine-fishermen—Privileges accorded to Drifters—The Seine or Sean—Ground-seines in Estuaries—Construction and Use of the Seine—The Tucking-seine— Independence of Steam—Fish caught in the Ground-seine—The Trammel —Other kinds of Nets—Capture of Fish by Hook and Line—Cost of Bait for Long-lines—Difficulty of getting Bait at Plymouth and Milford—North Sea Cod-fishery—Floating Cod-chests—Hand-lining for Mackerel—Long-lining—Line-fishing for Soles—Complaints against Trawlers—Different patterns of Crab- and Lobster-pots—Baits and Method of Use—Two kinds of Shrimp—The Shrimp-trawl—Maryport —Shrimping with Horse and Cart—Oysters—Whelks—Cockles— Mussels—Boiling Lobsters and Crabs—Tainted Living Lobsters— Smoked and Cured Fish.

THE production of the fish that we eat is in many respects different from the production of our meat, bread, or vegetable foods, bearing a closer analogy to

those processes by which man extracts metals from the
earth. Both operations, mining and the fisheries, entail
a continual drain on the resources of nature, without
any corresponding effort to replace the stock. Since
the hatching experiments so far conducted by biological
establishments in Europe and America cannot be said
to affect the supply, it may be said that the fisherman
reaps without sowing. Nor can his methods be compared in any respect with those of the farmer. Centuries
of thought and failure have gone in the successful
breeding and selection of cows for milk and bullocks
for beef, while the fruits and vegetables that figure on
our tables are equally the result of the gardener's art
in editing the cruder products of nature. In so far as
both departments are concerned in the production of
food for man, the association of the Fisheries and
Agriculture under one Minister has much in its favour.
On the other hand, when we remember how important
a part efficient harbours must play in the prosperity of
our fisheries, the recent joint control of the two at the
Board of Trade was also not wholly illogical. Our
mining industry, with its inspectors and assistant
inspectors, is under the Home Office. In the Australian colonies there are Ministers of Mines. These
sometimes take charge of agriculture as well, but in
most colonies the two interests are departmentally dis
tinct. If we had a Minister of Mines, it might be
possible to give him control of the fisheries as well.
The two industries have, as already indicated, much in
common. An illustration of this analogy may be cited
in the prevailing apprehension of the exhaustion of the
plaice or sole. By this is meant, not that there will be
none of these fish left in the depleted sea, but that
over-fishing may tend to bring about a condition similar

to that of a mine that no longer pays for the working. It is evident that, with the mining machinery at present in use, hundreds of thousands of tons of gold must be left lying in the earth, because it lies too deep for extraction at a profit. Not even the employment of Chinese labour will affect this residue. So, with the valuable food fishes of our seas, the grounds near home, which were once productive, may no longer yield fish enough to pay for working over them with the trawl. Our trawlers are therefore compelled to fish further and further from home, until, at the present day, they operate over two thousand miles of latitude, bringing within the immense sphere of their operations coasts as far apart as those of Iceland in the north and Portugal to the south. So that, when we say that the plaice is exhausted in our bays, we do not mean that there are no plaice left, but merely that these are either so few or so small that it does not pay the owner or captain of the trawler to fish for them. Inshore waters, rightly regarded as exhausted, or fished out, from the point of view of the skipper of a steam-trawler, a costly vessel to buy and work, and therefore needing large returns, may still be profitable to the smaller sailing-smacks; and even when these no longer find it worth while to fish them, the small hooker may long continue to make a modest living.

The point which we have, at the outset of this chapter on production, to keep before us is that the fisherman, like the miner, takes all and replaces nothing. Unless compelled to do so by law, he is even reluctant either to leave certain bays lying fallow for a period, or to return to the sea such small fishes as are practically unmarketable. He is the most wasteful worker of a wasteful race. The Anglo-Saxon perpetually jeopardises his own welfare by over-production, and the fishing industry holds out greater temptations to over-produce than most. Shareholders in the big northern trawling syndicates are human and look for dividends. Their directors are in many cases enlightened men who have made a life-study of the problems of the sea, and of whom a number have even served their time on board of trawlers; but, although they know well the evils of over-trawling, they cannot use their knowledge in mollifying discontented half-yearly meetings. The captains and mates employed on their fleets are paid by results, and therefore they bring ashore as much fish as they can cram in their holds. The fisherman is, no doubt, a greedy creature, catching more than he can sell, and daily overloading the shops of London fish-mongers, the surplus being given away or sold at a nominal cost each evening. Yet he leads a dog's life, one that would ill suit those who live in luxury ashore and blame him for his lack of forethought and restraint. If Adam Smith, before writing so smoothly of the ' agreeableness or disagreeableness of the employment' as a factor in determining wages, had studied the fishing industry, he might have arrived at different conclusions. Fawcett and other economists have regarded the eight hours day as a fair maximum for those who toil in Cornish mines, but I know many labourers in Cornish bays who, with almost as much discomfort and with quite as much danger, work uncomplainingly for nearer eighteen. From the skipper to the ship's boy, they all carry their life in their hands; and that life, reckoned by its comfort, is worth very little. They get no sympathy, for the seaside-going public judges them by the longshore imitations, who profit by its credulity and whine for alms. Until the authorities at our watering-places treat these unredeemed loafers on the same basis as other mendicants, it will never be generally recognised that the real fishermen do not come in contact with the tourist, nor, if they did, would they ask for money. Theirs are the strenuous life and the mean reward. The fish which cost the greatest labour fetch the lowest price. It may take a dozen small trawl-fish to fetch the price of a single red mullet; it may take two hundred to equal the value of a salmon. Yet the salmon netsmen need never take their feet off the ground, while the red mullet is caught in shallow water and in a net which fishes while its owner lies abed.

In the present chapter an attempt will be made to describe the appearance and manner of working of the nets used in British seas. As this book is, however, intended for those who wish to form a general idea of how our fishing industry is conducted, and not for the technical reader, only the first principles of each are here given. The actual manufacture and curing of the nets are dealt with in more technical handbooks by Mr. Cunningham and other authorities, and have little interest for those to whom the present work is addressed.

Broadly speaking, one of two principles governs the working of every kind of net used for taking sea-fish. The net may either be small in the mesh and catch the fish, dead or alive, as in a sack, the principle of the trawl and seine; or it may have a large mesh which catches in the gills of the fish and strangles it, as the drift-net. The trammel, a fourth pattern of considerable importance, may be said to work on a compromise between the two. These principles must be differentiated in connection with two other alternative methods of fishing. The trawl and seine seek the fish, scooping them up against their will; the drift-net and trammel lie in wait for them, though, whereas the latter is absolutely stationary, the former does move through the water in order to meet the shoals half-way.

An attempt was made in the first chapter to group the fishes not on the basis of their biological affinities, but rather according to the method of their capture. This means considerable dovetailing of the naturalist's groups, for it classifies the herring and mackerel as fish of the drift-net; the plaice, skate, and cod as victims of the trawl; and the red mullet and sea-trout, which are captured side by side in the trammel. Some of our food fishes are taken by more than one method, the difference being generally a matter of season. Thus, at one time of the year, the mackerel and pilchard are taken in the drift-net; at another, in the seine. The red mullet, though mostly caught in trammels, is also found in the trawl when the latter moves fast enough over the right ground. Cod and haddock among round fish, as well as plaice and halibut among flat, are caught both in the trawl and on the hook. A lively controversy rages round which method provides the finer fish. On the one hand, it is argued that a fish must be in good condition when feeding, and this gives the preference to fish caught by the line-fisherman. The trawl, says the latter, sweeps up every fish, sound or unsound. The trawl-fisherman, on the other hand, contends that if the fish is hungry enough to take a baited hook, it is also often lean, and that the fish taken in his net are too well fed to take baits. On the whole, the former proposition, in favour of hook-fish, involves the sounder logic, but it is doubtful whether both are not open to almost equally serious objections.

1. **The Trawl** is by far the most important and destructive net yet devised. So far as the United

Kingdom is concerned, the trawl is in general use only in England and Wales. At a few growing Scotch fishing ports, such as Aberdeen and Fraserburgh, the trawl has come to stay, but in Scotland and Ireland the proportion of men and lads employed on herring-drifters and hookers is far in excess of those engaged in trawling. Some comparison of the figures may be gathered from the statistics of 1901, which showed that the hands employed on trawlers of one kind or another (including shrimp-trawlers) in England and Wales more than equalled those engaged in all other kinds of fishing. Without counting the shrimp-trawlers, the actual figures were 15,690 on trawlers, against 15,893 for all other kinds of fishing, and the hands employed in shrimp-trawling would give a handsome balance in favour of the former. In Scotland and Ireland, on the other hand, for the same year, less than 20,000 hands were paid aboard trawlers, as against nearly 50,000 in other fishing vessels.

The origin of English trawling is variously ascribed to Barking and Brixham, and, whatever historic importance is due to the Thames port, it is certain that the glory remains with the men of Devon, the most venturesome, roving pioneers anywhere known in the fishing industry. There are two patterns of trawl-net—the older beam-trawl, used only on board sailing smacks belonging to a few ports like Lowestoft, Ramsgate, and Brixham, and the more modern otter-trawl, used on the steam-vessels of Hull, Grimsby, Fleetwood, and all the largest centres of the industry. Comparison between the efficiency of the two rival forms of trawl is not easy. The otter-trawl, which was invented by Mr. Hearder, of Plymouth, and improved upon by Mr. Scott, of Granton (see diagrams, p. 43), and others, has undoubted advantages over the other, which will presently be appreciated when both have been described. Yet, when Holdsworth, writing thirty years ago, refused to take the otter-trawl seriously, except for amateurs fishing from yachts, he recognised its uselessness on sailing vessels; and it must be remembered that he could not foresee the coming developments in steam-fishing. On the sailing smack the otter-trawl is still far less efficient than the beam-trawl, for it is found very difficult to maintain the regularity of speed and strain necessary to its proper working. It is, moreover, unsuited to much rough ground, which

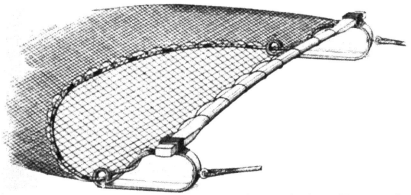

[*From a plate lent by Mr. W. Hearder*

BEAM-TRAWL.

the beam-trawl fishes with ease, and it is altogether less efficient than the older pattern in the capture of the smaller flat fish. At the same time, it is by no means impossible to use the otter-trawl on sailing-boats.

(*a*) **The Beam-trawl.**—The beam-trawl is so called from the beam of beech, oak, or elm, from 30 to 45 feet long, employed to keep the mouth of the net open. In both trawls the net is practically the same, a triangular bag, which may be 80 feet long, and which is open at either end. It is made of well-tarred hemp twine, and is broadest at the mouth. The mesh of the net is about 4 inches square at the mouth, and only

1¼ inch at the "cod" or narrow end. The spread of the mouth, when open at its widest, would, in a large beam-trawl, be between 150 and 200 square feet. The beam is made fast to the upper edge of the net, and is kept clear of the ground with the aid of stirrup-shaped trawl-heads of iron, one at each end. A ground-rope is attached to the lower part of these trawl-heads, and also to the lower edge of the mouth of the net. This keeps the mouth wide. The net is towed over the ground by a very powerful warp, which consists of 150 fathoms, or more, of 6-inch rope, with a length of strong chain at either end. To this are made fast the bridle-ropes, also attached to the trawl-heads. (See diagram.) While the trawl is fishing, the cod-end [1] is tied up. When it is hauled on board, so that the great bag of fish hangs over the deck, the cod is untied and the contents fall out on the deck. It will be understood that different parts of the trawl do not all bear the same strain and brunt of the work. The 'belly' of the trawl bears the worst, and, although it is strengthened by pieces of old net known as 'rubbing pieces,' it has to be renewed three or four times during an average year's fishing. When it is remembered that a large trawl may weigh one or two tons, some idea may be formed of the heavy burden borne by the under part, the friction with the ups and downs of the sea-bed being enormous. The upper part lasts, without accident, a whole year. The weight of weed, stones, and other débris falls chiefly on the cod-end; and, when pressed upon by these, the soles find their way into the blind pockets in the wings.

In shooting the trawl, the boat sails full speed ahead. When there is only one trawl, it is hauled on the port

---

[1] 'Cod' is an old Anglo-Saxon word denoting a bag, or purse, and the term has no reference to the fish of that name.

side. On some parts of the coast the smacks carry two trawls, shooting the second on the starboard quarter as soon as that on the port has been hauled. Elsewhere, the second trawl is carried only as a reserve in case of breakage ; while a third plan is to carry a spare net only for use with the same beam. In other countries, local customs vary from ours. The Dutch of some ports, for example, use two trawls at once, one in front of the other. As a converse case, some of the Spaniards use two boats to each trawl, the mouth of the net being kept stretched open between them.

The cod-end is lowered first, and then the beam is let down very carefully, the trawl-heads lowermost, as in any other position the net would not work. The fore-bridle is slacked away, the whole beam lowered at once in the water, and as soon as more way is got on the vessel the trawl sinks in the right position for fishing. The trawl is towed with the tide, the tow-rope being so adjusted that the net may drag lightly over the ground. The duration of each haul depends on the nature of the bottom and on a variety of other conditions. An average haul over good ground might last six hours. In order to understand the manner in which the trawl catches flat fish, it must be borne in mind that these fish lie on, or in, the sand, and, when disturbed, rise a foot or so in the water. The ground-rope of the trawl then sweeps under them, and they pass over it and so into the net. A stiff breeze is required for towing, for the pressure of water in the net takes as much as five or six knots (nautical miles, *i.e.* each equivalent to 1·15 mile) off the way of the boat, and unless the trawl moves faster than the tide, the mouth of the net is not properly extended. An average pace for the trawl itself is about two knots an hour, and, as already stated, the duration of the haul on good ground would be about six hours. Three hours on hard ground, or five on mud, would also be average hauls; but there are many considerations of a technical and local nature which determine this. The depth at which it is best to trawl is also influenced by the strength of the tides and by the whereabouts, as far as is known, of the fish. Trawling for commercial (as distinguished from dredging for scientific) purposes is not carried on at a much greater depth than fifty fathoms; and the best, indeed, may be said to lie within the thirty-fathom limit.

When the time comes to haul the trawl, the warp is slacked, and the vessel consequently comes round head to wind. The warp is then got on the winch. Contrary to what might be expected by those who have not witnessed the operation, this is considerably easier in that unpleasant condition of the sea known as 'loppy,' for every lurch of the vessel then sends several fathoms of the rope slack, and these can be wound on the winch quickly and easily. As soon as possible the beam is swung alongside, and the back-end and fore-end are successively hoisted and made fast. The final proceeding is to gather in the net, slip the cod-line, and let the mass of fish and weed fall out on the trawler's deck.

The beam-trawl, worked in the manner described, survives at Lowestoft, Ramsgate, and Brixham. These ports, as is elsewhere explained, are peculiarly suited to the more primitive method for several reasons, the chief being their remoteness from the coalfields and consequent disadvantage in respect of steam-fishing, as well as their proximity to home grounds, easily reached without the aid of steam, and yielding returns which, though not perhaps large enough to compensate the greater expense of steam-craft, represent a sufficient margin of profit to pay the smack-owner. The Brixham smacks of the larger class are, I suppose, the finest sailing vessels anywhere engaged in fishing. Ketch-rigged, they can weather anything in the Channel, and they have before now led the way to new grounds in the North Sea on the one side, and in the Bristol

A TYPICAL SMACK.

Channel on the other. Such a smack would measure rather over 70 feet between the perpendiculars, and the tonnage would be about fifty-two. The beam of the trawl carried on a vessel of this class would be about 47 feet in length. The smaller Brixham smacks, which are cutter-rigged, and known as 'Mumble-bees,' are not more than half the size; and the beam of their trawl would be well under 40 feet.

(b) **The Otter-trawl.**—The introduction of steam into trawling vessels has revolutionised an industry that, until the last quarter of the nineteenth century, showed a tendency to run in a groove. The installation of steam was no sudden innovation. Partial dependence on its assistance paved the way for its complete adoption. Smacks becalmed off Plymouth and other sailing ports still avail themselves of an occasional tow when the skippers are anxious to catch the early market. Elsewhere the fishing-boats stay out on the grounds and send their catch to market by fast steam-carriers. Residents of Sunderland can remember a yet further stage of advance, in which the trawler, her nets down,

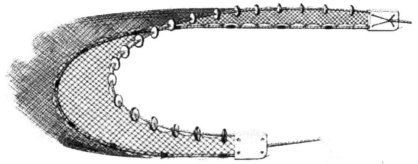

[*From a plate lent by Mr. W. Hearder.*

OTTER-TRAWL.

was towed slowly over the fishing-grounds on days when there was not sufficient wind to take her along. Then, no doubt, it occurred to the enterprising owner of some tug-boat to fit out a trawl, so that she might catch fish for market when towing was slack. In fact, it is on record that when the Cornwall Sea Fisheries Committee closed the inshore bays, so that fishing near home was no longer a paying concern, many of the Falmouth paddle-boats, which had been fitted out for trawling, returned to their old occupation of towing. Even the sailing trawlers of Ramsgate and elsewhere use steam-winches to haul the net, and the owners are compensated for this labour-saving appliance with an extra share of the money earned by the catch.

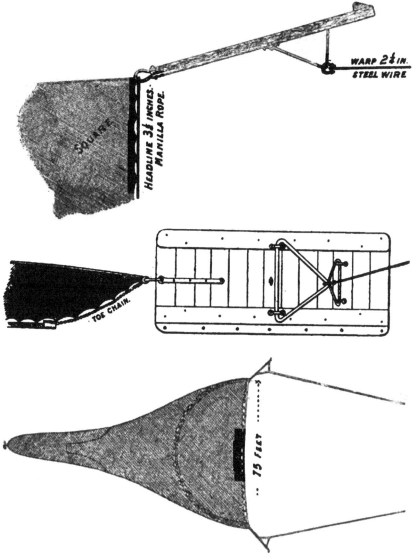

[*Reproduced by permission of the Marine Biological Association.*

THE OTTER-TRAWL, AS IMPROVED BY MR. SCOTT, OF GRANTON.

At first, steam-trawlers were propelled by paddles, and a few obsolete paddle-trawlers may still be seen in Scarborough harbour and at one or two other ports;

but they are relics only of a bygone age, entirely superseded by the modern screw-trawler, an iron vessel of
perhaps 120 feet long, carrying not less than sixty tons
of coal and five tons of ice, and costing, with all nets
and gear, as much as £5,000.

One of the most important changes brought about
by the advent of the steam-trawler has been the
alteration in the pattern of the trawl itself. The beam
is dispensed with, the mouth of the net being kept open

STEAM-TRAWLERS.

by the kite-like action of two heavy 'otter' boards of
deal or elm, each about 10 feet long, 5 feet broad, and
3 or 4 inches thick. These are heavily sheathed with
iron and, when drawn quickly through the water, they
fly apart and effectually stretch the mouth of the net.
A new pattern of otter-board has lately been designed
and tried, but with what success I have not been able to
ascertain. In it, the heavy wooden boards are dispensed
with. The relative merits of the rival patterns have

already been alluded to. It is obvious that the otter-trawl has the advantage of packing within smaller compass, since there is no unwieldy beam, while the risk of the latter breaking under sudden strain is also eliminated. It is also found practicable to keep the head-line further off the ground, thereby giving greater efficiency in catching round fish; and it is said to be possible to have the mouth of the net nearly twice as wide, in fact to a spread of 300 or 400 square feet. The coming of the otter-trawl, which must be regarded as chiefly of advantage in steam-fishing, since it can be worked under sail only with some difficulty and uncertainty, has been rapid during late years, for even as recently as ten years ago it was regarded as a novelty in Scotch waters.

A peculiar form of trawl, chiefly used for shrimps on the Lincolnshire coast of the Wash, may here be mentioned in passing. It is sometimes drawn in shallow water by a horse. There are neither beam nor otter-boards, the mouth of the net being kept open by the action of two sticks which, like the otter-boards, fly apart when the net is in motion. The trawl is essentially, in its existing forms, a ground net. This imposes considerable limitations on its catching power, particularly for scientific purposes; and Mr. H. M. Kyle has designed a new pattern, modelled on the ordinary umbrella, for use in mid-water as well, the mouth of which may have a spread of 850 square feet.[1]

The wonderful development of steam-trawling at the Humber ports and elsewhere, has led up to conditions radically different from those which survive at peaceful old trawling centres like Brixham. Neither

[1] See *Publications de Circonstance* (Committee of International Explorations), No. 6.

covets the state of the other. Hull's fishing prosperity was founded by men from the West country, and on sentimental grounds alone the present leaders of the industry in both Hull and Grimsby are friendly to Brixham; but their business instincts would chafe at the picturesque stagnation of the sleepy Devon port. The sailing ports, on their side, regard with suspicion the over-capitalising of the more progressive centres of the industry, and rejoice in their own slow and sure prosperity. The element of personal ownership, the family associations and close relations of the older sailing centres, are obscured in the busy North-country centres, where powerful fishing syndicates control the industry and seek returns on their capital on the most distant fishing-grounds ever visited by British trawlers.

Apart from an occasional towing fee, the profits of a steam-trawler are all in the catch, while in the sailing-trawler there is not even the variety of a towing fee. The most considerable expenses of the steamer are in coal and ice, though an allowance is made in the cost of each voyage for stores, as well as for repairs to both hull and machinery. The bunkers are filled with coal on the maiden voyage and subsequently replenished as required, but on no single voyage, I think, does the vessel use her full complement of coal. Other expenses go towards insurances and a sinking fund for depreciation. Of the wear and tear of the trawl-net something has already been said. Nor does the vessel herself last for ever. Ten or fifteen years may be regarded as a good life; twenty years as rare.

It will now be necessary to give some idea of the wages or shares on which our fishermen work. The statement was made at the beginning of this chapter that they work harder than many of their more pitied fellows on land; and it will now be shown, without any further comparisons, that their wage is approximately as low as is compatible with the nature of their dangerous calling. The profit-sharing system, advocated by Schultz-Delitzsch and other sound economists, obtains in the Cornish drift-net fisheries and, in fact, on many parts of the South coast. In the steam-trawling of the Humber ports, however, the owners now seem to prefer paying as many as possible by regular wage. It was an attempt on the part of the owners to pay their men a lower fixed wage and a higher royalty on results which brought about the Grimsby strike, of which a brief account is given in Chapter VI. Making some allowance for local variation of custom, it is usual to pay the skipper and mate of a trawler wholly by results, while the engineers and deck-hands receive fixed wages, independent of the success or otherwise of the voyage, though at Hull all the deck-hands receive poundage in addition to fixed wages. When the share system is adopted, all expenses are first paid, and these include coal, ice, commissions, harbour dues, fresh water, porterage of the fish from the landing-stage to the market, and some other charges. The remainder would then be divided in a certain number of shares, perhaps fourteen, of which the master (indifferently known as captain or skipper) may receive one and three-eighths, the mate one, and the owners the rest. Out of this they have to pay three engineers (including a fireman), three deck-hands and a cook. The first engineer receives about £2 5s. a week, the second engineer £1 15s., and the trimmer 16s. The deck-hands receive a weekly wage and a poundage, and the owners find food for all hands except the master and mate, both of whom pay their share.

Example is better than theory; and the subjoined tables, which apply respectively to a steam-trawler and steam-drifter, and for which I am severally indebted to the late Mr. W. H. Storey, of North Shields, and a gentleman at Great Yarmouth, will illustrate the system of payment in practice.

PRINCE LINE STEAM-TRAWLERS

WAGEMEN'S ACCOUNT ' ....

Engineer
    8s. per day = £ ....
Less Advances—Shields...............
                Aberdeen ....
                Grimsby ....

Deck Hand
    5s. per day = £ ....
Less Advances—Shields...............
                Aberdeen ....
                Grimsby ....

Second Engineer
    6s. 6d. per day = £ ....
Less Advances—Shields...............
                Aberdeen ....
                Grimsby ....

Deck Hand
    5s. per day = £ ....
Less Advances—Shields...............
                Aberdeen ....
                Grimsby ....

Trimmer and Deck Assistant
    5s. per day = £ ....
Less Advances—Shields...............
                Aberdeen ....
                Grimsby ....

Cook
    3s. 4d. per day = £ ....
Less Advances—Shields...............
                Aberdeen ....
                Grimsby ....

BALANCES

                £   s.   d.

....
....
....
....
....
....

Total   ...   . £

Signed ....

Wages paid up to   Port   ....

Steam =   Date ..   .. , 190 .

SHAREMEN'S ACCOUNT ....

190   £   s.   d.

.... Gross Sale at ....

.... ,,   ,, ...

.... ,,   ,, ...

.... ,,   ,, ...

.... ,,   ,, ...

Less Expenses :   £   s.   d.

Commission, Dues, Dock Passes, Boxes, Towage,
    Labour, Watching, Water, &c.......................

Ice—Shields................ ; Aberdeen................ ;
    Grimsby ....

Coals—Shields............. ; Aberdeen................ ;
    Grimsby ....

Stores consumed............ ; River dues............

Cook..................... ; Trip money.................

Dan gear replaced .... ; Large baskets.........

Extra deck hand's wages...... ; Coal checker......

Less Advances :   14 £

3rd Hand—Shields .... }   3rd Hand   1   £

         Aberdeen .... } £   Mate   . 1¼

         Grimsby .... }   Master   1⅛

2nd Hand—Shields ....

         Aberdeen .... } £   Total   3½ £

         Grimsby .... }

Master   —Shields ....

         Aberdeen .... } £

         Grimsby .... }

(Sharemen's balances : 3rd Hand, £......; Mate, £......;
    Master, £......).. £

      Add Trip Money for Wagemen (if any) ....

                       Balance .... £

Coals left on   Signed ... .

Ice left on –   Port......   ..   . .

Steam –   Date ...   . 190 .

'LONGMAN,' SCOTCH VOYAGE, 1903.

VOYAGE COMMENCED, MAY 10 } 92 days.
VOYAGE ENDED, AUGUST 10 }

Expenses.

                              £   s.   d.

Commission *   .   .   .   .   .

Harbour dues   .   .   .   .   .   .

Landing and labour   .   .   .   .   .

Coals (say 95 tons)   .   .   .   .   .

Stores   .   .   .   .   .   .

Provisions .   .   .   .   .   .

Cartage   .   .   .   .   .   .

Tanning   .   .   .   .   .   .

Spoilt nets .   .   .   .   .   .

Sundries—allowance, labour, &c.   .

          * Salesman's 5 per cent. on gross sales.

                                           E

The expenses of the herring voyage, under the above heads, are then deducted from the gross earnings, and the balance is divided into sixteen shares, of which the owners take nine and the crew seven. This is allotted as follows :—

Crew.	Share.
J. Smith, *Master*	1⅞
A. Robinson, *Second hand*	1⅝
B. Jones, *Engineer*	1¼
A. Black, *Stoker*	⅞
J. Wood, *Hawseman*	⅞
A. Cotton, *Net-stower*	⅞
A. Gunnel, *Waleman*	⅞
A. Brown, *Younker*	⅞
J. Bull, *Younker*	⅞
J. Cook, *Boy*	⅞
Engine	1
Total	85 Doles †

† *I.e.* eighths.

At the end of the voyage each man is paid the balance due to him after deducting any advances, or ' allotments,' previously made by the skipper or owners, and also a small agreed contribution (about a shilling) to the Royal Provident Fund.

Three methods are in vogue : payment entirely by wage ; payment entirely by share ; and payment on a combined basis of either a fixed wage and poundage for all hands, or a fixed wage for the crew and poundage for the master and mate. Local custom sanctions various modifications of each and all of these arrangements. Sometimes, for instance, trawlers find themselves becalmed out at sea and are unable to continue trawling. Instead of wasting precious time, they then cut up some of the rougher fish for bait and put out hand-lines for ling, or cod, or pollack. The fish thus caught is shared on a different system from that regulating the partition of the trawl-fish ; and this, seeing that so much more individual skill and labour go to the capture of fish on a hand-line, is obviously an equitable arrangement. Where, for example, the trawl-fish makes 7 shares, of which the owner and boat take 3, the line-fish makes only 5, of which the owner gets but $1\frac{1}{2}$. On the larger drift-boats the herring, mackerel, or pilchard sometimes makes 11 shares, of which the owner takes $5\frac{1}{4}$, the master $1\frac{1}{4}$, the men 1 each, and the boy $\frac{1}{2}$. On hookers it is usual for the fish to make $5\frac{1}{2}$ shares, of which the owner and master take $1\frac{1}{4}$.each and the men 1 each.

It is perhaps unnecessary to offer any lengthy criticism of these various methods. In theory the ideal arrangement is for the workmen to supply all the capital and to take all the profits. The Cornish drift-net fishery furnishes an example of harmonious working on this basis, for the men who form the crew bring their own nets, and where some contribute more nets than others the profits are divided accordingly. In the mackerel season, for instance, a large Cornish drifter would carry seven men and a boy, and the catch makes 17 shares, the boat and gear taking 2, the nets $7\frac{1}{2}$, the men 1 each, and the boy $\frac{1}{2}$. When, as is often the case, the master is also the owner, he, of course, takes his ' body ' share as a working member of the ship's company, in addition to the 2 earned by his boat. He is thus labourer and capitalist in one. It is only, however, in certain ports of Cornwall that this ideal system of co-operation obtains. In others, the expenses of the season are first cleared, after which the owner and boat together take one-half of the net profits, the men dividing the rest. If the owner stays ashore, instead of working, he pays a master 5s. a week over and above his share. The system by which the men are paid a fixed wage, while the master and mate get a poundage on results, is also equitable, since it is in great measure on the judgment of the two officers that the success of the catch depends. In theory, the division of profits between employer and employed is an ideal basis. Where, however, the element of risk enters into the transaction, the employee may be worse off in the long run with a share of the profits than if, good times and bad alike, he received a fixed wage. As fishing is the most uncertain of industries, a combination between the fixed wage and the poundage, such as is contrived at Grimsby, is preferable. The men are at any rate sure of a living wage, and with hard work and good luck they may make a considerable sum besides.

The smack is gradually disappearing before the more modern steam-trawler, although it survives at the three ports already named, besides fishing side by side with the steam-trawler at others, like Plymouth and Fleetwood. The steam-trawlers in our ports are probably a thousand more, and the smacks a thousand less, than they were ten years ago. Tradition and sentiment may have something to do with the persistence of the smack at these ports, though expediency has more. Hull and Grimsby on the east, or Fleetwood on the west, lie within easy distance of the North-country coal-fields, whereas at the ports of Suffolk, Kent, or Devon, coal is more expensive. Lowestoft, Ramsgate, and Brixham, moreover, have at their doors fishing grounds which yield sufficient profit to repay the small investor in smacks, whereas the steam-fishing syndicates have to send fleets forth to Iceland and the Faroes in order to pay a dividend on their immense outlay. The Brown Ridges and Leman Banks are within easy reach of Lowestoft. Ramsgate still makes good catches just beyond the Goodwin Sands. Even the smacks at Brixham, though they fare forth to the Bristol Channel during half the year or more, can catch a very fine quality of soles and other prime fish on the Spion Kop ground and elsewhere between Berry Head and Portland.

The dual claim of Barking and Brixham to the honour of having originated trawling, and the preponderance of evidence in favour of the more western port, have already received notice. What is at any rate known is that the Brixham men took this method of fishing early in the nineteenth century eastward to Rye; then, still working round the coast, to Harwich, Lowestoft, and Yarmouth. And then came the accident which led to the foundation of the trawling industry in the Humber. Between 1830 and 1840 the Brixham boats were working the Dogger Bank, and during the summer season they were in the habit of running with fresh fish into Scarborough and there realising good prices from the visitors. One day a sudden gale sprang up, as is not unusual on the north-east coast, and dispersed the fleet, one being separated widely from the rest. When the master of this vessel hauled his damaged trawl, it was to find it, even in the upper part, so thickly 'meshed' with fine soles that these fish were obviously in quantity on that spot. To find the ground again he had to enlist the aid of navigators from the Tyne, and the result of a haul exceeded his fondest expectations. The ground was named the Silver Pit and has since been famous. The secret could not be kept, and the Silver Pit was soon frequented by trawlers from all parts. Scarborough, though a good market, particularly in the holiday season, lacked resources in stores and repairs, and this defect led to the migration of the trawling industry to the Humber.

Hull was its first home, and then some of it crossed the water to Grimsby, not only relieving the pressure on the accommodation of the senior port, but also moving nearer to the open sea and being more independent of the Humber fogs. To-day, the two ports flourish in friendly rivalry. There is trade enough for both, and the somewhat different conditions under which the industry is conducted at each will be explained in a subsequent chapter.

With the advent of steam came the introduction of ice, and between them, not long before 1860, they revolutionised the fishing industry. The modern fishing of the remote Iceland grounds is not fifteen years old, for it was in 1891 that the first Grimsby steam-trawler visited Iceland, making a good catch of plaice and haddock on the Ingol's Hoof ground. The latest discovery of new grounds takes us to the Bristol Channel; and again the Brixham men were the pioneers, finding new fields for their energy in the closing decade of the nineteenth century.

The trawl catches a greater variety of fish than any other form of net. Turbot, brill, plaice, soles, lemon-soles, dabs, witches, megrims, solenettes, flounders, and halibut; skate, cod, ling, hake, and whiting; gurnards, conger eels, red mullet, and other kinds are all the more or less regular harvest of the trawl. Even mackerel and herrings, commonly the business of the drift-net, are taken in the trawl under certain conditions of season and speed, though not as a rule in sufficient quantity for the market. If the afore-mentioned mid-water trawl, devised by Mr. Harry Kyle for scientific purposes, were adapted to commercial fishing, the mackerel and herring could doubtless be caught in remunerative quantity, though such an extension of its efficiency would bring the trawler into more heated rivalry with the drifter than ever. Trawling is pursued both day and night, a preference for either being determined by local conditions. The advantage of one or the other, according to circumstances, may be illustrated by four typical cases. Night is preferred by the trawlers from both Poole and Brixham; by the former, because the water in Bournemouth Bay is so shallow that the trawl would be seen by the fish in daylight; by the latter, because more soles are caught in the dark, and soles fetch the best price in the Brixham market. On the other hand, day fishing is given the preference at Plymouth, and on parts of the Cornish coast it is compulsory. The Plymouth trawlers fish by day, because that port has a special market for rough fish, which is mostly caught by day. In Cornwall the drift-nets for pilchards and mackerel take precedence of trawling, and as they can fish only by night, the trawler is by local law compelled to confine his operations to the daytime.

It is not difficult to understand why so successful a fisherman as the trawler should be disliked by the other classes of fishermen who work the same grounds and compete in the same markets, while the steam-trawler, in proportion to its greater success, is even more hated than the smack. The various enactments, either actually in force or under discussion, for his repression are considered in a later chapter, but the main charges brought against him may here be summarised.

These are four in number :—

1. That he destroys undersized flat fish;
2. That he disturbs the spawning-grounds;
3. That he fouls the sea-bed with débris;
4. That he damages other classes of fishing-gear.

1. That the trawl-net does destroy quantities of undersized and immature (for the distinction between these terms see Chapter I.), flat fish is beyond doubt. Such destructiveness is inseparable from its structure and from the fact that it fishes on the bottom. The small flat fish, alarmed by the sudden approach of the looming net, rise just above the sand and are then scooped into the bag. The weak part of the prevalent outcry is that it overlooks the small shrimp-trawler, who can also be extremely mischievous in this respect. The scientific staff of the Lancashire Sea Fisheries Committee has published some interesting evidence on the subject. It appears that one shrimp-trawl, working in the Mersey, took 10,000 baby plaice in a single haul, while another in the same district brought up over 250 small soles, 900 tiny dabs, nearly 300 unmarketable whiting, 18 little skate, and some hundreds of useless plaice. When to this is added the fact that all this waste fish was accompanied by only twenty quarts of shrimps, some estimate may be formed of the terrible destruction for which such agency is responsible.

2. The accusation of disturbing the spawning grounds holds true in one case only, for we have long known that, with the single exception of the herring, all our food fishes deposit floating eggs, which disperse in the upper strata of the water and are consequently out of reach of the trawl. Herring spawn, then, is alone disturbed by the trawler, and that only at a single season, in which he follows the haddock that are feeding on the spawn.

3. As to fouling the bed of the sea with débris, it is clear that, before dumping such rubbish down in one spot, he must have taken it up from another. On many parts of the coast, and notably in Devon, the line-

fishermen regard the way in which he ploughs up the submarine fallows as a direct benefit to the fishing grounds.

4. That the trawler damages other classes of nets, as well as lines, is undeniable. I have heard of cases near the Start, in which trawlers have trespassed within the territorial limit and carried away lobster-pots. At the same time, the lobster-pots and trammels themselves are not above blame in this respect, for they lie hidden in the path of the drift-nets, with no tell-tale corks to betray their whereabouts when the tide runs strong.

, A French committee recently appointed to consider the relations between the steam-trawler and other classes of fishing craft, declined to impose the suggested tax of 10 francs per ton with a view to handicapping steam trawling in respect of other methods. The committee found four objections to the proposed tax: that the steam-trawlers did not compete with the smacks on the same grounds; that they caught a different class of fish; that, fishing in deeper water, they did less injury to the small fish than the smaller nets inshore; and that they brought in so much fish that the market price was kept down, to the benefit of the consumer.

Thirty years ago Holdsworth doubted any serious development of steam-fishing and any general introduction, for commercial purposes, of the otter-trawl. Yet trawling has developed with the aid of steam more during the thirty years since Holdsworth wrote than during twice the period preceding, and it is evident that the end is not reached. Future advance may be rather in the direction of discovering new grounds than in the introduction of further mechanical improvements in the gear, though even in this department new experiments are continually tried. The relative importance of the ports also varies from time to time, as new

centres attract to themselves the bulk of the trade,
while older fishing towns, with a great history behind
them, fall into decay.   This is the inevitable result of
opening up new grounds.   The history of Great Yarmouth and Milford during the past ten years illustrates
these changes.   In Holdsworth's time the Welsh port,
now the most prosperous fishing centre on the west side
of the island, was not seriously regarded as a fishing
port at all.   Yarmouth, on the other hand, had a
trawling fleet that was in its day the envy of Lowestoft
and other neighbouring ports, and that fleet came under
the hammer in 1903 without finding a bidder.   Yet
Yarmouth has wisely diverted its energies to the drift-
fishing, and thereby remains one of the first herring
ports in the kingdom.   The possibilities of opening up
new trawling grounds are very wide.   As an inlet of
the Atlantic, the Bristol Channel has great resources,
but it is not inexhaustible.   There is apparently no
limit to modern trawling enterprise.   During the closing
weeks of 1903 attempts were made by both England
and Sweden to establish a fishery in South African
waters, and French trawlers also visited the coast of
Senegal.

2. The principle of the **drift-net** has already been
briefly indicated.   It is, with some modifications, what
Americans call a 'gill-net.'   A hanging wall of large-
meshed net drifts at night across the path of the
shoals.   The herring, mackerel, sprat, or pilchard strike
against it, and, in endeavouring to force their way
through, are caught by the gills and suffocated.   On the
Irish coast hake are caught in drift-nets, and cod are
taken in the same manner on the banks of Newfoundland.   Whatever may be said of the fish taken from the
trawl, every single fish caught in the drift-net is killed

in the act, and to this fact may perhaps be traced the saying, 'Dead as a herring.' Four fishes only (if we except hake and such vermin as sharks, which find their way into the nets in pursuit of the shoals) are taken on the English coast in the drift-net, which has the drawback of taking fish of only one size. This is why the anchovies in our seas are not caught in the drift-nets, and this also is why the fishermen have to carry a separate ' fleet ' of nets for mackerel, herring, or pilchard. It may be that if our fishermen used a smaller mesh they would catch the younger pilchards of the size so successfully prepared by the French as sardines. The neglect of the anchovy is a regrettable waste, which has exercised the attention of many biologists attached to the Marine Biological Association in the Plymouth Laboratory, but the results of their investigations do not appear to have given any stimulus to the enterprise of our fisherfolk. In these days of preferential tariff war it seems strange that we should continue to buy our anchovies from Gorgona and other ports in the Mediterranean, when the fish has been caught, along with sprats, at places so far apart on our coast as Southport, Mevagissey, Torquay, Dover, the Wash, and the Moray Firth. Yet, though anchovies are in all probability plentiful in our seas, there is no established fishery for them between the Mediterranean and the Zuyder Zee.

The drift-net varies somewhat on different parts of the coast. Those used in Scotland are of fine cotton, the reason for this being that the Scotch coast is rocky and the water clear, and finer nets are therefore required than in the more muddy water of the Norfolk coast. The finer Scotch nets, when tried by Yarmouth boats in their own waters, gave indifferent results. Some idea may be formed of the prodigious captures of herrings in that part of the country from the fact that some 600,000,000 herrings have been landed at Yarmouth in a single year. Each boat carries for the drift-fishing a 'fleet' of nets, and this may consist of any number between twelve and a hundred, according to local custom and the individual length of the nets. In the large centres, like Mevagissey, on the south-west coast, the measurements and number of the nets are, with some variation, approximately as follows :— .

Net to Catch	Length (in fathoms)	Depth (in fathoms)	Mesh (in inches)	No. of Nets in a 'Fleet'
Pilchard . .	40–60	4	$\frac{9}{10}$	16
Mackerel . .	20–30	$2\frac{1}{4}$	$1\frac{3}{4}$	80
Herring . .	40–60	$4\frac{1}{4}$	1	16–20

At Yarmouth, however, the average 'fleet' would number 160.

The upper edge of the drift-net is kept in position by a line of corks; the lower edge is weighed down in some cases with a foot-rope, in others with a roll of old net laced on the lower edge, while sometimes the lower edge of the net hangs free of any such encumbrance. Each boat shoots its fleet of nets and then drifts at the end of them and to leeward. The mast is stepped; and the lugger is either blown along by the wind or driven by the tide, whichever is the stronger, till the nets stretch tight. When fishing for mackerel, the upper edge of the net drifts close to the surface of the water; in the pilchard or herring fishery, on the other hand, the upper edge lies several fathoms below the surface. The nets are exposed to entanglement with sunken lobster-pots and trammels below, and to the keels of passing steamers above. Against the damage done by the former there is neither remedy nor redress. As a precautionary measure against passing vessels, however, the nets are provided with a footrope, too far below the surface to be caught in any passing keel, by which the damaged nets can be hauled on board. Bad weather does not, as a rule, affect the nets when fishing, but an eddy or stream of tide is apt to tear them in shallow water, a casualty above all likely to happen in August, when the pilchards are for the most part caught at a depth of only eight or nine fathoms. The nets have to be tied close up, so as to hang just below the surface, and a sudden gust of wind will sometimes do great damage. Earlier in the season the risk from this source is much less, for the pilchards then lie out in the deeper water, the net hanging seven fathoms down, and the coble-strap four, well out of harm's way. The foregoing particulars apply chiefly to the Cornish fishery, and not to those of the East Coast and Scotland, which are conducted on a larger scale.

Unlike the trawler, the drifter can fish on any kind of ground, and his harvest is among the most restless fishes in our seas. At the same time, the herrings are generally caught on identically the same ground at each season of the year. He may either endeavour to ascertain the whereabouts of the shoals from the colour of the water or from the movements of the gulls and cormorants, or he may shoot his nets on chance. More often, perhaps, he fishes 'blind,' guided each evening in his choice by the direction of the wind and by the state of the tide. On dark, still August nights in Cornwall, I have known the men on the pilchard-drivers stamp heavily with their sea-boots on deck, which has the effect of frightening any pilchards that have been drifting motionless near the boat, and causing them to dart about in the phosphorescent water. I never knew this manœuvre lead to a great catch, though in winter it certainly does so, as enormous catches of from 50,000 to 100,000 have been made in this way. Sailing-drifters are put out of action by either dead calm or heavy weather, and for this reason steam has likewise invaded the drift-net fishing, and steam-drifters are as familiar to-day as steam-trawlers. Many of the Scotch herring

A STEAM-DRIFTER, GREAT YARMOUTH.

boats were helpless in the still, misty weather which was so prevalent in the summer of 1903, while the Galway fleet, on the other hand, failed from scarcity of fish. The Scotch boats, however, which fished off Scarborough during September, landed more herrings than they had done for years, and the Douglas herring season of 1903 was also up to the average.

A first-class steam-drifter, as built to-day at Yarmouth, would cost, all found, from £2,300 to £3,300, and would measure 74 feet over all. For some years the tendency was to construct iron vessels, but Yarmouth owners give the preference to wood as a material, for they find that it throws less strain on the fragile nets than the heavier iron. In the 'Fish Trades Gazette,' (May 14, 1904) some account was given of the trial of a new and comparatively inexpensive form of steam-drifter. The experiment was made in the Moray Firth, on the Banffshire coast, and was apparently successful. The new model was constructed on sailing-boat lines, but with a rounded stem and propeller.

Steam was introduced in drifting in the same way as in trawling. It is sometimes insisted, by way of contrasting the two, that steam power helps the drifter only in moving backwards and forwards between the fishing-grounds and the market, whereas the trawler actually catches the fish with its aid. This, though accurate in the main, needs one qualification. Sometimes the drifter moves too quickly through the water, so that the nets are debarred from being properly shot. On sailing drifters this fault is remedied in a rough and ready way by throwing overboard a baulk of wood, which acts as a brake and takes a certain amount of way off the vessel while the nets are being shot, and in some cases a rude raft of timber is constructed as a breakwater or to keep the boat's head to sea in heavy gales of wind. On steam-drifters, however, a few turns of the propeller correct the rate at which the boat and nets move, so that the latter act as efficiently as possible.

The advantages of steam in drifting, as in trawling, are mainly a question of the proportion of profits to outlay. So long as fish are plentiful and lie too far from home to be reached conveniently in sailing-boats, a steam-drifter with all the latest improvements may be a sound investment, since, under these conditions, it commands a monopoly of the local market. When, however, the fish are so scarce that the entire season's catch cannot compensate the owners of so costly a craft, or when they lie so close to port that the sailing fleet is on an equal footing with the steamers, then, in these circumstances, the owner of one or two luggers may realise a better return on his modest investment than the shareholders in the steam syndicates.

Our drift-net fishermen do not use any bait to attract the shoals of fish into the nets. The pilchards enter the bays in Cornwall to feed on the weed-spores, copepoda, or entomostraca, and the fleet is guided to the shoals by the oily appearance of the water, or by the calls of the seafowl. The sardine fishermen of Nantes, Bordeaux, and Belle Isle, whose sufferings enlisted widespread sympathy a couple of years ago, use a strong-smelling bait known as *rogue* or *roque* and consisting of dried offal and cod's roe. This they import in large quantities from other countries, obtaining it from both Norway and Newfoundland, and they cast it on the waters, shooting their nets as soon as the fish have gathered to the feast. Seeing how difficult the shoals are to find in some seasons, it is surprising that this aid to fishing should not have crossed the Channel. Our fishermen are, however, men of conservative instincts, regarding any innovation with suspicion. Reference has been made to the manner in which the drift-nets suffer from hidden trammels and lobster-pots. The drifters themselves are also offenders in this respect. A drifter sometimes bears down on the small hookers, sweeping his nets right across the lines, so that, unless promptly hauled, these are torn away. Even in Cornwall they do not of right take the same precedence as the seine-nets, yet, as the more ancient method, they are privileged in those waters, and all trawlers give way to the drifter by day, in addition to which they are practically debarred from fishing at night, the drifter's harvest time.   This right of way in the daytime severely handicaps the trawler, which, with its net down, is to all intents and purposes as hampered as a vessel at anchor.

3. The **seine**, or **sean**, may be regarded as a trawl

THE SAND-EEL SEINE, TEIGNMOUTH.

worked for surface- or shallow-water fish.   In fact, the Scotch call it a ' trawl' on many parts of their coast.

There are two kinds of seine, the boat-seine (sometimes known as ' tucking ' seine) and the ground-seine. The former is used with two boats, or even three, and can be worked at some distance from land.   The ground-seine is used, with the aid of one boat only, close to the beach, or in what the Americans call a ' strand-fishery.' In either case the seine is pulled as quickly as possible in a circle, so as to enclose a shoal of fish.   In some cases the actual position of the shoal is ascertained by watchers posted on high cliffs to command a view of the sea. In others the net is ' shot blind' where the shoal is supposed to be. This is the usual plan with the ground-seine; and in estuaries like that of the Teign, in Devonshire, immense quantities of sand eels and launce are taken in this way every day throughout the summer. This also is the principle of salmon-fishing in estuaries. There is a peculiar mode of seining for sprats in Torbay, in which several boats join in shooting the nets round the fish, which are finally hauled in a large boat moored close inshore.

The ordinary seine, used at St. Ives for pilchards, at Sennen for grey mullet, at Looe for mackerel, is a net of one hundred fathoms or so in length. In the bunt, as the middle portion is called, the net may be some ten fathoms deep, but it tapers to narrow wings. As this is one of the nets which enclose the fish alive, the mesh is smallest in the bunt. Of the other nets already described, it will be remembered that the trawl crushes the fish to death, while the drift-net strangles them.

The upper edge of the seine has corks at intervals to keep it in position. In the middle is either a large cork or a bunch of smaller corks, sometimes known as the ' master cork,' and useful as a guide to the position of the net. The lower edge is weighed down with pipe-leads strung along the rope. The mode of fishing is simple. It is to-day what it was in the days of the ancient Greeks, to whom this pattern of net can be traced; and in those ages fish were so plentiful in the Mediterranean that there was no need for any more complicated engine of capture. Pilchard-seines are quite distinct from those used for mullet or mackerel. The mesh is only $\frac{1}{2}$ inch, the length 190 fathoms, the depth ten fathoms. Each of the two boats takes one extremity of the seine, and they then row round the shoal in opposite directions, moving away from each other at right angles. One or more shorter nets, known as 'stop-nets,' are sometimes used as well when a very large shoal is to be inclosed, but these are removed as soon as the fish can be guided into the one large net. As soon as the ends of the net have been brought together, the boats are rowed inshore, and the net is moored in shallow water. Then the 'tucking-seine,' about half the length of the other, and furnished with a deeper bunt, is brought into use. It is drawn in under the imprisoned fish, which are then raised to the surface and dipped out in baskets, the quantity removed depending either on the requirements of the master-seiner, or the bulk which they are able to handle.

When the pilchards are close to the land, the seine, though simple, is a most effective mode of capture. In August 1903, a Cadgwith seine inclosed an immense shoal of these fish, estimated at 200 hogsheads, or about 600,000 fish, which were sold to a Mevagissey buyer at 15s. per thousand. Some of the traditions of St. Ives, the headquarters of the pilchard seine-fishery, preserve records of even greater catches. On one occasion, in the early seventies of the nineteenth century, as many as 24,000,000 fish, or 8,000 hogsheads, were inclosed at one haul. Unfortunately, this immense quantity of pilchards was too heavy to remove from the nets until it had rotted. It was in consequence never utilised as food, but was finally carted away for manure.

The seine-net is interesting, not merely by reason of its antiquity, but also because it successfully defies the modern invasion of steam. The rowing-boat is, in fact, inseparable from inshore seining. Sailing-boats could only with great difficulty be manœuvred round a moving shoal. Steamers, which would possibly perform that portion of the work even more effectually than boats propelled by oars, could not run ashore with the end of the net. Nor, indeed, would the ordinary harvest of the seine pay for the upkeep of even small steamers specially built. The primitive rowing-boat is in keeping with the primitive seine, and to the artist at any rate, as he contemplates the busy scene in St. Ives Bay, it will seem good that one spot, at least, is sacred from the devouring steamer, protected from either competition or disturbance by economic considerations, as well as by local regulations of great antiquity.

The ground-seine works on the same principle, though it is a still simpler contrivance. One boat only is used, and it carries one end of the net round the shoal, or round the spot on which the shoal is assumed to be, the other end being kept ashore. The boat is rowed in a circular course, eventually returning with its end of the net to a point on the shore near where it started. The men step ashore, holding the rope, and gradually approach their fellows, who haul the other end on land. In this way the two ends are brought together, and all the fish within the narrowing circle find their way into the bunt. If the net is working over rough or uneven ground, one man sometimes returns in the boat to the end furthest from the shore, so as to free it whenever it gets foul of the bottom. He also splashes with an oar in the water with a view to keeping the frightened fishes within the net. The fish chiefly caught in the ground-seine are bass, grey mullet, sand-eels, sprats, and small flat fish, and I have also seen in one haul of such a net salmon, mackerel, turbot, dog-fish, monk-fish, and shad.

4. In all the foregoing types of net the fisherman goes to the fish. With the trawl and seine he sweeps up everything in his path. With the drift-net he meets the fish half-way, catching only those which swim against his net. The **trammel** catches fish on an altogether different principle. It is, in fact, a fixed trap for use during the night. Other fixed engines are in use in our seas, for the Cornish fishermen sometimes moor their drift-nets for the herring close inshore, on the principle of the fixed nets prohibited for salmon-fishing. The trammel is, however, a more complicated device. It has the two recommendations of fishing at

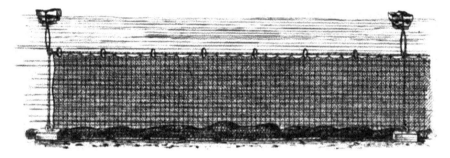

[*From a plate lent by Mr. W. Hearder.*

TRAMMEL.

night when its owner is ashore, and of working ground too rocky for either seine or trawl. It consists of three parallel walls of net, the two outer measuring about fifty fathoms long and two deep, while that in the middle is about twice as long and twice as deep. The mesh of the outside nets is 5 or 6 inches from knot to knot, allowing large fishes to swim through unhindered. The mesh of the middle net is only about 1 inch from knot to knot, in consequence of which none but the smallest fishes can pass through it. The middle net hangs in loose folds between the shorter nets on either side, and the latter are so placed that their mesh corresponds.

When a fish swims against the trammel, what happens is this. It passes through the outer net and strikes against the centre one, but cannot pass through it, as the mesh is too fine. Baffled by this unexpected obstacle in its path, it makes a dash for the large hole in the third net, on the further side, carrying with it the loose net. We now have a blind pocket, with the desperate floundering fish a prisoner. If it makes a dash for liberty, it only draws the walls of its prison closer. Advance and retreat are equally impossible. A very powerful fish will sometimes swim, with the merciless bag still about it, through the adjoining large mesh, which imprisons it more tightly than ever. The most valuable fish taken by this means is the red mullet, though the trammel also catches bass, plaice, and even lobsters, so that its victims are of diverse size and shape. The figure, for which I am indebted to Mr. Hearder, of Plymouth, shows only a side view of the trammel. To appreciate its action, it must be seen from either end.

The remaining nets in use on our coasts may be regarded as designed to suit strictly local conditions. Such are the well-known 'stow-net,' used for whitebait at Leigh and elsewhere in the Thames estuary; the 'brat-net,' used for turbot (known locally as 'brat') at Craster and elsewhere on the Northumbrian coast; and the weirs and stake-nets, which are conspicuous on the shores of the Bristol Channel, as well as in some other parts of the country.

The **stow-net**, which is worked from a smack, may be likened to an immense fixed trawl. It consists of a triangular bag, 50 or 60 yards long and 30 feet wide at the mouth. The mesh varies somewhat in different parts of the net, being rather over 1 inch square at the mouth to $\frac{1}{2}$ inch at the further end. The stow-net is worked on the ebbing tide, by either day or night. The vessel is anchored in the tideway, and the net streams out astern, one man staying on deck as lookout. When the tide is at its lowest, he calls all hands and the net is hauled, the mouth being closed by an ingenious chain arrangement. It is then brought on deck amidships with a grappling-hook, and the contents removed. The '**trim-nets**' used in the mouth of the Nene for catching eels, smelts, and flounders are not unlike small stow-nets.

The '**brat-nets**' of Northumberland are practically fixed drift-nets, which hang in slack folds, and in these the turbot get entangled. **Stake-nets, weirs,** and **hedge-baulks,** as they are called on the coast of Lancashire, all catch fish on the principle of the sieve. They are fixed below high-water mark, and the ebbing tide leaves the fish stranded against a wall of net or wattled stakes.

The nets described in the foregoing pages are the outcome of centuries of experiment and improvement. Some, like the seine, have altered but little from what they were in olden time, while others, like the otter-trawl, are comparatively modern. Net-fishing is, and always must be, the mainstay of the market.

The capture of fish with **hook and line** is too simple to need any long description. The fishing-lines used on a large scale for commercial purposes are very different from the delicate tackle employed by those who fish for sport. Hooking is done on either hand-lines or long-lines. The latter, which are not held in the hand when fishing, may extend to five or six miles in length when several are joined end on end, carrying five or six thousand hooks and using a large quantity of bait. Pilchard, herring, mackerel, squid, whelks, and other articles are used, and on the Devonshire coast and elsewhere the bait difficulty is at times acute. A long-line of 8,000 fathoms, with 5,000 hooks, might in times of scarcity cost as much as £10 to bait. The North Sea line-fishermen have access to the prolific shellfish beds of the Wash; but Plymouth has to procure bait from Falmouth, and, in the spring of the year, mostly pilchards from Mevagissey; while the Milford steam-liners—steam has invaded even this branch of fishing—have often to telegraph to Yarmouth for herring or to Ireland for mackerel. A favourite bait with the Plymouth fishermen is composed of a piece of squid and a piece of pilchard over it. This acts on the same principle as the combined pilchard and mackerel bait, also used with great success in those waters. The pilchard is oily and attractive, but easily removed from the hook. The fish, having bitten it off, returns to the tougher squid or mackerel that remains, and is caught.

The hand-line, used in the North Sea for cod and halibut, and in the English Channel for whiting, bream, and pollock, carries only two or three hooks. For any of these fish the boat is anchored, and the baits are worked near the bottom. For mackerel the boat is kept under sail, and the baits are drawn through the water at varying depths below the surface, a method known as plummeting, whiffing, or railing. In either case heavy leads, weighing from one to six pounds, are used, the speed of the boat in mackerel-fishing being sufficient to keep the lead off the bottom. The lines used are stout, not so much for the sake of strength as because a finer line would cut the fisherman's fingers with the constant hauling. The tackle generally used on hand-lines takes the form of a bent sprool of wire soldered into the lead and carrying a hook depending from either extremity. In some patterns the wire is curved in a half-circle; in others it is bent at right angles. At some ports the fishermen do not solder the lead to the wire, but fasten it on with a loop of leather, while another form of hand-line has several crossbars at intervals up the line. Where there is tide enough to keep the baited hooks away from the main line and clear of the crabs and mud, the wire is dispensed with altogether, its place being taken by a ' sid-strap ' of finer line furnished with swivels to prevent fouling. The size of the hook is determined by the size of the mouth of the particular fish which it is intended to catch, and the manner of fishing is as follows. The hooks having been baited, the lead is allowed to sink until it strikes the bottom. A fathom or so of line is then hauled in, and the fisherman grips the line firmly between the thumb and forefinger of the right hand. As soon as he feels a bite, he strikes smartly and hauls in the fish before it can struggle off the hook. The cod taken in this way in the North Sea are often transferred alive to wells, and are even kept in floating chests until wanted for market. I have seen flat fish kept in the same way by the German fishermen in the Baltic, and it is a pity that some of our undersized flat fish cannot be similarly preserved until fit for consumption.

Hand-line fishing for mackerel is conducted on different principles. The difference is that between the trammel and the drift-net. The stationary net, like the anchored line, catches the stationary fish ; the migratory mackerel must be sought either in the drift-net or on a line which, like it, moves through the water. Moreover, the mackerel has a habit, not shared by the majority of ground-fish, of darting at any bait that is pulled away from it. Consequently, it is taken on baited hooks dragged astern of a boat under sail. The lead takes the form of a plummet, and, when in action, it hangs below the line. This arrangement enables the fisherman to feel the slightest bite, even with his boat sailing quickly through the water and with a line eight or ten fathoms long. The heavier the lead, the shorter the line used. The bait is a pear-shaped piece of mackerel, cut in a peculiar way from the side of the tail and known as a ' float ' in Devonshire, as a ' snade ' in Cornwall, and as a ' last ' on some other parts of the coast. To be effective, the bait must be cut from a freshly caught mackerel, and on Monday mornings, before the first has been caught, the fishermen use either a bright tinned spinner, or a ' float ' from a pilchard. This, however, is easily torn off the hook, and they gladly exchange it for a mackerel ' float ' at the first opportunity. Three lines commonly are used, one over either quarter, and a third, lighter than the others, over the stern. When more are used, they are passed out over booms, or bobbers, of ash or cane fixed on the gunwale. These keep the lines 15 feet or so clear of the boat, and branch-lines enable the fishermen to haul each fish on board when caught. Fishing single-handed in this way, it is surprising how easily one man controls four or six lines, with several fish fast at a time. One at least is left trailing astern until the other hooks are baited, as this keeps the shoal in pursuit. When the mackerel shoals break up, and the fish go to the bottom, numbers are taken on ground-lines used as for bream or whiting.

On some parts of the coast flat fish are extensively caught with hook and line, and there is a regular hook-fishery for soles off Scarborough. Long-lines catch most of the fish, being laid across the tide at sunset, their whereabouts marked by buoys and flags, and taken up again next morning. As already mentioned, steam has been adapted to the requirements of line-fishing, and on the East Coast and at Milford steam-liners are elaborately fitted out for the Iceland halibut fishery, the great flat fish being tethered by the tail in wells, and thereby prevented from doing themselves injury. In the English Channel, where Folkestone is a prosperous centre of this fishing, lining is carried on in yawls. The advantage of steam in line-fishing is easily understood. The long-lines cannot be properly hauled on board a sailing-boat, unless the wind blows against the tide, and it may easily happen that this condition is so long postponed that the lines have to be left down until the dogfish have robbed all the hooks. The steamer is independent of such vagaries of wind and weather, and therefore does the work far better. When long-lines are shot on smooth ground also worked by trawlers, they are occasionally carried away by the sweeping-net. When the culprit can be identified, litigation ensues, and the trawler is usually acquitted. A case of the kind came before the Aberdeen courts in September 1903. The evidence was conflicting, and the Sheriff pronounced a decree of *absolvitor*. The pursuers alleged culpable and negligent steering and claimed damages to the extent of £7 10s., but failed to sustain their case.

A few marketable fish are occasionally taken in the

shrimp-trawl, or even in the lobster-pots ; but the fore-going methods may be said to supply between them the whole of the British-caught sea-fish in the market.

Crabs, lobsters, and prawns are taken in variously shaped traps or pots. The commonest pattern, such as that in use at Selsey, resembles a beehive of cane or wicker. At Cullercoats, and elsewhere on the north-east coast, preference is given to a more elaborate trap

A CULLERCOATS CRAB-POT.

of net stretched on hoops. In any case the trap, or pot, is baited with pieces of gurnard or other fish, slung on cross-lines, and is then left overnight among the rocks. Every morning the crabbers go the round of their pots, two in each coble, haul the pots and remove the crabs or lobsters, which are then taken alive to market, their claws being tied to prevent them fighting. The pots are then rebaited and lowered on the same spot, corks marking the whereabouts of the lines.

Here and there on the Yorkshire coast, and also at Folkestone, open hoop-nets are preferred, particularly for prawns. If properly hauled, a proceeding which requires special knowledge, these are very efficient. As all these crustaceans, but particularly the prawns and lobsters, are found in the rock pools, the centres of the fishery must be sought on the rocky portions of the

THE SHRIMPER.

coast. Among the most important are Cullercoats in Northumberland, Filey in Yorkshire, Sheringham and Cromer in Norfolk, Selsey in Sussex, Lulworth in Dorset, and Gorran, Porthloe, and Mousehole in Cornwall. There is a large tract of suitable ground in the neighbourhood of Tenby, but Wales has no really important lobster-fishery.

Shrimps, on the other hand, live on soft ground, and are consequently caught on a large scale in such

sheltered muddy estuaries as those of the Thames and
Mersey, while the Wash is another important centre of
the shrimp-fishing.   There are two shrimps in our
markets, the brown (*Crangon*) and the pink (*Pandulus*),
the latter being in some parts popularly misnamed a
'prawn,' of which it is, however, a near relation.   The
small-meshed trawl and the push-net are the two chief
methods of taking shrimps.   The latter is the more
familiar at our seaside resorts, consisting of a net on a
square frame, pushed along with the aid of an ash-pole.
Shrimp-trawls are worked in shallow water by small sailing boats.   Yarmouth and Maryport have considerable
fleets of these shrimp-trawlers, which are also conspicuous in the Thames estuary and at Fleetwood.   The
shrimp-trawl is also worked, in the shallowest water,
with the aid of a horse and cart, a method common to
Lincolnshire and Lancashire.

The craft and gear employed in fishing for oysters,
whelks, cockles, and mussels differ so widely from those
hitherto referred to, and the whole fishery for these
molluscs is altogether conducted on principles so much
more approximating those of farming, that it is not
proposed to include any detailed account of them in the
present volume.   The nearest approach to other fishing is
seen in the 'trotting' for whelks on the coast of Essex,
a method by which the molluscs are taken on baited
lines, though hooks are unnecessary, so firmly do the
whelks cling to their prey.   Baited pots are also used
for whelks with success, the principle being the same
as in the pots set for lobsters and prawns.   Oysters
and mussels are dredged, and cockles are raked
by hand, particularly in muddy estuaries like those
of the Exe and Teign.   In the Lancashire district

they are taken with engines known as 'craams' and 'jumbos.'

We have now glanced at the means by which fish is produced at the seaside. The process of placing it on the market belongs to the domain of distribution and is separately considered in the next chapter. The greater part is retailed fresh, but there is also a considerable trade in manufactured fish and shellfish. The simplest form is the boiled shrimp, which is caught, cooked, and brought to market (as at Yarmouth) in one and the same boat. Crabs and lobsters are usually boiled ashore, and the underground boiling-house at Billingsgate market enables the salesmen to boil their lobsters at the modest charge of 1s. 6d. for a large basket, 9d. for a smaller basket, or 3d. for ten. On the recommendation of Dr. Klein, a steamer has recently been erected as an experiment. The process is considered both cleaner and more efficient. Lobsters are preferably bought alive, with the object of knowing that they are perfectly fresh; but I am assured by Mr. Johnson, chief inspector to the Fishmongers' Company, that even a living lobster, which has been packed in close company with others which are dead and tainted, may be a fit subject for condemnation. Among the fish proper which are treated in various ways for the market, the most common are haddocks, herrings, and pilchards. All three are familiar in the smoked form, particularly the first two, while the pilchard is also treated with olive oil and sold in tins as a Cornish sardine. This involves no deception, for the pilchard and sardine are one and the same fish. Unfortunately the sprat is also preserved in the same way, and it is not thought necessary to give it its own name.

There is also an export trade in smoked mackerel and in tinned limpets, which will be more fully dealt with when we come to an account of Mevagissey, the Cornish port at which these delicacies are prepared.

PRAWN-NETS AND CORKS.

CHAPTER III

DISTRIBUTION

Billingsgate—Harbours owned by Railway Companies—Exports and Imports—Transport by Land and Sea—Hull Carriers at Billingsgate—'Single Boating' and 'Fleeting'—Billingsgate and Shadwell—Harbours—Fishing Centres without a Harbour—Qualifications of a Fishing Harbour—War Office at Plymouth and elsewhere—Ice—Salt—Coal—Home Grounds—Natural Harbours—Drift-net Ports—Centres of Crab, Lobster, and Prawn Fisheries—Work done by the Railways—Strain on the Companies' Resources—How Steam has aggravated the Difficulty—Owner's Risk Note—Returned Empties—A Possible Remedy—Billingsgate—Inspection by Fish Meters—Condemned Fish—The Fishmongers' Company—The National Sea Fisheries Protection Association—Charter relating to the Inspection of Fish.

WE have in the foregoing pages considered the conditions under which fishes live in the sea, and the engines with the aid of which man takes them out of it for his own uses. It is, however, obvious that a haddock or a halibut trawled on the Iceland banks, or a mackerel suffocated in the drift-nets off the south-west coast of Ireland, has to travel some distance by sea and land before it can appear on the table of a London restaurant. This chapter will endeavour to give an outline of the immense machinery of transport, of storage, and of market facilities for sale involved in a transaction apparently simple.

Billingsgate Market, more than any other fishing centre, is the focus of the whole activity of fish distribution in this kingdom. Even where the line of least resistance might seem to run wide of the metropolitan market, it is surprising how consistently the bulk of the fish consumed in this country travels from catcher to consumer by way of Billingsgate. Here and there a seaport town like Plymouth consumes, during certain seasons of the year, a considerable amount of the fish landed daily at its quays, but this self-supporting condition is the exception and not the rule. Such of our colonies as are already fostering their fish-

[*Photo, A. S. Rudland.*

BILLINGSGATE MARKET.

ing industry are not yet troubled with these problems of distribution. During a residence in Sydney I remember eating for breakfast fish landed at the Wooloomooloo Market at daybreak, while the hotels at Melbourne or Brisbane furnished snapper or garfish caught by local fishermen the same day. This simple and satisfactory traffic is, however, compatible only with a very early stage of development; and when, in the not far distant future, engineering has rendered that waterless waste in the interior of Australia habitable, great cities will spring up inland, and the problems of distribution by rail will have to be solved there as they are here. The newly established trawling industry of South Africa may in like manner find its first profits in Cape Town and Durban, but a larger prosperity can

WAITING TO UNLOAD.

only be attained by the tapping of inland markets along the spreading railroad.

So immense is the daily transport of fish in this country that all the great railway companies keep special departments busily occupied with this branch of traffic alone. In fact, the railways may be said to have contributed as much to the modern development of the fish trade as either steam-trawling or the introduction of ice. Time was when, as his grandson has often told me, Tucker, of Christchurch, sent the famous salmon of that fishery to Grove, of Charing Cross, by coach, and when shrimps, previous to about 1856,[1] came from Leigh to London each night by cart. The fishing industry, as we now know it, had practically no existence in those days. The most remarkable development of facilities for distribution is noticeable at such fishing centres as are partly controlled by a railway company; and where, as in the case of Hartlepool, Grimsby, Lowestoft, or Milford, the latter has proprietary rights in the harbour, the genius of the carrying agent has achieved results little short of marvellous.

The case of the last three is sufficiently interesting to suggest a somewhat more detailed notice of their recent growth.

Grimsby has, under the fostering hand of the Great Central Railway Company, and by the energy of its resident traders, come to the front as our leading fishery port only during the last fifty years. Going back exactly that period, we find that in 1854 Grimsby despatched just 453 tons of fish. In 1882 the total was 56,000 tons; in 1892, 78,225 tons; and in 1902, at the end of which year the port owned over 500 trawlers, mostly under steam, the output reached the enormous figure of 165,510 tons. With the disastrous strike, which was a serious set-back to the industry, not only locally but all over the country, it will be necessary to deal later. It is here sufficient to say that the ill-effects of that upheaval have not even now entirely ceased to make themselves felt, but there is every indication that Grimsby is recovering from the shock of economic disturbance, and that it will only with difficulty be ousted from its premier position among the fishery ports of the world. The work of the railway company, which is

[1] See Murie's *Thames Estuary Sea-Fisheries*, Pt. I. p. 21.

what more immediately concerns us in the present chapter, is prodigious. In an average busy day the Great Central officials are concerned in the despatch of two or three hundred fish-waggons, conveying 700 or 800 tons of fish, while as many as 1,153 tons have actually been sent away in one day. This, reduced to other terms, means between 4,000 and 5,000 small parcels and 18,000 and 20,000 packages, while a similar number of returned empty packages must be dealt with in the day's work.

The development of Lowestoft has been achieved by the Great Eastern Railway Company. It is no secret that Lowestoft harbour failed lamentably in its original purpose, which was to secure the monopoly of the Dutch cattle trade. The labour and capital, however, which were fruitlessly sunk in the ineffectual encouragement of one industry, have immeasurably benefited another ; and Lowestoft, also an important centre of the East Coast herring fishery, has completely absorbed the trawling trade from its once more prosperous neighbour, Yarmouth.

Milford Haven, somewhat confusingly renamed ' Old Milford' by the Great Western Railway authorities, has now, thanks entirely to the Railway Company, assumed the leading position in the Bristol Channel. In 1890 the yearly despatch of fish amounted to under 10,000 tons ; in 1903 the yearly output was 24,000 tons. Primarily a trawling station, Milford has also a bright future as a mackerel port, and this wholly because the Company had the foresight to respond to its requirements in this respect and to provide a special quay and slip on which so perishable a fish as mackerel may be landed at any stage of the tide, a most important consideration.

Although the chief problems of distribution dealt

with in this chapter are concerned with fish both produced and consumed at home, it must not be forgotten
that there is a large export and import trade.   Herrings
and pilchards are our chief exports, the herrings to
Protestant markets in Germany, and the pilchards to
Catholic buyers in Italy ; and it is rather interesting,
in view of the programme recently submitted to the
country by Mr. Chamberlain, that we send Italy the raw,
or practically raw, pilchard and receive back the manufactured ' sardine,' which is only a pilchard of a more
tender age.[1]   Of fresh trawl-fish we send little abroad
nowadays, the once regular packing of such fish for the
French market, which in former days was supplied from
both Hastings and Brighton by the daily packet between
Newhaven and Dieppe, having been stifled by two
agencies.   In the first place, the French Government
imposed heavy duties with a view to encouraging the
home industry ; in the second, the time allowed for
transport by *Grande Vitesse* proved too slow for the
conveyance of fresh fish.   The only regular British export trade of any importance, in addition to that already
mentioned, is a yearly consignment of spring herrings
from Stornoway to the North Russian ports, though
from time to time an abnormal glut in the home market
is relieved by specially arranged freights.   Thus, the
famous landings of herring at Yarmouth and Lowestoft
in the autumn of 1902 found an outlet at Dantzig, Stet-
tin, Königsberg, and other Baltic ports ; and it has
before now happened that when the master of a steam-
trawler found, on entering the Humber with a large
catch, that the Hull market was overstocked, and that
prices were ruling too low to be remunerative, he some-

---

[1] The imported sardine is, of course, the product of native Mediterranean
fisheries not our own older and larger pilchards in other guise.

times steamed away to Rotterdam and there realised a
better price for his owners and, since he had a share
in the sales, for himself. This, however, is a very rare
occurrence nowadays. (The lobsters and crayfish caught
by Breton crabbers on the Cornish coast, and taken

[*Photo, A. S. Rudland.*

THE DUTCH EEL-BOATS, BILLINGSGATE.

over to France three times a week by one of their fleet,
have clearly no connection with British exports. They
are caught by foreigners for foreigners, and, nominally
at least, outside our territorial limits.)

Herrings figure very largely in the fishery returns
of the United Kingdom, whether we look at the catch

or at the imports or exports. Roughly, one-third of the 10,000,000 cwt. landed at British ports in 1902 is described as herrings. Taking away the quarter of a million tons of fish exported, and, adding the hundred thousand tons imported from other maritime nations, we find that in 1902 no less than £9,297,000[1] worth of fish was consumed in the United Kingdom. Here, then, we have a yearly value of not far short of ten millions sterling in an industry about which comparatively few intelligent people seem to care for information.

To the imports, by the way, should be added the eels brought to Billingsgate by the old Dutch eel-boats, as well as the foreign oysters imported for either food or breeding purposes.[2]

Great as is the enterprise involved in catching all this fish, the activity called for in distributing it throughout the country is even more stupendous. In the ordinary way, it is disposed of as rapidly as possible after capture, and even dried fish can hardly be assigned to the class of foodstuffs that buyers hold for a rise. I recollect, however, one case in which, the Cornish market of that year being glutted, some pilchards were held back and palmed off on the Italian buyers next season, small quantities being packed in with the fresh fish of the year. The buyers of Leghorn and Genoa are not, however, devoid of intelligence, and the trick was discovered, with the result that the port from which these tainted pilchards were shipped was regarded with such disfavour for many years that it is doubtful whether honesty would not in the long run have proved a better policy.

[1] This represents the value of the fish on landing.

[2] Mr. Cunningham, on one occasion, found common sprats cleverly disguised as ' Norwegian anchovies,' a fraud against which the public ought to be protected by the Merchandise Marks Act.

The fish which we eat in London or in the provinces is caught by our fleets all over the North Sea and English Channel, as well as in and beyond the Bay of Biscay, off the coast of Iceland, and on many grounds in the Bristol Channel and Irish Sea. In such extraordinary fashion does it fly round the coast and up and down the land on its way from the net to the fish-kettle that many of its migrations after capture savour of paradox. As a few cases in point, the following may serve : Grimsby and Hull, which undoubtedly receive more fish by sea than any other score of fishing ports in the Kingdom together, must yet take daily trucks of fish by train from Milford, while the latter port receives fish caught by English boats within sight of the Irish coast, and then sends it back by the Cork or Waterford mail-boats, to be consumed on the tables of Limerick and Tipperary. A Scotch dealer in Hull takes (or, until recently, took) loads of partly cured cod by sea to Scotland, and thence re-exports it to buyers in Devonshire. The populous town of Bournemouth, which must lie three times as far by rail from Hull and Grimsby as it does from Plymouth, buys nine-tenths of its daily supply of fresh fish from the Humber or from Billingsgate, and one-tenth only direct from the Devon market. This, no doubt, is because the supply from the north is more constant than that from the west. When last at Brighton, I saw mackerel, which had been sent by rail all the way from Cornwall, competing successfully with other mackerel landed the same morning on Brighton beach from the boats. Most of the foregoing cases are sufficiently intelligible, but the last may call for a word of explanation. It happens that the mackerel landed at Brighton by the boats in the spring of the year are large in size, and they have, moreover, having been caught a great distance from the Sussex coast, been some days in ice. The Cornish mackerel, on the other hand, which come by train from Mevagissey viâ St. Austell, are not only smaller (and on that account alone preferable to the hotel caterers), but also fresher, for they were in all probability swimming in the sea only thirty-six hours before reaching Brighton station. So much therefore are they in demand, in small quantities, at the Sussex resort, that it may pay to send small consignments by a devious railway route instead of to Billingsgate in the ordinary way.

If we were to follow a turbot on its journey from the Bay of Biscay to the table of a London club, we should have to travel by sea to Plymouth Barbican or Milford Dock ; thence by Great Western or South Western to Paddington or Waterloo ; thence by van to Billingsgate. With the arrival of the fish at the central market, it may be regarded as having been produced and distributed, and with its ultimate consignment to the shop of the retail dealer, and subsequently to any one of a million homes, this volume has no concern. On a very limited scale, at the seaside itself, the middle-man is dispensed with, the fishermen hawking their own fish from door to door, or even selling them retail on the beach. In a letter addressed to his mother from Leyden, in 1765, the first Earl of Malmesbury described a similar primitive arrangement at Catwyck, in Holland, 'a multitude of small craft, on the very edge of the sea, with their sailors turned *sellers* instead of *catchers* of fish .   '

Fish is brought to Billingsgate both by rail and steamer—the former for expediency, the latter for cheapness. As it is the most perishable of foodstuffs, the railway companies absorb most of the carrying trade; and the only water-borne fish which still reaches Billingsgate, in addition to the afore-mentioned Dutch eels, is that which is delivered by the Hull carriers. This is done under what is known as the 'fleeting' system. There are two methods of bringing fish back to port. In the first, each fishing-boat brings her own catch, and this, known as the 'single-boating' system, is adopted by such ports as Grimsby, Lowestoft,

[*Photo, A. S. Rudland·*

HULL CARRIERS AT BILLINGSGATE.

Ramsgate, Brixham, and Plymouth. In the second, the main fleet remains out on the grounds, sending the catch periodically to market by fast sailing or steam carriers. This, which is called the 'fleeting' system, was formerly in favour at Yarmouth, when that port yet had a flourishing trawl-fishery, and is still preferred at Hull; and the three Hull fleets contribute between them the bulk of the yearly tonnage (about 40,000 tons) of water-borne fish credited to Billingsgate. Shadwell market also received water-borne fish in the days ot its prosperity, but of Shadwell this aspect of the fish trade has seen nothing since the autumn of 1899. The delivery by Hull steamers at Billingsgate amounted in 1902 to upwards of a million boxes of fish, and the fleets out in the North Sea still employ this direct means of communication with the London market, the steamers employed in the work of carrying being yet known as 'cutters,' a survival perhaps of the days in which

THE EARLY MARKET.

Hewitts and other owners actually employed fast-sailing cutters to carry fish from the fleets.

Three important agencies are concerned in the distribution of fish : **harbours; railways;** and the **inland markets,** which connect the first with the second. Following this course, we will now devote some attention to the harbours, to the railway carriage of fish, and to the facilities for disposing of it at Billingsgate market. That once accomplished, as has been said above, our present interest in it ceases.

I. HARBOURS

If we admit that efficient and well-preserved harbours round the coast are among the first conditions of a prosperous fishing industry, we shall find very little reason to criticise the recent association of fisheries and harbour departments under one roof. This, however, would perhaps imply an admission that our fishery harbours are efficient, and that would be a very daring proposition. Of the thirty or forty fishery harbours of any consequence on the coasts of England and Wales, just seven might be passed over by a lenient critic, while the rest are hopelessly inadequate, whether at low water, in bad weather, or at all times and under every condition. It must however be borne in mind that a few of our ancient fishing centres on the Sussex coast, such as Hastings, Brighton, and Selsey, have facilities for landing fish on the open beach in lieu of harbour accommodation. The first-named, it is true, has part of a harbour in a state of arrested development, but, when I last visited the town, the scheme showed little promise of early completion, and local opinion was evidently divided on its merits.

The qualifications of a fishery harbour are somewhat more complicated than those of harbours devoted solely to passenger or mail traffic. Proximity to the actual fishing grounds is of less importance in this age of steam than was the case when the red-winged fleets crept home to port with each day's catch. On the other hand, however, we have, among other necessary conditions of prosperity, accessibility to Billingsgate by a direct route, easy entry and exit at all states of the tide, ample accommodation and frontage, covered wharves and markets, and cheap supplies of coal, salt, ice, and fresh

water.   The ideal fishery harbour, which has no existence, would combine all these conditions in a high
degree.   The seven above indicated as coming nearest
to these requirements are North Shields, Hull, Grimsby,
Lowestoft, Plymouth, Milford, and Fleetwood.   All that
can in the immediate future threaten the industrial
prosperity of these ports is the covetous hand of the
War Office.   Plymouth, indeed, already suffers from
this cause.   The Government yards tempt hands from
the smacks by the inducement of a more regular wage ;
the Government dredgers have before now deposited
their rubbish on the inshore fishing grounds ; and shells
from Government forts occasionally endanger the lives
of those on board fishing vessels.   Dover, which has to
all intents and purposes ceased to be a fishing centre,
has fallen entirely under the hands of the War Office.
As some compensation, the Government works doubtless
employ much of the labour which was formerly more
profitably employed in bringing back splendid fish from
the Varne, but the fishing has gone to Folkestone, and
will never return.   Milford Haven, on the other hand,
enjoys a wonderful immunity from the Government,
and the promise of further abstinence was held out in
the recent Report on the Berthing Accommodation for
H.M. Warships.

Of our remaining fishery ports, however, many are
absolutely useless at spring low tides, a disability aggravated by the recent tendency to construct larger fishing
vessels.   Nor are the local authorities always alive to
the needs of the case.   When I was at Whitby, a tidal
harbour that must need unremitting dredging to keep
it in order, I found that the only dredger belonging to
the harbour trustees was away on hire.   Scarborough,
though better protected by its Castle Hill from the

north-easterly gales so dreaded on that coast, has a harbour little superior at low tide to that of Whitby; while other cases of harbours practically useless on the ebb tide may be seen at Margate, Ramsgate, St. Ives, Padstow, Swansea, Pwllheli, and Maryport. Pwllheli is, however, to be improved in the near future.

As regards accessibility to the nearest railway station, the greatest facilities are, as might be expected, found

BRIXHAM TRAWLERS IN PORT.

in the harbours owned by the railway companies themselves. Hartlepool, Grimsby, Lowestoft, and Milford have already been named in this respect; while others, not actually owned by the companies, but equally well placed, are those at Whitby, Swansea, Padstow, and Fleetwood. Elsewhere, on the other hand, we find the nearest station either remote from the harbour, or reached only by a hilly or circuitous route.

Scarborough and Brixham severally illustrate these two objections. The passage of the dripping herring-carts through the chief thoroughfare of Scarborough, on their way from the fish-quay to the depôt of the North Eastern Railway, has more than once given rise to serious disagreement between the fish trade and those who depend on a 'good season' of visitors. Brixham has no fashionable *clientèle* to offend in this way, but the terminus of the Great Western branch line can be reached only from the harbour by a distressing zigzag ascent of great steepness ; and it seems remarkable that this progressive company should not serve so important a trawling harbour with, at any rate, some form of hydraulic lift whereby the boxes of fish might be despatched to the waiting trucks with less labour and less loss of time. If Hastings and Brighton handled greater quantities of fish than is the case, the inconvenient distance between their fish-markets and railway stations would also make itself felt ; but a yearly output of 1,000 tons or so throws no very serious strain on their resources.

Some of our smaller south coast fishing ports are even worse situated with regard to the nearest station. Selsey Beach must be a good mile by road from the terminus of the steam-tram which runs to Chichester, where the shell-fish has to be transferred to the London, Brighton and South Coast line. Looe sends its mackerel by a similar light railway to Liskeard, where it is re-loaded on the Great Western trucks. Mevagissey, a mackerel and pilchard centre of some importance, must be six miles or more from St. Austell,[1] the road leading over some appalling hills which preclude anything but

---

[1] This station, which lies inland, was credited in the old Board of Trade returns with Mevagissey's fish.

a walking pace. The much talked of light railway between Mevagissey and the Great Western main line would doubtless develop the local fish-trade, as the trains which brought down the clay would take back mackerel and pilchards, and much fish would thus be transported to better markets that under the present primitive conditions is distributed among the hamlets and farmhouses by 'Jowders.'[1] Newlyn, one of the most important mackerel centres in the kingdom, is without a railway station, and during the brief period of its greatest activity an endless procession of fish-carts may be seen and heard clattering backwards and forwards along the Penzance parade to the nearest terminus. With the exception of the carters themselves, all concerned would benefit by the extension of a light line down to the harbour.

Allusion has already been made to the obviously greater importance of proximity to the fishing grounds in the case of sailing trawlers or drifters. Conversely, it is found that the old smack persists, unmoved by modern innovations, at those ports which are conveniently placed for trawling near home. The reason is that they are far less costly in both build and up-keep than the steam-trawlers, while the comparatively small catches made on the home grounds, which would be useless to the latter, sufficiently repay the small investor. It is merely a question of fishing near or far, and the steam-trawlers of Hull fish the Ingols Hoof ground, off Iceland, with no more effort than that which takes the smacks out of Lowestoft to work the Swarte Bank, in the North Sea.

Natural harbours are not in every case superior to those on which capital has been expended with

[1] See footnote on page 318.

H

judgment. Lowestoft Harbour has many advantages over that of Yarmouth ; yet at the latter the Corporation had the estuary of a river ready to its hand. Such large natural havens as The Wash and Milford Haven, or the estuaries of the Humber, Thames, and Mersey, will always attract fishing-fleets in bad weather, but the home fisheries may in time be practically ruined by over-trawling, traffic, or pollution.

A ready and cheap supply of ice, salt, and, where

ICE FOR THE SMACKS.

steam-trawlers are catered for, coal, has been mentioned as among the conditions of success in a fishery port, and the liberal use of ice is certainly the most important factor in the distribution of fish from distant grounds. Ice does not alter the character of fish as it does that of meat, and, even if it did, the growing requirements of the nation could never be supplied without drawing on the further grounds; and the fish trade, therefore, uses ice in immense quantity. Not many years ago our ice was still imported entirely from Scandinavia, but the more recent invention of new plant for its manufacture has enabled some of our ports to be self-supporting, producing sufficient for their purpose in the local ice-factories. Brixham favours both, manufacturing some and importing the rest. At Grimsby I was shown over a factory which can turn out 300 tons of ice every day ; and at Milford there are two, one of which has a daily output of 70 tons. The ice is generally crushed at the factory and conveyed down a sloping shaft on board the vessels lying alongside.

The salt used on board our fishing-boats comes chiefly from the mines in Cheshire, so that in the matter of salt as well as coal the northern ports have the advantage in price. The suggestion has already been made, in the preceding chapter, that the remoteness of the coalfields from such ports as Ramsgate and Brixham may in part be responsible for the persistence of the sailing smack. Similarly, Milford and Swansea trawlers have the advantage of the coalfields of South Wales.

As our fishing ports will be considered in greater detail, it is here only necessary to draw a general distinction between those which are used by trawling-fleets and those devoted to the drift-net or other fisheries. Trawling is the chief source of supply of almost all our fish, with the four exceptions of the mackerel, the herring, the sprat, and the pilchard; and Hull and Grimsby stand far above all the rest of our trawling ports, Hull, though rightly reckoned second to Grimsby, catching at times as much as 15,000 tons (a third of which is despatched by sea to Billingsgate) in a month. In estimating the relative importance of, say, the first ten trawling ports, the proper basis of comparison is the

strength of the resident fishing-fleets. To compare
them by the yearly quantities of fish landed at each is
a fallacious method of testing their fitness, for an
element of chance and even of custom may enter into
the results. Thus, Hull would get no credit for sending
the third of its fish by water to London. Brixham
would similarly suffer from the fact of its smacks landing
their entire catch at Milford during about six months
of every year, while the Welsh port would also include
in its returns all the mackerel brought there by Newlyn
luggers. It might perhaps be argued that if Milford
is so much more convenient than either Brixham or
Newlyn as to attract so great a quantity of the fish
caught by their boats, it should take credit for its
superiority; and so, to a certain extent, it should. At
the same time, the number of fishing-boats actually
belonging to the port is, on the whole, a more satisfactory standard of comparison; and on this basis the
first ten ports would probably stand somewhat as follows, though continual migrations of fishing craft from
one port to another render the order liable to revision
at any time: Grimsby, Hull, Lowestoft, and North
Shields would rank first four; then Brixham and Ramsgate; lastly, Boston, Plymouth, Milford, and Fleetwood.

With the exception of Milford, the conditions of
which are somewhat peculiar, the chief ports for drift-
boats lie on the open coast. The reason of this is that
estuaries like that of the Humber offer no attraction to
such fishes as the mackerel and herring, which constitute the harvest of the drifter. The chief centres of
drift-net fishing south of the border are Whitby, Scarborough, Yarmouth, Mevagissey, Newlyn, Mousehole,
and St. Ives, here given in their geographical order

from north-east to south-west; and, though two of
these (Whitby and Yarmouth) lie on small estuaries,
they will all be found on the open coast. The fish
taken in drift-nets are more perishable than those
caught in the trawl, a difference due to physical
qualities, and not to the methods of capture. They
are therefore, as a rule, landed at the port nearest the
fishing grounds and conveyed away inland as expeditiously as possible by train. Mackerel caught on the

A TRAWLING PORT.

Scilly grounds are daily despatched to Penzance by the
mail steamer, and the winter herring taken by Mevagissey boats in Bigbury Bay are landed at Plymouth
Barbican. If proximity to the grounds is a convenience
to the drift-boats, it is an absolute necessity for the
crabbers, whose small open boats are unsuited to adventure far from home. The centres of the crab, lobster,
and prawn fishery will therefore be found on rocky
coasts, close to suitable ground. This rule applies to

several in Northumberland and Yorkshire, two in Norfolk, one in Dorset, half a dozen in Devon and Cornwall, and one in Wales. The single important exception is Selsey Beach, where the coast is flat and the foreshore is of shingle.

II. Railways

Only a small quantity of the fish landed on our coasts is actually eaten within sight of the sea, and

HOW THE FISH COMES TO BILLINGSGATE.

even then, as already indicated, it is by no means necessarily consumed at the port of landing. Fear of pirates and invaders in olden time, and, more recently, convenience in working the coal mines and other natural resources of the land, have decreed that the chief centres of population shall lie inland. In a Commonwealth like Australia, where the interior can be rendered fit for a white population only by engineering operations of great magnitude, the large cities still lie on the coast; but it is only a question of time and money for the growing population to reside in the heart of that continent.

In England, however, special fish-trains are run every day of the week from the coast to the capital, conveying thousands of tons of fish either in boxes or else in open 'machines' or tanks, a system which has the twofold advantage of saving the fish from excessive handling and also mitigating the grievance of returned empties, to which more detailed reference will presently be made. The companies carry much of this enormous bulk of fish without fault or accident, both prime (soles, turbot, whitebait, salmon, and red mullet) and what is rather unpleasantly termed 'offal,' such as cod, hake, plaice, haddock, herring, and lemon-sole. (The term 'offal' has, however, no offensive meaning, and is a relic only of the days when soles and turbot were more plentiful than they are to-day, and when consequently many of the rougher kinds, now eagerly bought up for food, were, owing to want of railway facilities, thrown away as rubbish.)

The total weight of fish (reckoning the boxes and ice) carried every year by the railway companies reaches not far short of half a million tons. A valuable memorandum of this was annually issued by the Fisheries Department of the Board of Trade; and Lord Onslow might with advantage avail himself of the new administration of the Fisheries by introducing here and there a little necessary revision. If I may venture to indicate two of the several cases where, at any rate, an explanatory footnote would be welcome, it will be found that in the old returns (1902) Penzance is credited with

10,000 tons of fish, the bulk of which was unquestionably Newlyn mackerel, while, as a still more serious
error, the mackerel from Mevagissey and the shell-fish
from Gorran Haven are credited, in a total of 350 tons,
to St. Austell, which, although it lies several miles from
water, thus figures as a ' port.'

The great strain thrown at times on the resources
of the carrying companies would paralyse any but an
almost perfect organisation. The special demand during
Holy Week is an annual trouble. On the Wednesday
before Good Friday the Great Central Railway has
before now had to despatch from Grimsby 372 trucks,
containing some 25,000 packages of fish weighing
1,153 tons. On the day before Good Friday 1902,
the Great Western Railway received at Paddington
270 tons of fish which had, in the early hours of the
morning, before the immense holiday passenger-traffic
had yet flooded the great terminus, to be carted off to
Billingsgate. This sudden demand for rolling-stock,
always a crucial matter, has of late years been aggravated in a curious way by the development of steam-
fishing. In the old days the approaching smacks were
sighted hours before they could get alongside the fish-
quay, and the station master consequently had ample
time to telegraph up and down the line for extra
waggons and locomotives, according to the likely
requirements of the coming fleet. Nowadays, however,
a puff of smoke is seen off the nearest headland, and in
a few minutes the steam-trawler or drifter is alongside,
impatient to discharge her catch.

When we consider that the railway companies have
practically made the fish trade what it is, any serious
friction between the two would seem uncalled for. On
the other hand, we have to bear in mind that in making

the fish trade the companies have also made themselves, and the carriage of fish is so enormous an asset to at least three of the chief companies, that any alternative route, by sea or road, would seriously affect their dividends. As a matter of fact, the need of transporting such perishable merchandise as expeditiously as possible precludes the probability of any serious rival of the companies appearing in the near future; yet, when we consider the strides made of late years in motor traction by road, such a menace is not beyond the bounds of practical politics, and the companies cannot therefore afford to ignore the grievances that form the subject of interminable correspondence, of conferences under the auspices of the Fishmongers' Company, of petitions to the Fisheries Department, and of often indecisive litigation in the Courts.

These grievances are two in number, and they turn upon what are known respectively as the Risk-note and Returned Empties. The risk-note is the more serious trouble of the two. Certain maximum rates were fixed for the carriage of fish in 1891, these being arrived at by a meeting of delegates deputed by the Board of Trade to hear the case as between the public and the railway companies in respect of the maximum rates for the conveyance of fish and other material. The recommendations made by this body were subsequently submitted to Parliament, varied, and finally confirmed. As far back, however, as the passing of the Carriers Act of 1830 there has always been an alternative arrangement whereby the sender could, if he so pleased, consign his wares at his own risk on a lower scale of charges, paying the higher freight only if the carrier took all risk. A later Act of 1854, as illogical and distracting a document as can be unearthed, even from the dusty shelves of Parliamentary procedure, virtually disallows the exemption implied in the risk-note, and leaves the decision in each case to the Judge. When, therefore, the trade found that the cheaper kinds of fish would not bear the rates fixed by the Board of Trade, the railway companies fixed a still lower charge, at which merchants could send fish at their own risk.

Below is given the form of risk-note retained by the Great Central Railway. The other companies formerly used the same note, but they have since adopted one considerably less drastic, claiming exemption only 'from all liability for loss, damage, misdelivery, delay, or detention, *except upon proof that such loss, damage, misdelivery, delay, or detention arose from wilful misconduct on the part of the Company's servants.'*

To The Great Central Railway Company _____ _____190 .

    In reference to the above [1]   *request that all Merchandise, for which there are alternative rates by Passenger Train or other similar service, delivered by*   *or on account at any of your stations for carriage by railway may be carried at the Reduced Rates (where and so long as such rates exist), except when specially consigned at the higher rate; and in consideration of your charging such Reduced Rates,*   *agree to relieve you and all other Companies or persons over whose lines the Merchandise may pass, or in whose possession the same may be during any portion of the transit, from all liability for loss, damage, misdelivery, delay, or detention from whatever cause arising.*

    And   *further agree that this Agreement shall apply to traffic consigned to*   *from stations on other Companies' lines when the rate charged for the carriage of*

---

[1] This is merely a statement of the lower rate having been arranged, and sets forth that this form must be signed by all wishing to take advantage of it.

such traffic is a Reduced Alternative Rate.   *also*
agree to the conditions on the back hereof.

This Agreement shall continue in force from the present
date until   *signify in writing to the contrary.*
Provided nothing therein shall prevent   *during its*
continuance from sending or receiving any particular con-
signment at the higher rate, should   *at any time*
so direct in writing.

The conditions on the back of the document read as
follows :—

General Conditions.

1. *All goods delivered to the Company will be received*
   and held by them subject to a lien for money due to
   them for the carriage of and other charges upon such
   goods, and also to a general lien for any other
   moneys due to them from the owners of such goods
   upon any account, and in case such lien is not satis-
   fied within a reasonable time from the date upon
   which the Company first gave notice to the owners
   of the goods of the exercise of the same, the goods
   may be sold by the Company by auction or otherwise,
   and the proceeds of sale applied to the satisfaction
   of every such lien and expenses.

2. *All perishable articles refused by the Consignee, or at*
   the place to which they are consigned, or consigned
   to a place not known by the Company's agents or
   servants, or insufficiently addressed, or not paid for
   and taken away within a reasonable time after
   arrival, if addressed to be kept till called for, may
   be forthwith sold by auction or otherwise, without
   any notice to the Sender or Consignee, and payment
   or tender of the net proceeds of any such sale after
   deduction of freight charges and expenses shall be
   accepted as equivalent to delivery.

3. *In respect of goods consigned to places beyond the*
   limits of the Company's free delivery, the responsi-
   bility of the Company will cease when such goods

have been delivered over to another Carrier in the usual course for delivery.

4. *In all cases where the Company's charges are not pre-paid, the goods are accepted for carriage only upon the condition that the sender remains liable for the payment of the amount due to the Company for the carriage of such goods, without prejudice to the Company's rights, if any, against the Consignee or any other person.*

5. *In respect of traffic of every description which loses weight in transit through drainage, evaporation, or any cause beyond the Company's control, carriage shall be paid upon the weight ascertained at the sending station.*

To the ordinary intelligence it seems impossible that anyone signing an exemption worded in this manner could go before the Courts with any reasonable expectation of an award of damages in case of accident. If wilful negligence were proved, the Judge might find the company guilty of a breach of contract, but who is to prove wilful negligence? It is capable of many interpretations, and one company was even accused of employing servants incapable of reading the consignment notes, which was held, not unreasonably, to be tantamount to wilful negligence.

The attitude of the companies in respect of this grievance is simple. They say that the trade wants to eat its cake and have it too, paying the lower rate, and also shifting the risk to the carriers. Any merchant, they say, who desires to send his fish at the company's risk is at liberty to pay the higher rate charged for the privilege. The merchants retort that the stress of competition renders the higher rate prohibitive; and that the difference is considerable (averaging about 1s. 4d. per cwt. on the Great Central) may be seen from the following table, for which I am indebted to Captain Barwick, Port Master at Grimsby :—

CHARGES PER CWT. FROM GRIMSBY PER GREAT CENTRAL.

Station	Ordinary rate	Owner's Risk	Station	Ordinary rate	Owner's Risk
	s. d.	s. d.		s. d.	s. d.
London	2 8¼	1 6	Bristol	4 2¼	2 5
Manchester	2 2½	1 9	Plymouth	5	3
Liverpool	2 11¾	2 0	Reading	1¼	2
Birmingham	3 3¼	2 3	Portsmouth	10¾	3
Sheffield	1 9¼	1 7	Edinburgh	6	3
Leeds	1 7¼	1 6	Dublin	9	3
Bradford	1 11	1 9	Cardiff	3¼	2

In the cases of the longer journeys over other companies' lines it will be seen that the difference between the two rates is proportionately heavy, and when the fish trade on one occasion objected that the difference was excessive, the companies pointed out that the ordinary rates had been fixed first, and that the obvious remedy would be to increase the special low rates until the discrepancy was removed. Formerly it was the practice of each individual company to deal with claims on their own merits, although there was a disinclination on the part of companies generally to recognise claims of any description. Now, however, a Claims Conference has been arranged by the Clearing House, and in the case of total loss or proved pilferage these are admitted. In this attitude they have been encouraged by some of the Judges, who admitted their inability to help anyone who could sign such an undertaking. The merchants, for their part, say that, as the higher rate is prohibitive, they have no choice but to sign.

Looking at the grievance in this light, it would appear that the objection is raised not so much to the literal interpretation of owner's risk as to the excessive ordinary rates of carriage sanctioned by the Board of Trade. The railway companies are surely entitled to charge the highest rates allowed by the law. They are commercial investments, not philanthropic institutions, and, even if they are the servants of the public, they are not expected to be its slaves. They are worthy of their hire; and if they have contrived to make themselves indispensable, they cannot be greatly blamed for fixing their wage as high as possible.

Were it not for the pressure of competition and the cutting down of profits, the charges for · carriage at ordinary rate could hardly be regarded as excessive, particularly when we remember the despatch with which fish has to be consigned, taking precedence of all other merchandise. The Great Eastern Railway Company carries a ton of prime fish from Lowestoft to Billingsgate at its own risk for 33s. 9d., while merchants consigning herrings at their own risk can actually send five tons from Yarmouth to London, a distance of more than 120 miles, at the seemingly absurd price of 12s. 8d. per ton.

Even at the lowest admissible rates it may not pay to send fish from the coast to London, and it may even in that case be sold near the coast for manure. This, on the face of it, reads as a wicked waste of cheap and wholesome food, but the carrying companies can hardly be held responsible for the relations between supply and demand. Nor are they to blame because now and then a Hull trawler steams across to Rotterdam with a catch of rough fish that would not have borne the railway rates to Billingsgate, or even because the merchants of Esbjerg, in Denmark, can send fish by sea to London more cheaply than Grimsby can send it by rail. Water carriage must always compare favourably with land carriage in the matter of cost, and where the fish will bear the longer time taken in the journey by sea there is no reason why it should not be so consigned. It must, however, be remembered that the maximum rates were fixed when the bulk of fish caught for the market was prime, and not the commoner kinds that predominate to-day. When fish landed by the Hull carriers at Billingsgate realises only a fraction over 1d. per pound, and the fish landed at Hull, including prime, realises under 1d. per pound, the railway rates are necessarily very high in proportion to the market value. As another case in point, it has been said that the railways are greatly to blame for the restricted development of the Scotch herring trade in the London market. Fresh herrings, we are told, can be sent from the North of Scotland to New York, or even to Australia, for much less than it costs to send them by rail to London, so that not more than 3 per cent. of the herrings landed at Wick or Fraserburgh ever reach the London shops. From the standpoint of the Scotch dealers this is undoubtedly a serious matter, but those who view it on broader grounds will see that it would be absurd to expect London to go all the way to Wick for herrings when Yarmouth, less than one-sixth of the distance by rail, can supply as many as the metropolis can consume. The fresh herring is not a favourite table-fish, and it is in its smoked or salted state that the species is chiefly valued in London. If thirty-three times the present number of Scotch fresh herrings from one district alone were to find their way to the London market, even if the railway companies carried them free of charge, it is unlikely that the demand for them would be sufficient to assure a profit.

The other grievance, which seems perennial, has to do with the handling of the empty boxes, tens of thousands of which have to be sent back to the coast for fresh consignments of fish. The quantity of empty boxes, baskets, barrels, and other receptacles requisitioned for the conveyance of fish by train is appalling. When the herring shoals move round the coast, with greedy fishing-fleets on their tracks, the railway companies

RETURNED EMPTIES.

find it as much as they can do to keep pace with a demand so migratory. The low intrinsic value of some of the packages so used only aggravates the difficulty, for it does not seem to be worth while labelling them properly so as to ensure their delivery at the right destination; in fact, many of the commission salesmen and retailers are very indifferent as to the ultimate disposal of the empties. Consequently there is a great leakage from this cause, large numbers not being returned at all, whilst others are dumped and carelessly left at railway depôts improperly addressed, and without being consigned or having the carriage-charges prepaid as required.

The offending empties therefore accumulate in very large numbers on every line. I have seen acres of returned empties stacked at Milford. At Grimsby I have walked up and down avenues alphabetically arranged in two groups, London and Provincial. It is estimated that a couple of million empties yearly find their way to Grimsby. The trade suggests that the railway companies are notoriously careless with these empties, refusing to give advice-notes of their arrival. Grimsby has, in fact, made a special study of the grievance generally, and it has been computed that Grimsby merchants alone suffer from loss, in one direction or another, not less than £15,000 a year. The companies, on their side, allege that the dealers are not sufficiently careful in addressing the packages, which they say are dumped down at the railway depôts anyhow, with utter disregard as to record or correct particulars. They also maintain that all empties handed to them properly booked and consigned, invariably reach their destination in due course.

However, a solution to this admittedly serious question has, it is hoped, at length been found, a company having been promoted, with its headquarters at Grimsby, with the express object of manufacturing a non-returnable empty, of any size required. This, having been tested by Grimsby fish-merchants, has been found to answer all essential requirements ; viz., it is sufficiently strong to stand one journey and it can be supplied at a price that should ensure its remunerative adoption by the trade. It is anticipated that this non-returnable box will do much to mitigate the loss which merchants have sustained in the past, and to allay the irritation such loss has up to the present produced in the trade.

This discontent on the part of the trade is greatly increased by sudden demands on the resources of the carrying agents. One day, for instance, four boats, their fish-holds only half full, may creep abreast into Lowestoft Harbour, and then the dealers have no use for either empties or rolling stock. The next day four hundred, crammed to the decks, may race for the quays, and the company is then anathematised if it be found unprepared.

III. BILLINGSGATE

· We have now glanced briefly at the harbours which first receive the fish from the boats and at the railway arrangements by which it is possible to bring the harvest of the sea within reach of London and other great centres. It only remains to conclude this survey of the means of distribution with some notice of Billingsgate Market, the converging point of all the carrying trade. This, the central market, has not escaped severe criticism, and its limited accommodation, together with the congestion of the hilly streets that converge on its approaches, is certainly in need of improvement. Whether any other site would be equally convenient for the terminus yards of the railways, the water-borne fish of the Hull steamers, and the shops of West End fishmongers, is another matter. At the same time, it is impossible to overlook the serious overcrowding in the vicinity of the market and the obstructions which impede the drivers of railway vans anxious to make quick deliveries. That this is a most serious loss in money to the companies is easily shown. A railway van may, under existing conditions, be kept idle for six or eight hours, waiting to discharge its fish. Such a van cannot carry more than two tons, and may contain even less. This means that it earns, at the outside, 8s. 4d. for the whole day's work, reckoned at 4s. 2d. per ton, since by the time it has stood eight hours outside Billingsgate, unloaded its fish and returned to the yard, very little of the working day remains. Seeing that the companies undertake to deliver the fish at Billingsgate at a fixed inclusive rate, which makes no allowance for such delays, they inevitably suffer considerable losses in the course of the year.

If the congestion at Billingsgate is grave even to-day, it is impossible to forecast what may be its condition in five years' time if the traffic continues to increase in proportion. Some idea of the growth of business may be formed from the following returns for three recent years :—

1900	.	.	.	.	.	187,684 tons.
1901	.	.	.	.	.	196,190 „
1902	.	.	.	.	.	216,183 „

It does not, therefore, seem unwarranted if the probable volume of trade at Billingsgate in the year 1909 be estimated at considerably over a quarter of a million tons.

Even now an endless stream of leather-hatted porters flows between the Hull carriers and the market. Each morning the Monument stands in such slippery heaps of fish as seem likely to deplete all the seas of Western Europe before the century is much older. The scene is indescribably fascinating to any-one interested in the fishing industry. Whether the observer mingles with the busy crowd, jostled by hurrying porters or by, white-coated salesmen, or whether he views the throng from the windows on the first floor, the market offers a wonderful sight.

The dealers are not wholly indifferent to personal

[*Photo, A. S. Rudland.*

THE PROCESSION OF PORTERS, BILLINGSGATE.

comfort. The dark and dank underground market is used only for [the storage of empties. Nor will they climb a staircase, so that the haddock market, origin-ally on the first floor, was moved to a ground floor across the road. One convenient room is used as a boiling-house, and here, for a small payment, lobsters are boiled ready for sale.

Considerable quantities of fish are sometimes condemned by Mr. Johnson and his assistant meters, who inspect under an old Charter granted to the Worshipful Company of Fishmongers. During 1902 upwards of 1,148 tons of fish (haddock, plaice, skate, whiting, herring, and shell-fish) were thus condemned, removed to the hermetically sealed tanks in the condemned barges, and disposed of by a contractor, who, in addi-

[*Photo, A. S. Rudland.*

THE ' CONDEMNED ' BARGE, BILLINGSGATE.

tion to the receipt of £250 a year from the Company, makes what he can out of selling the condemned fish after treatment, for manure. The profit on the latter transaction is not, however, very great, for not only has the introduction of artificial manures brought the market price of fish manure from £12 down to less than £5 per ton, but it takes five tons of fish to make one ton of manure, so great is the percentage of water.

Return of Fish condemned for one year to October 31, 1903.

	BILLINGSGATE MARKET				SHADWELL MARKET			
—	Delivered	Condemned			Delivered	Condemned		
1902	Tons	Tons	Cwt.	Qrs.	Tons	Tons	Cwt.	Qrs.
November	16,219	46	17	1	105	0	2	0
December	14,550	20	19	0	90	—		
1903								
January	17,047	20	6	1	87	—		
February	14,050	31	12	1	75	—		
March	18,288	34	1	3	51	—		
April	18,169	28	12	0	68	—		
May	19,712	136	9	2	69	—		
June	19,141	176	1	2	64	0	7	0
July	19,133	273	17	2	65	0	8	0
August	20,693	128	4	2	44	—		
September	20,214	301	10	3	41	—		
October	18,225	98	8	3	40	—		
Total.	215,441	1,297	1	0	799	0	17	0

Twelve months delivered 216,240 tons, of which 1,298 tons were seized, being at the rate of 1 ton in 166·6, or a little over ½ per cent.

The constitution of the Fishmongers' Company is in some respects peculiar. The history of the Company can be traced back to the end of the thirteenth century, for it took a leading part in the pageant that welcomed King Edward I. after his victory over Wallace at Falkirk. In addition to the administration of important trusts and the dispensing of much hospitality, the Fishmongers' Company is known to-day chiefly by the interest which it takes in every movement connected with the improvement of the sea or inland fisheries. Many such schemes have owed their inception to the Wardens, and more than one Society having these objects is allowed to hold its meetings at the Company's Hall.

The one with which we are here more immediately concerned is the 'National Sea Fisheries Protection

Association,' the honorary secretary of which is Mr. J. Wrench Towse, Clerk to the Company. It was established in 1882, and has for its objects :—

(a) *The protection of the interests of Smack Owners, Fish Curers, Fish Merchants, Boat Owners, Fishermen, and Fish Salesmen throughout the United Kingdom. The legal enforcement of their just claims, the due representation in Parliament and elsewhere of their requirements, and the promotion or opposition for their benefit of Legislative measures.*

(b) *The reduction of the rates and expenses of and incidental to the carriage of Fish, and the enforcement of prompt deliveries and the reduction of high rents and tolls ; also the abolition of monopolies which obstruct the natural development of the Sea Fish Trade.*

(c) *The promotion of improvement in Harbour accommodation for fishing.*

(d) *The prevention of frauds upon and by those engaged in the several businesses mentioned in clause (a) or any of them.*

(e) *The collection and circulation of statistics or other information relating to the several businesses mentioned in clause (a) or any of them.*

(f) *The consideration of all general questions which affect the interests of those engaged in the several businesses mentioned in clause (a) or in any of them, or which in any way relate to the Sea Fish Trade or Sea Fisheries of the United Kingdom, and the carrying out of the decisions arrived at.*

Between twenty and thirty companies and associations at the ports are affiliated to the Association, as follow ·—

Aberdeen Fish Trade Association.
Aberdeen Steam Trawl Owners' Association.
Boston Deep Sea Fishing and Ice Company.
Boston Fish Merchants' Protection Association.
Brixham Fishing Smack Insurance Society, Limited.
Flamborough Fishermen's Association.
Great Grimsby Fish Merchants' Association.
Great Northern Steamship Fishing Company, Limited.
Grimsby and North Sea Steam Trawling Company, Lim.

Grimsby Federated Owners' Protecting Society, Limited.
Grimsby Steam Fishing Vessels Mutual Insurance and
　Protecting Company, Limited.
Hull Fishing Vessel Owners' Association, Limited.
Hull Fish Merchants' Protection Association, Limited.
Humber Steam Trawling Company.
Liverpool Fish, Game, and Poultry Dealers' Association,
　Limited.
London Fish Trade Association.
Lowestoft Branch.
Moray Firth Fisheries Association.
North-Eastern Steam Fishing Company, Limited.
Port of Falmouth Chamber of Commerce.
Port of Hull Trawl Fishermen's Protective Society.
Port of Plymouth Fishermen's Insurance Society, Limited.
Ramsgate Fishing Vessels Mutual Society.
St. Mawes Branch.
Steam Tug and Trawlers' Protecting and Indemnity
　Association.
Suffolk Mutual Drift-net Fishing Boat Owners' Trade
　Protection Society, Limited.
Whitstable Branch.

Mention was made in the present chapter of the
inspection of fish carried out by the officials of the
Fishmongers' Company. As the extent of its powers
in this respect is sometimes under discussion, it may be
useful to subjoin the precise terms of that portion of
the Charter granted by James I., under which, for the
common good, that power is exercised.

Search of
Fish, and
to enter
Shops, &c.,
where the
same is, if
bad, to
seize and
dispose of.

*And moreover we will, and by these Presents for
Us, our Heirs and Successors, we grant to the
same Wardens and Commonalty of the Mistery
of Fishmongers of the City of London and to
their Successors, That the same Wardens and
the Assistants of the Mistery of Fishmongers of
the City of London aforesaid, and their Successors, which for the Time shall be from Time to
Time hereafter for ever, shall have, make and
use, within the City of London, and within the
Liberties and Suburbs of the same, and within*

our Borough of Southwark *aforesaid, at all convenient Times, the full and entire Survey, Search, Government and Correction, of all and singular Persons, Denizens and Strangers, and of all others whatsoever, of whatsoever Art or Mistery they shall be, selling or having, possessing or keeping, to sell, any salted Fish, salted Herrings, fresh Fish of the Sea, Salmons, Stock Fish, or any other Fishes whatsoever, within the same City of* London, *Liberties or Suburbs of the same City, or within the same Borough of* Southwark, *and the Liberties and Precincts of the same Borough : And that it shall be Lawful to the Wardens of the same Mistery for the Time being, and to every of them from Time to Time, and at all Times convenient, whensoever it shall seem good unto them, or any of them, to enter into any House, Shop, Ship, Cellar, Wharfe, and other Place and Places whatsoever, within the City and Borough aforesaid, or either of them, or within the Suburbs, Liberties or Precincts of the same City or Borough, or either of them, where any such salted Fish, salted Herrings, fresh Fish of the Sea, Salmons, Stock Fish, or other Fish whatsoever shall be laid, or house, wither the same be in Cask or without Cask, and to view, search, and survey wither the same be wholesome for Mans Body, and fit to be sold or no : And if the same Fish, either fresh or salt Herrings, Salmons, Stock Fish or other Fish whatsoever, by them or any of them, within the City, Borough, Suburbs, Liberties or Precincts aforesaid, in such Search shall be found to be unwholesome or corrupt, or unfit to be sold That then it shall be lawful to the same Wardens, of the Mistery of* Fishmongers *aforesaid, or to any of them, the same bad, unwholesome and corrupt Fish, from the Owners and Possessors thereof, as forfeit, to take and seize, and thereof to dispose and do, according to our Laws of* England, *and the Usages and Customs of the said City of* London *and Borough aforesaid, from Time to Time used and frequented.*

The wording of the foregoing may be open to the charge of obscurity, but it has been thought better to give it in its original form, as any controversy on the subject of the actual powers assigned to the Company cannot well be settled otherwise than by reference to the original terms of the Charter.

We have now followed the fish from the sea into the nets, and thence to the hold of the trawler ; to the markets on the coast ; thence by rail to Billingsgate, where, under proper inspection by the official meters of the Fishmongers' Company, it is distributed among the retail dealers, who sell direct to the public. At Billingsgate we leave it, and must now go back to the catching stage, in order to take notice of some of the existing and proposed laws regulating such operations, and also of the extent to which biological investigation may in the near future come to the aid not so much of the catcher as of the legislator, who is anxious, for the fisherman's own sake, to control his rapacity.

CHAPTER IV

LEGISLATION

Fishery Laws—Private Ownership—Territorial Limits—Act of 1868—Act of 1877—Act of 1883—International Convention—'Sea Fisheries Regulation Act, 1888'—Creation of Sea Fisheries Districts—Ports outside such Jurisdiction—Endeavour to include Yarmouth and Lowestoft—How a District is Created—Acts of 1891 and 1894—Limits and Bye-laws of the Sea Fisheries Districts of England and Wales—Other Laws—Foreign Fisheries Legislation—Portmarks—Proposed Protection of Spawning Grounds—Close Time for Herring and Mackerel—Objections to these Proposals—Laws to Check the Trawler—Closure of Selected Areas—Extension of the Three-mile Limit—Increase in the Mesh of the Trawl—Prohibition of Landing and Sale of Undersized Flat Fish—Lord Onslow's Bill—Opposition and Amendment—Fishery Board for Scotland—Good work done by it—Fisheries Administration in Ireland—Report of the Committee on Ichthyological Research.

No great industry can be properly regulated without the aid of laws specially framed for its conduct in the interests of all concerned. The laws are generally of two kinds: there are general laws which apply to the whole country, and there are supplementary, or even contradictory, bye-laws, which operate only within the districts for which they were enacted. The element of private ownership, which enters into the laws made for the regulation of mining and agriculture, has but a small part in our sea-fisheries. On the other hand, legislation for that industry is peculiarly complicated by international difficulties absent from the other two, the territorial limits of each maritime state forming a more or less imaginary water frontier, across which it is difficult to prove trespass, and scarcely less difficult to frustrate. Within the three-miles territorial line, fishing rights belong to the nation. There is no private ownership in the sea or, for the matter of that, in the fisheries of tidal waters, except in rare instances.[1]

The object of this chapter being to set forth the terms and principles of modern sea-fisheries laws, there will be no need to go back into the past beyond the Act of 1868, the basis of much later legislation. Among

[*Photo, A. S. Rudland.*

THE FISHMONGERS' HALL.

the objects of that Act were, besides the repeal of much obsolete legislation, the stricter registration of fishing-boats, the control of the oyster fisheries, and an understanding with France on certain matters of common interest. The Act also had a more local interest in the special protection which it extended to

---

[1] The private ownership claimed in several Norfolk Broads regarded by angling and yachting experts as tidal, rests on other grounds than those on which certain exclusive rights of fishing in parts of the sea are based, and is not entitled to further consideration in a work dealing only with our sea-fisheries.

the Cornish seine-nets between July and November, trawlers and drift-nets being prohibited from fishing within two miles of the land or from anchoring within half a mile of a seine-boat.

The next Act, that of 1877, is commonly cited as the 'Oyster, Crab, and Lobster Act, 1877.' In this, for the first time, legislators appear to have recognised the serious position of 'crustacea,' and the facilities which the haunts and habits of crabs and lobsters afford for depletion by wasteful fishing uncontrolled by proper laws.

Generally speaking, and with certain exceptions in favour of undersized crabs caught for bait,[1] the Act prohibits the taking or sale of :—

Edible crabs under 4¼ inches across the broadest part of the back.

Crabs in spawn, variously known as 'berried,' 'seed,' 'spawn,' or 'ran' crabs.

Crabs that have just cast the shell, variously known as 'soft,' 'white-footed,' or 'glass' crabs ; or as 'casters.'

Lobsters under 8 inches from tip of beak to end of tail, when spread as flat as possible.

More recent legislation, in the form of bye-laws passed by some of the subsequently created sea-fisheries districts, has tended in the direction of still further protection. On the South Coast, for instance, from Hayling Island to the Land's End, as well as on the coast of West and North Wales, Lancashire, Northumberland, and Cumberland, the minimum size for crabs is raised to 5 inches ; and on some other parts of the coast the minimum size for lobsters is 9 inches. Berried lobsters, of which no mention is made in the original Act, are protected throughout the year in Lincoln,

---

[1] A subsequent Act of 1884 empowered the Board of Trade to protect undersized crabs unconditionally.

Kent, Essex, Lancashire, and Cumberland; and in Northumberland from April to July. The only extension of the Act is in Lincolnshire, where berried crabs, instead of being for all time protected, enjoy immunity only from November 1 to June 30.

The penalties enforced by the original Act are £2 for the first offence and £10 for subsequent offences, with forfeiture of unfit or undersized crabs and lobsters.

Passing mention may be made of the Act of 1883, which had somewhat different aims from the rest. It established, in fact, a kind of Convention between the nations bordering on the North Sea for the more effectual policing of the high seas outside the three-mile limit, the formulation of recognised regulations for lettering and numbering all fishing vessels, the protection of drifters and hookers against trawlers (the increase in the numbers of which was apparently viewed with apprehension), and sundry other matters of common import.

The most important Act of all, however, in its bearing on existing laws is that commonly known as 'The Sea Fisheries Regulation Act, 1888,' the outcome of which was the creation of sea-fisheries districts for the local control of sea-fishery matters. The bye-laws of the twelve existing districts are given later in this chapter. It may here be noted that the whole coast is now partitioned off under districts, with two exceptions; of these the first is the coastline of part of Norfolk and of Suffolk, between the limits of the Eastern on one side and the Kent and Essex on the other; the second is a portion of the shores of the Bristol Channel, embracing bays in Somersetshire, Gloucestershire, and Monmouthshire. With regard to the proposals for including the outlying fishing ports of Yarmouth and Lowestoft in the Eastern district, Mr. C. E. Fryer conferred with representatives of various bodies, heard *ex parte* statements, and recommended an extension of the Eastern district to Covehithe, which would bring the ports in question under proper jurisdiction without in any way interfering with the existing powers of the Suffolk and Essex conservators. The proposal met with strong opposition from the fishing centres in question, which still, at the time of writing, remain outside the jurisdiction of any district. To this freedom they cannot lay claim on account of their size, for Hull and Grimsby, both of which have far outstripped the more southern ports, are within the North-Eastern district. Cardiff, on the west side of the island, shares this independence of district control, though whether the Board of Agriculture and Fisheries will long rest content with these two gaps in the otherwise continuous chain of local government authority round the coast of England and Wales has yet to be seen.

The manner in which the Board of Trade used to proceed when petitioned to create a new district may be illustrated by the circumstances which attended the formation of the Devon Sea Fisheries District in 1892. In this case the application was made by the Devon County Council, and Mr. A. D. Berrington, then Inspector of the Fisheries Department of the Board of Trade, was sent down to hold inquiries and sound local opinion at Plymouth, Brixham, and Dorchester. The original petition included Dorsetshire, but the town clerk of Plymouth took exception to the extension of the proposed district so far east, on the ground that the two counties, though neighbours, had no community of fishing interests. Moreover, he contended, with scarcely less reason, that harmonious working would be difficult between centres lying so far apart as the eastern ports of Dorset and the western ports of Devon. The rivalry between the two counties went to such extremities that, in order to shift the centre of gravity to the advantage of his county, the spokesman for Plymouth recommended the addition of Cornwall (purposely ignoring the fact that Cornwall already had a Sea Fisheries Committee of its own), while Dorchester retaliated by proposing the addition of Hampshire. Had Cornwall been added, then Plymouth would have been the geographical centre of the district, while a similar honour would have fallen to Dorchester with the inclusion of Hampshire. Eventually, though not until instructive argument had combated considerable opposition on the part of the fishermen, a draft order was issued for the creation of the Devon Sea Fisheries District, having a coastline of about 130 miles, while Mr. Berrington concluded his report with a recommendation that Dorset and Hampshire be included in a separate district, a suggestion that has since taken shape under the name of the Southern Sea Fisheries District. The petition sometimes originates differently, while the establishment of some of the districts has been more strongly opposed, but the case of the Devon district will serve to illustrate the general procedure.

The Act of 1888 empowered these districts to frame bye-laws :—

(*a*) To prohibit or regulate methods of fishing.

(*b*) To set apart areas for oyster-breeding.

(*c*) To prohibit the capture of undersized or unfit crabs, even for bait.

(*d*) To prohibit the deposit of rubbish or other mental material.

(*e*) To repeal or amend bye-laws.

These bye-laws, however, required confirmation by the Board of Trade before they became valid. The districts further had the right to appoint fishery officers, with full powers of search, or even of seizure, within the district, and they were also obliged to furnish the Board of Trade with statistics or other information in respect of fishery matters.

An Act of 1891 increased the power of the committees, extending moreover to any injured party the right to take legal proceedings under the bye-laws. This right had hitherto been vested only in the fishery officers.

A later Act of 1894 dealt with the more effective protection of shell-fish.

The system of fisheries districts has been objected to in Scotland on the ground of local expenditure. In Ireland there are obvious reasons, mainly fiscal, why it would not work. The expense of protecting the coast waters of the different maritime counties is, under the present system, borne by the counties themselves. That useful work is often done in the way of protecting the inshore waters may be gathered from a single instance within the jurisdiction of the Eastern District, the officers of which, one night in the summer of 1903, caught no fewer than seven large steam-trawlers two miles inside the territorial limits, and penalties were inflicted amounting to £174. One obvious drawback to the working of the system is that wealthy inland centres, like London, contribute nothing, and this in spite of the fact that, being the greatest consumers of fish, they have, if only indirectly, the largest stake in the welfare of the industry. Another criticism of the system is the unavoidable lack of uniformity in the regulations now in force around the coast. The case of spawning

K

lobsters, protected all the year in Lincolnshire, but only during five months in the neighbouring county of Yorkshire, has already been noticed in this chapter. What is to prevent the capture of berried lobsters off Grimsby between February and August and their sale at Hull ? While some measure of local control is unquestionably preferable to absolute *laisser faire*, it would be most beneficial if the Minister of Agriculture and Fisheries could see his way to co-ordinate the laws which at present conflict within territorial waters. The proposal recently put forward by Professor Herdman, that the existing districts should be merged in three separate divisions corresponding with the East, South, and West coasts, would probably work more satisfactorily. The districts themselves were the product of a period in which the decentralisation of authority was very popular.

For the sake of reference, I here give the complete bye-laws at present in force in the twelve sea-fisheries districts (see Map, facing p. 1), which are named in their geographical order.

NORTHUMBERLAND SEA FISHERIES DISTRICT.

(*From the Border to the Tyne.*)

Trawling is hereby prohibited within the limits of the Northumberland Sea Fisheries District.

Provided that this Bye-law shall not apply to any person trawling for scientific purposes, under the written authority in that behalf of the Local Fisheries Committee, signed by their Clerk, and in accordance with any conditions contained in that authority.

Any person who shall commit a breach of this Bye-law shall, on summary conviction, be liable for each offence £20   to a penalty not exceeding Twenty Pounds, and in the case of a continuing offence to a further penalty not £10   exceeding Ten Pounds for every day during which the offence continues, and in any case, to a forfeiture of any fishing instrument used or sea fish taken in contravention of, or found in the possession of a person contravening this Bye-law.

The following Bye-laws shall apply to the whole area of the Northumberland Sea Fisheries District, except in the cases to which the provisions of the 13th section of the Sea Fisheries Regulation Act, 1888, apply: Provided that nothing in these Bye-laws shall apply to the removal of Crabs or Lobsters for scientific purposes, or for stocking or breeding purposes, by any person acting under the written authority in that behalf of the Local Fisheries Committee, signed by their Clerk, and in accordance with the conditions contained in that authority.

(1) No person shall remove from a Fishery any Lobster which measures less than nine inches from the tip of the beak to the end of the tail when spread as far as possible flat.

(2) During the months of April, May, June, or July, in any year, no person shall remove from a Fishery any Lobster carrying any spawn attached to the tail or other exterior part of the Lobster whether known as 'Berried Lobster,' 'Seed Lobster,' or by any other name.

(3) Any person who takes any Shellfish, the removal of which from a Fishery is prohibited by any Bye-law in force in the district or the possession of which is prohibited by any Act of Parliament, shall forthwith redeposit the same without injury as nearly as possible in the place from which it was taken.

Any person who shall commit a breach of the above Bye-laws, or any of them, shall be liable to a penalty not £20 exceeding for any one offence the sum of £20, and in the £10 case of a continuing offence the additional sum of £10 for every day during which the offence continues, and in any case to forfeiture of any fishing instrument used or any sea fish taken in contravention of or found in the possession of a person contravening the said Bye-laws or any of them.

K 9

NORTH EASTERN SEA FISHERIES DISTRICT.

(From the Tyne to Donna Nook Beacon.)

1. Within the North Eastern Sea Fisheries District, except as may be otherwise provided by the 13th Section of the Sea Fisheries Regulation Act, 1888, a person shall not use in fishing for sea-fish any trawl or trawl net or any net having a beam which is pulled or pushed or otherwise propelled along or over the bottom of or in the sea, or along or over the sea shore, or any seine net, sand-eel net, sparling net, haffle net, or offal net.

Provided that this Bye-law shall not apply to :—

(a) Any person using a net for scientific purposes, under the written authority in that behalf of the Local Fisheries Committee for the District, signed by their Clerk, and in accordance with the conditions contained in such Authority.

(b) Any person using, within so much of the North Eastern Sea Fisheries District as lies between a straight line drawn true East from Castle Eden Dene and a straight line drawn true North-east from Skinningrove Beck, a push net for taking shrimps or prawns, or any person using in any other part of the said District a net for taking shrimps or prawns, with a beam not exceeding 8 feet in extreme length, and raising and clearing the net not less than once in every half-hour.

(c) Any person using, within that portion of the river Humber which lies between a straight line drawn from the entrance to St. Andrew's Dock to the Northern extremity of the Pier at New Holland, and a straight line drawn from Spurn High Lighthouse to Donna Nook Beacon, between the 1st day of March and the 31st day of October both inclusive, in any year, a trawl or trawl net for taking shrimps or prawns, with a beam not exceeding twenty feet in extreme length, such trawl or trawl net being pulled by or from a sailing or row boat, or by a horse or other animal, and being raised and cleared not less than once in every hour.

(d) Any person using in connection with a sailing or row boat, within the area enclosed by a straight line drawn true South-south-west, from the South Landing near Flamborough Head, and a straight line drawn true South-east from the seaward extremity of the North Pier of Bridlington Quay Harbour, between the 1st day of February and the 30th day of September, both inclusive, in any year, a trawl or trawl net, with a beam not exceeding twenty-two feet in extreme length, and raising and clearing the net not less than once in every half-hour.

(e) Any person using for taking sand-eels for bait a net constructed without any purse or pocket and not exceeding 108 feet in extreme length, and 12 feet in extreme depth the central portion whereof to the extent of not less than 12 feet in length, and for the full depth of the net consists of closely textured netting.

(f) Any person using, between the 21st day of July in any year, and the 21st day of March in the following year, for taking sparling, a net made of material not thicker than cotton twine of thirties yarn, twisted nine ply, and the meshes of which net are not less than six-tenths of an inch, measured from knot to knot, when the net is wet.

2. Within so much of the North Eastern Sea Fisheries District as lies (a) between a straight line drawn true East from the Lighthouse on the Heugh at Hartlepool, and a straight line drawn seaward along and in continuation of Coatham Pier, (b) between a straight line drawn true East from Kilnsea Beacon and a straight line drawn true East from Donna Nook, or (c) between a straight line drawn true North-East from Upgang Beck and a straight line drawn true North-East from Saltwick Nab, to the extent seaward of 1590 yards from the base of the Whitby Cliffs, except as may be otherwise provided by the 13th section of the Sea Fisheries Regulation Act, 1888, a person shall not use in fishing for sea-fish any trammel net.

3. Any person committing a breach of either of the preceding Bye-Laws shall be liable to a penalty not exceeding for any one offence the sum of Twenty Pounds, and, in the case of a continuing offence, the additional sum of Ten Pounds

for every day during which the offence continues, and in any case to forfeiture of any fishing instrument used, or fish taken in contravention of, or found in the possession of a person contravening the Bye-Law.

4. So much of section 8 of the Fisheries (Oyster, Crab and Lobster) Act, 1877, as provides that a person shall not be guilty of an offence under that section if he satisfies the Court that the edible crabs found in his possession, or alleged to have been sold, exposed for sale, consigned for sale, or bought for sale, were intended for bait for fishing, shall not apply within the North Eastern Sea Fisheries District.

1. The following Bye-Laws shall apply to the whole area of the North Eastern Sea Fisheries District, except in the cases to which the provisions of the 13th Section of the Sea Fisheries Regulation Act, 1888, apply. Provided that nothing in these Bye-Laws shall apply to any person fishing for, taking, or removing sea fish for scientific purposes or for stocking or breeding purposes, under the written authority in that behalf of the Local Fisheries Committee, signed by their Clerk, and in accordance with the conditions contained in that authority.

2. No person shall remove from a fishery any lobster which measures less than nine inches from the tip of the beak to the end of the tail when spread as far as possible flat.

3. Any person who takes any shellfish, the removal of which from a fishery is prohibited by any Bye-Law in force in the District, or the possession of which is prohibited by any Act of Parliament, shall forthwith redeposit the same, without injury, as nearly as possible in the place from which it was taken.

4. Between the 1st day of September in any year, and the 31st day of January in the following year, both inclusive, no person shall fish for or take any edible crab or lobster.

5. Any person committing a breach of any of the foregoing Bye-Laws shall be liable to a penalty not exceeding for any one offence the sum of Twenty pounds, and in the case of a continuing offence the additional sum of Ten pounds for every day during which the offence continues, and in any case to forfeiture of any fishing instrument used or sea fish taken in contravention of or found in the possession of a person contravening such Bye-Law.

At a Meeting of the Joint Committee for the said North Eastern Sea Fisheries District, held at York on April 22, 1903, in exercise of the powers vested in the said Committee

by the Sea Fisheries Regulation Acts, 1888 to 1894, and the
Regulations of the Board of Trade made thereunder, and of
every other power or authority in anywise enabling the said
Committee in that behalf, the following Bye-Laws were made,
viz. :—

Sea Fisheries Regulation Acts, 1888 to 1894.

North Eastern Sea Fisheries District.

No person shall remove from the Oyster, Mussel, and
Cockle Fishery in the Estuary of the River Tees, as defined
by the Tees Fishery Order, 1902, any mussel which measures
less than two inches in length.

Any person committing a breach of the preceding Bye-
Law shall be liable to a penalty not exceeding for any one
offence the sum of £20, and in the case of a continuing offence
the additional sum of £10 for every day during which the
offence continues, and in any case to forfeiture of any fishing
instrument used or sea fish taken in contravention of or found
in the possession of a person contravening the Bye-Law.

Bye-Laws regulating the taking of Cockles within the
above District, made by the North Eastern Sea Fisheries
Committee on the 21st of October, 1903, and confirmed by the
Board of Agriculture and Fisheries on the 2nd of January
1904:

1. No person shall use any instrument for the purpose
   of taking Cockles other than a rake or other like
   instrument not exceeding twelve inches in length,
   and having spaces of not less than three-quarters
   of an inch between the teeth.
2. No person shall remove from a Fishery any Cockle
   which will pass through a gauge having an oblong
   opening of three-quarters of an inch in breadth
   and two inches in length.
3. Any person committing a breach of either of the
   preceding Bye-laws shall be liable to a penalty
   not exceeding for any one offence the sum of £20,
   and in the case of a continuing offence the additional sum of £10 for every day during which the

offence continues, and in any case to forfeiture of any fishing instrument used, or sea fish taken, in contravention of, or found in the possession of, a person contravening the Bye-laws.

[*Note.*—The Tees Bye-laws are still before the Board of Agriculture and Fisheries, and will not be confirmed in time to include them here.—F. G. A.]

EASTERN SEA FISHERIES DISTRICT.

(*Donna Nook Beacon to Happisburgh.*)

The following Bye-Laws shall apply to the whole area of the Eastern Sea Fisheries District, unless otherwise specified and except in the cases to which the provisions of the 13th Section of the Sea Fisheries Regulation Act, 1888, apply.

Provided that nothing in these Bye-Laws shall apply to any person fishing for sea fish for scientific purposes under the written authority in that behalf of the Local Fisheries Committee, signed by their Clerk and in accordance with the conditions contained in that authority.

1. Within that portion of the Eastern Sea Fisheries District which lies between a line drawn true North from Wells Lifeboat House and a line drawn true North-East from Happisburgh Lighthouse, no person shall use any trawl net in fishing for sea fish. Provided that this Bye-law shall not apply to any person using, between a line drawn true North-East from Cromer Lighthouse and a line drawn true North-East from Happisburgh Lighthouse, a trawl net for taking shrimps or prawns, with a trawl beam not exceeding 10 feet in extreme length.

2. Within that portion of the said District which lies North of a line drawn true East from the Coast Guard Station at Gibraltar Point.

    (*a*) No person shall use any trawl net in fishing for sea fish except in accordance with the following regulations :—

        1. The net shall not be used in connection with any vessel other than a sailing or row boat.

        2. The net shall be raised and cleared not less than once in every hour.

3. The length of the trawl beam shall not exceed 22 feet, and if two or more trawl nets are used in fishing at the same time from the same boat, the total length of the trawl beams together shall not exceed 22 feet.

(b) Between the first day of December and the last day of February following, both inclusive, no person shall use any trawl net in fishing for shrimps or prawns.

3. No person shall use in fishing for sea fish any otter or beamless trawl.

4. No person shall use in fishing for shrimps or prawns any trawl net otherwise than from a boat unless such net be raised and cleared not less than once in every half hour and the contents forthwith sorted and sifted into the sea at a place where the water is at the time not less than 6 inches in depth.

5. No person shall fish for or take any smelts or sparling between the first day of April and the thirty-first day of August, both inclusive in any year.

6. No person shall fish for or take any mussels between the first day of May, and the thirty-first day of August, both inclusive in any year.

Provided that any person holding a written authority in that behalf, signed by the Clerk to the Committee, may, during the month of May, subject to any conditions contained in the authority, remove mussels from one part of the Eastern Sea Fisheries District to another part thereof for stocking or breeding purposes.

7. No person shall take any mussel of a less size than two inches in length.

Provided that any person holding a written authority in that behalf, signed by the Clerk to the Committee, may, subject to any conditions contained in the authority, remove mussels of a less size than two inches in length from one part of the Eastern Sea Fisheries District to another part thereof for stocking or breeding purposes.

8. No person shall use any instrument for the purpose of taking mussels other than a rake or other like instrument not

exceeding eighteen inches in width, and having spaces of not less than one inch between the teeth.

9. No person shall use any instrument for the purpose of taking cockles other than a rake or other like instrument not exceeding twelve inches in length, and having spaces of not less than three-quarters of an inch between the teeth.

10. Within that portion of the said District which lies between a line drawn true East from the Coast Guard Station at Gibraltar Point, and a line drawn true East by North and true West by South through the Lower Light Beacon on the Benington Sand (except in cases to which the provisions of the 13th Section of the Sea Fisheries Regulation Act, 1888, apply) no person shall remove from the fishery any cockle which will pass through a gauge having an oblong opening of three quarters of an inch in breadth and two inches in length.

11. No person shall fish for or take any periwinkles between the 1st day of May and the 31st day of August, both inclusive in any year from the following portions of the district :—

    (a) The Toft Beacon Scalp.
    (b) The Mare Tail Scalp.
    (c) The Gat Sand Scalp.
    (d) The Old South Middle Scalp.
    (e) The Herring Hill Scalp.

12. So much of section 8 of the Fisheries (Oyster, Crab and Lobster) Act, 1877, as provides that a person shall not be guilty of an offence under that section if he satisfies the Court that the edible crabs found in his possession or alleged to have been sold, exposed for sale, consigned for sale, or bought for sale were intended for bait for fishing, shall not apply within the Eastern Sea Fisheries District.

13. Between the first day of November and the 30th day of June following, both inclusive, no person shall remove from a fishery any crab of the kind locally known as the 'white-footed' crab.

14. No person shall remove from a fishery

    (a) Any lobster carrying any spawn attached to the tail or other exterior part of the lobster, whether known as 'berried' lobster, 'seed' lobster, or by any other name.

    (b) Any lobster which has recently cast its shell and is still in 'soft' condition, whether known as 'soft' lobster, or by any other name.

15. Any person who takes any crab or lobster, the removal of which from a fishery is prohibited by this Bye-Law, or the possession of which is prohibited by the Fisheries (Oyster, Crab and Lobster) Act, 1877, shall forthwith re-deposit the same in the sea as nearly as may be in the place from which it was taken.

16. The deposit or discharge of any solid or liquid substance detrimental to Sea Fish or Sea Fishing is hereby prohibited.

> Any person who shall commit a breach of any of the foregoing Bye-laws shall be liable to a penalty not exceeding for any one offence the sum of twenty pounds, and in the case of a continuing offence the additional sum of ten pounds for every day during which the offence continues, and in any case to forfeiture of any fishing instrument used or sea fish taken in contravention of or found in the possession of a person contravening such Bye-laws.

Boston Fishery Order, 1897.

The following are the description and limits of the fishery comprised in this Order (hereinafter called 'the fishery') as shewn on plans deposited at the Board of Trade, namely :

> All those parts of the foreshore and bed of Boston Haven and estuary known as Boston Deeps, situate within the county of Lincoln, containing an area of 122 square miles, or thereabouts, and bounded as follows, that is to say : To the west and north by the line of ordinary high water mark from the point where the northern bank of Dawes Mere Creek intersects the old Roman bank in the parish of Gedney, to a point on the western bank of the River Witham, opposite Hobhole Sluice, thence by an imaginary line to Hobhole Sluice, and thence by the line of ordinary high water mark to the Coast Guard Station at Skegness, such boundaries being within or adjacent to the several parishes of Gedney, Holbeach, Frampton, Wyberton, Fishtoft, Freiston, Butterwick, Benington, Leverton Leake, Wrangle, Friskney, Wainfleet and Skegness.   To the

east and south by an imaginary line drawn from the last-named point to the Outer Knock buoy situated at the lower end of a sand known as the Outer Knock Sand, thence by an imaginary line drawn across two sands known as the 'Dog's Head Sand' and the 'Long Sand' to the Roger buoy, situated at the south-west point of a sand called the 'Roger Sand,' and known as the 'Roger Point,' thence by an imaginary line drawn to the 'Gat Buoy,' situated to the south of a sand known as the 'Gat Sand,' thence by an imaginary line drawn in a south-westerly direction along the north-western side of the Wisbech Channel to the Bachelor's Beacon and thence along the northern side of Dawes Mere Creek (but not including the said creek) up to the old Roman bank in the parish of Gedney at the point of intersection first mentioned.

The following Bye-Laws are in force _only_ within the limits of this Order.

1. No person shall dredge, fish for, or take any Mussel except

(*a*) By hand or

(*b*) With a dredge, not exceeding 3 feet in width, used from a sea-fishing boat, when the Mussel bed is covered with water at least 4 feet deep or

(*c*) With a didle or rake, not exceeding 3 feet in width, used from a sea-fishing boat, when the Mussel bed is covered with water at least 4 feet deep ;

and no person dredging, fishing for, or taking Mussels shall cause any sea-fishing boat to be so berthed or grounded as to injure any Mussels.

2. No person shall remove from the Fishery or from one part of the Fishery to another part thereof any Mussel less than 2¼ inches in length.

Any person dredging, fishing for, or taking any Mussels in contravention thereof or in contravention of any of the provisions of the Boston Fishery Order, 1897, is liable to a penalty not exceeding 20*l.* for each offence and to forfeiture of any Mussels so taken or a sum equal to the value thereof.

Licenses to dredge, fish for, or take Mussels on payment of the prescribed Tolls, can be obtained from Mr. H. Donnison, Fishery Inspector, Boston.

KENT AND ESSEX SEA FISHERIES DISTRICT.

(*Dovercourt to Dungeness.*)

1. The following Bye-laws shall apply to the whole area of the Kent and Essex Sea Fisheries District, unless otherwise specified, and except in the cases to which the provisions of the 13th Section of the Sea Fisheries Regulation Act, 1888, apply.

2. No person shall use in fishing for flounders or soles any net having more than 30 rows of knots to the linear yard, except that for a length of 10 feet from the cod end there may be not more than 36 rows of knots to the yard.

3. No person shall use in fishing for smelts any net having more than 72 rows of knots to the linear yard, or any net more than 60 fathoms in length, measured along the head-rope.

4. No person shall use in fishing for garfish any net having more than 54 rows of knots to the linear yard, except that in the middle of the net for a space of 20 fathoms there may be not more than 72 knots to the yard.

5. No person shall use in fishing for shrimps, prawns or eels any trawl net having more than 108 rows of knots to the linear yard, except that for a length of 8 feet from the cod end there may be not more than 144 rows of knots to the yard.

6. Except as is hereinbefore provided, no person shall use in fishing for sea-fish any trawl net having more than 36 rows of knots to the linear yard.

7. No person shall use in fishing for sprats any stow boat net having more than 72 rows of knots to the linear yard, except that at the enter and in the sleeves there may be not more than 108 rows of knots to the yard.

8. No person shall use in fishing for sea-fish any net having more than 144 rows of knots to the linear yard.

9. No person shall take or fish for whitebait between the first day of August and the thirtieth day of October following, both inclusive.

10. No person shall remove any culch from any oyster ground.

11. No person shall remove from a fishery any berried lobster.

12. No person shall use the method of fishing known as 'trotting' except with lines baited with fish, other than soles, plaice, dabs, or flounders.

13. No person shall use two or more nets placed behind or near to each other, or cover the nets with canvas, or use any other artifice in such manner as to practically diminish the mesh of the nets, and all measurements referred to in the foregoing Bye-laws shall be measurements made when the net is wet.

14. Any person acting in contravention of any of the above Bye-laws shall, on summary conviction, be liable for each offence to a penalty not exceeding 5l., and in the case of a continuing offence the additional sum of 3l. for every day during which the offence continues, and in any case to the forfeiture of any fishing instrument used, or sea-fish taken in contravention of, or found in the possession of any person contravening such Bye-law.

15. The deposit or discharge of any solid or liquid substance detrimental to sea-fish or sea-fishing is hereby prohibited. Provided that this Bye-law shall not apply (1) to the deposit or discharge of refuse by the Lords Commissioners of the Admiralty in the River Thames below 'The Mouse' lightship and near the 'Mouse Sand,' or (2) to the deposit by any other person with the consent in writing of the Committee given under the hand of their Clerk and confirmed by the Board of Trade, of any such solid or liquid substance on an area shewn on a chart referred to in the consent, and in accordance with the conditions laid down in that consent. Any person acting in contravention of this Bye-law shall on summary conviction be liable for each offence to a penalty not exceeding 20l., and in the case of a continuing offence the additional sum of 10l. for every day during which the offence continues.

ADDITIONAL BYE-LAW.

No person shall fish for or take periwinkles or winkles otherwise than by hand picking.

Any person acting in contravention of the above Bye-law shall, on summary conviction, be liable for each offence to a penalty not exceeding 5l., and in the case of a continuing offence the additional sum of 3l. for every day during which the offence continues, and in any case to the forfeiture of any fishing instrument used, or sea fish taken in contravention of or found in the possession of any person contravening such Bye-law.

SUSSEX SEA FISHERIES DISTRICT.
(*Dungeness to Hayling Island.*)

1. The following Bye-laws shall unless otherwise specified, apply to the whole area of the Sussex Sea Fisheries District, except in the cases to which the provisions of the 13th Section of the Sea Fisheries Regulation Act, 1888, apply.

2. In that part of the Sussex Sea Fisheries District which lies within a line drawn across the entrance to Chichester Harbour from East Head to Black Point, no person shall use in fishing for sea fish any stake or stop net except in accordance with the following conditions:—

> (a) During the period between the commencement of the last hour before low water and the expiration of the first hour after low water, no stake or stop net shall be placed or maintained across, or partly across, any channel or creek.
>
> (b) In the case of any channel or creek, or any part thereof which becomes dry at low water, no stake or stop net shall be placed or maintained across, or partly across, any such channel or creek or part thereof during the period between the commencement of the last hour before the tide leaves such channel or creek or part thereof, and the expiration of the first hour after the tide has begun to re-enter the same respectively.

3. No person shall take or fish for periwinkles between the First day of May and the Thirty-first day of October following, both inclusive.

4. The deposit or discharge of any solid or liquid substance detrimental to sea fish or sea fishing is hereby prohibited : Provided that this Bye-law shall not apply (1) to the deposit by the Lords Commissioners of the Admiralty within the area coloured pink on the chart marked S, 753, 1894, in the possession of the Board of Trade, of refuse dredged or excavated in the course of any Admiralty works within the Dockyard Port of Portsmouth, or (2) to the deposit by any other person with the consent in writing of the Committee, given under the hand of their Clerk and confirmed by the Board of Trade, of any such solid or liquid substance, on an

area shown on a chart referred to in the consent, and in accordance with the conditions laid down in that consent.

5. After the Thirty-first day of May, 1895, no person shall use in fishing for sea fish, other than Prawns and Shrimps, any trawl net having more than thirty rows of knots to the yard, measured when wet.

6. Any person who shall commit a breach of any of the foregoing Bye-laws shall be liable to a penalty not exceeding for any one offence the sum of Twenty pounds, and in the case of a continuing offence the additional sum of Ten pounds for every day during which the offence continues, and, in any case, to forfeiture of any fishing instrument used, or sea fish taken in contravention of, or found in the possession of a person contravening any of the said Bye-laws.

7. No person shall use in fishing for sea fish any seine or draft or tuck net having more than thirty rows of knots to the yard, measured when wet, except during the months of May, June or July, in any year, when a net, having not more than thirty-six rows of knots to the yard, measured as afore-said, may be used. Provided that this Bye-law shall not apply to any person fishing for sprats during the months of November, December or January, with a net having not more than ninety rows of knots to the yard, measured as aforesaid, or to any person fishing for sand eels for the purpose of bait, during the months of May, June, July or August, in any year between the hours of sunrise and sunset in any Sub-District, within any area or areas approved for that purpose by the Local Fisheries Committee and designated on a map signed by the Clerk of the Committee, and deposited at his office, such areas not to exceed in the aggregate in the case of each Sub-District one half of a square mile.

This Bye-law shall apply to the whole area of the Sussex Sea Fisheries District, except as above provided, and except in the cases to which the provisions of the 13th Section of the Sea Fisheries Regulation Act, 1888, apply.

Any person who shall commit a breach of this Bye-law shall be liable to a penalty, not exceeding for any one offence, the sum of twenty pounds, and in the case of a continuing offence the additional sum of ten pounds for every day during which the offence continues, and in any case to forfeiture of any fishing instrument used or sea fish taken in contravention of or found in the possession of a· person contravening the Bye-law.

SOUTHERN SEA FISHERIES DISTRICT.

(Hayling Island to Western Boundary of Dorset.)

1. The following Bye-laws shall apply to the whole area of the Southern Sea Fisheries District, except in the cases to which the provisions of the 13th Section of the Sea Fisheries Regulation Act, 1888, apply : Provided that nothing in these Bye-laws shall apply to any person removing any sea fish for scientific purposes, or for stocking or breeding purposes, under the written authority in that behalf of the Local Fisheries Committee, signed by their Clerk, and in accordance with the conditions contained in that authority.

2. No person shall use any instrument for taking Oysters between the Fifteenth day of May and the Thirtieth day of September in any year, both days inclusive.

3. No person shall take Periwinkles between the First day of May and the Thirty-first day of August in any year, both days inclusive.

4. The deposit or discharge of any solid or liquid substance detrimental to Sea fish or Sea fishing is hereby prohibited. Provided that this bye-law shall not apply (1) to the deposit by the Lords Commissioners of the Admiralty within the area coloured pink on the chart marked S.2041, 1894, in the possession of the Board of Trade, of refuse dredged or excavated in the course of the execution of any Admiralty works within the Dockyard Port of Portsmouth ; or (2) to the deposit by the said Lords Commissioners within the area coloured pink on the chart marked S.1485, 1894, in the possession of the Board of Trade, of refuse dredged or excavated in the course of any Admiralty works within the Harbour or Roads of Portland ; or (3) to the deposit by any other person with the consent in writing of the Committee, given under the hand of their Clerk and confirmed by the Board of Trade, of any such solid or liquid substance on an area shewn on a chart referred to in the consent and in accordance with the conditions laid down in that consent.

5. No person shall use in fishing for Sea fish any trawl-net in connection with a vessel which is for the time being propelled otherwise than by sails or oars.

6. No person shall remove from any fishery any Oyster which will pass through a circular ring of Two Inches in

internal diameter, or any Culch or other material for the reception of spat, that is to say, of the spawn or young of any kinds of shell fish.   Any such Oyster, Culch, or other material for the reception of spat which may be lifted while fishing or otherwise, shall at once be re-deposited as nearly as may be on the same fishing ground.

7. No person shall use in fishing for Sea fish any kind of Trawl Net in those portions of the Southern Sea Fisheries District which lie within : (a) A straight line drawn from the landward end of Folly Pier in the Isle of Portland to White Nose (or White Nore) Head, or (b) A line drawn true South from the Chapel on St. Alban's Head until it reaches a point three nautical miles beyond ordinary low water mark, and thence continued in a Westerly direction parallel to and at a distance of three nautical miles from the general line of the coast at ordinary low water until it reaches the line hereinbefore first mentioned.

8. No person shall remove from a Fishery—

(a) any Lobster measuring less than nine inches from the tip of the beak to the end of the tail, when spread as far as possible flat.

(b) any edible Crab measuring less than five inches across the broadest part of the back.

9. No person shall take periwinkles except by hand-picking.

10. Any person who takes any shell fish, the removal of which from a fishery is prohibited by any bye-law in force in the district, or the possession of which is prohibited by any Act of Parliament, shall forthwith re-deposit the same, without injury, as nearly as possible in the place from which it was taken.

11. Any person offending against any of the foregoing Bye-laws shall be liable for any one offence to a penalty not exceeding Twenty Pounds, and in the case of a continuing offence the additional sum of Ten Pounds for every day during which the offence continues, and in any case to forfeiture of any fishing instrument used or Sea fish taken in contravention of or found in the possession of a person contravening the Bye-law.

DEVON SEA FISHERIES DISTRICT.

Southern Division : Eastern Boundary of Devon to Rame Head ; Northern Division : Western Boundary to Eastern Boundary of Devon.

1. The following Bye-laws shall apply to the whole area of the Devon Sea Fisheries District, except where otherwise specified, and except in the cases to which the provisions of the 13th Section of ' The Sea Fisheries Regulation Act, 1888,' apply. Provided that nothing therein or herein contained shall apply to a person fishing for sea fish or removing shell fish solely for scientific purposes, or for stocking or breeding purposes, under the written authority in that behalf of the Local Fisheries Committee of the District, signed by their Clerk, and in accordance with the conditions contained in that authority.

2. The deposit or discharge of any solid or liquid substance detrimental to Sea Fish or sea fishing is hereby prohibited, provided that nothing in this Bye-law contained shall affect the power of any Sanitary or other Local Authority to discharge sewage from any outfall in use on the 27th June, 1893.

3. No person shall use in fishing for Sea Fish any kind of Trawl Net in connection with a vessel which is for the time being propelled otherwise than by sails or oars.

4. No person shall remove from a Fishery :

> (a) Any Lobster measuring less than 9 inches from the tip of the beak to the end of the tail when spread as far as possible flat ;
>
> (b) Any edible crab measuring less than 5 inches across the broadest part of the back.

5. Any person who takes any Shell Fish, the removal of which from a Fishery is prohibited by any Bye-law in force in the District, or the possession of which is prohibited by any Act of Parliament, shall forthwith re-deposit the same without injury in the water, and as near as possible to the place from which they were taken.

6. No person shall use in fishing for sea fish :

> (a) Any Trammel Net exceeding 65 fathoms in length.
>
> (b) Any Trammel Net in such manner that any portion thereof shall be joined to, or shot or worked within a distance of 100 yards from any portion of, any other net whatsoever.

7. No person shall use in fishing for Sea Fish any kind of trawl net within any of those portions of the Devon Sea Fisheries District which lie to the landward side of the following lines, respectively :—

(a) A line drawn straight from the Southernmost extremity of Rame Head to the Mewstone off the mouth of the River Yealm, and thence straight to the seaward extremity of Bolt Tail ;

(b) A line drawn straight from the seaward extremity of Bolt Head to the seaward extremity of Prawl Point ;

(c) A line drawn East by a quarter South straight from the seaward extremity of Prawl Point, and keeping Prawl Point open of the Start, until it intersects a line drawn South-West by a quarter South straight from the seaward extremity of Berry Head, keeping open Downend Point, and continued along such last mentioned line until it reaches Berry Head ;

(d) A line drawn straight from the Lighthouse on the Breakwater at Brixham to the seaward extremity of Hope's Nose ;

(e) A line drawn straight from the seaward extremity of Hope's Nose to the seaward extremity of Straight Point ;

(f) A line drawn straight from the seaward extremity of Straight Point to the seaward extremity of Beer Head ;

Provided that this Bye-Law shall not apply to any person fishing for shrimps or prawns from a vessel or boat for the time being propelled only by sails or oars, and not exceeding five tons gross register, with a shrimp net having a beam not exceeding eight feet in length measured between the trawl heads or irons and raising and clearing such shrimp net at least once in every thirty minutes.

8. Within that portion of the Devon Sea Fisheries District which lies to the landward side of a line drawn from the Coastguard Station at Exmouth straight to the Mount Pleasant Inn, in the parish of Kenton, no person shall use in fishing for Sea Fish :

(a) Any kind of Trawl Net or Trammel Net ;

(b) Any net having a mesh through which a square gauge of 1¼ inches measured across each side of the square or 6 inches measured round the four sides will not pass without pressure when the net is wet.

9. Within that portion of the Devon Sea Fisheries District which lies to the landward side of a line drawn from the Flagstaff at Turf straight to the south-eastern extremity of Woodbury Road Station on the London and South-Western Railway, no person shall use in fishing for Sea Fish any net between the 1st day of September and the 15th day of April following, both inclusive.

10. Within that portion of the Devon Sea Fisheries District which lies to the landward side of a line drawn along the south side of the Starcross Pier to the eastern extremity thereof, and thence continued straight to Courtlands Beach Gate, no person shall use any net for fishing for Sea Fish between noon on Saturday and 6 o'clock on the following Monday morning.

11. Within those portions of the Devon Sea Fisheries District which lie to the landward side of a line drawn from Lord Clifford's House at Shaldon straight to the Lighthouse at Teignmouth, no person shall use in fishing for Sea Fish any net having a mesh through which a square gauge of 1¼ inches measured across each side of the square or 6 inches measured round the four sides will not pass without pressure when the net is wet.

12. Any person who shall commit a breach of any of the foregoing Bye-Laws shall be liable to a penalty not exceeding, for any one offence, the sum of Twenty Pounds, and in the case of a continuing offence, the additional sum of Ten Pounds for every day during which the offence continues, and in any case to forfeiture of any Fishing Instruments used or Sea Fish taken in contravention of, or found in the possession of a person contravening, any of the said Bye-Laws.

CORNWALL SEA FISHERIES DISTRICT.

(Rame Head to Northern Boundary of Cornwall.)

Steam Trawling is hereby prohibited within the limits of the Cornwall Sea Fisheries District.

Any person offending against this Bye-law shall, on summary conviction, be liable for each offence to a penalty not exceeding Twenty Pounds, and, in the case of a continuing offence, the additional sum of Ten Pounds for every day during which the offence continues, and, in any case, to the forfeiture of any fishing instrument used, or sea fish taken in contravention of, or found in the possession of a person contravening this Bye-law.

No person shall remove from a fishery any edible Crab which measures less than five inches across the broadest part of the back. Provided that this Bye-law shall not apply to any person removing any such Crab for scientific purposes, or for stocking or breeding purposes under the written authority in that behalf of the Local Fisheries Committee, signed by their Clerk, and in accordance with the conditions contained in that Authority.

This Bye-law shall apply to the whole area of the Cornwall Sea Fisheries District except in the cases to which the provisions of the 13th Section of the Sea Fisheries Regulation Act 1888 apply.

Any person acting in contravention of this Bye-law shall be liable to a penalty not exceeding for any one offence the sum of Twenty Pounds, and in the case of a continuing offence, the additional sum of Ten Pounds for every day during which the offence continues, and in any case to forfeiture of any fishing instrument used or sea fish taken in contravention of, or found in the possession of a person contravening this Bye-law.

GLAMORGAN SEA FISHERIES DISTRICT.

[Nash Point to Worm's Head.]

1. The following Bye-laws shall apply to the whole area of the Glamorgan Sea Fisheries District, except in the cases to which the provisions of the 13th Section of 'The Sea Fisheries Regulation Act, 1888,' apply.

2. No person shall use any artifice or device so as practically to diminish the size of the mesh of any net.

3. No person shall use

    (a) Any net for taking shrimps or prawns having a mesh through which a square gauge of $\frac{3}{8}$ of an inch measured across each side of the square, or $1\frac{1}{2}$ inches measured round the four sides, will not pass without pressure when the net is wet ;

(b) Any stop net for taking sprats having a mesh through which a square gauge $\frac{9}{16}$ of an inch measured across each side of the square, or $2\frac{1}{4}$ inches measured round the four sides, will not pass without pressure when the net is wet;

(c) Any trawl net for taking sea fish, other than shrimps or prawns, having a mesh through which a square gauge of $1\frac{1}{2}$ inches measured across each side of the square, or 6 inches measured round the four sides, will not pass without pressure when the net is wet; or

(d) Any net not hereinbefore specified for taking sea fish having a mesh through which a square gauge of 1 inch measured across each side of the square, or 4 inches measured round the four sides, will not pass without pressure when the net is wet.

4. No person shall use any trawl net having a beam of greater length than 40 feet between the trawl heads or irons.

5. No person shall use any trawl, shank, bow, hand or hose net having a less circumference than one hundred meshes.

6. No person shall use any trawl net for taking shrimps or prawns having a less circumference than one hundred and sixty meshes.

7. No person shall use any stop net for taking sprats between the 1st day of December and the 31st day of August following, both inclusive.

8. No person shall use any stake or stop net in fishing for sea fish except in accordance with the following regulations :—

(a) The site of the net shall be marked by poles, perches, or buoys visible above the surface at high water of spring tides, and such poles, perches, or buoys shall be maintained so long as the stakes of the net continue in position.

(b) No portion of the net shall be at a less distance than 10 yards from any portion of another stake or stop net or of any fishing weir.

(c) A pool shall be provided and maintained in connection with each stake or stop net, and such pool shall be at least 12 inches in depth at low water during the months of May, June, July, August, September and October in every year, and at other times of the year not less than 6 inches in depth ; and such pool shall be at least three-fourths of the size of the cage provided in connection with such stake or stop net ; provided that in any case such pool shall not in area be less than 36 square feet.

9. No person shall use in fishing for sea fish any weir the butt whereof is not constructed with apertures through which a square gauge of 1 inch measured across each side of the square, or 4 inches measured round the four sides, will pass without pressure (when the butt is wet).

10. No person shall take cockles, except (a) by hand, or (b) with a rake not exceeding 12 inches in width, and having teeth not less than ¾ of an inch apart.

11. No person shall take mussels, except (a) with a dredge, (b) by hand, or (c) with a rake not exceeding 3 feet in width, and having teeth not less than 1 inch apart.

12. No person shall take mussels during the months of May, June and July in any year, provided that any person holding a written authority in that behalf, signed by the Clerk of the Committee, may, during the month of May, subject to any conditions contained in the authority, remove mussels from one part of the Glamorgan Sea Fisheries District to another part thereof for stocking or breeding purposes.

This Bye-law shall not apply to the area of the Swansea Fishery Order, 1892.

13. No person shall deposit or discharge any solid or liquid substance, detrimental to sea fish or sea fishing.

14. Any person who shall commit a breach of any of the foregoing Bye-laws shall be liable to a penalty not exceeding for any one offence the sum of 20*l*., and in the case of a continuing offence, to the additional sum of 10*l*. for every day during which the offence continues, and in any case to forfeiture of any fishing instrument used or sea fish taken in contravention of or found in the possession of a person contravening any of the said Bye-laws.

15. No person shall use in fishing for sea fish any trawl net in connection with a vessel propelled otherwise than by sails or oars : Provided that this Bye-law shall not apply to

any person fishing for sea fish for scientific purposes under
the written authority in that behalf of the Local Fisheries
Committee, signed by their Clerk and in accordance with the
conditions contained in that authority. This Bye-law shall
apply to the whole area of the Glamorgan Sea Fisheries
District, except in the cases to which the provisions of the
13th section of the 'Sea Fisheries Regulation Act, 1888,'
apply. Any person who shall commit a breach of this Bye-
law shall be liable to a penalty not exceeding for any one
offence the sum of 20*l*., and in the case of a continuing
offence the additional sum of 10*l*. for every day during which
the offence continues, and in any case to forfeiture of any
fishing instrument used, or sea fish taken in contravention of
or found in the possession of a person contravening the Bye-
law.

16. The following Bye-laws shall apply to the whole area
of the Glamorgan Sea Fisheries District, except in the cases
to which the provisions of the 13th section of the 'Sea
Fisheries Regulation Act, 1888,' apply : Provided that nothing
in these Bye-laws shall apply to any person fishing for sea fish
for scientific purposes, or for stocking or breeding purposes,
under the written authority in that behalf of the Local
Fisheries Committee, signed by their Clerk, and in accordance
with the conditions contained in that authority.

(1)—No person shall remove from a fishery any cockle
which will pass through a gauge having an
oblong opening of ¾ of an inch in breadth, and
not less than 2 inches in length.

(2)—Any person who takes any shell fish, the removal
of which from a fishery is prohibited by any
Bye-law in force in the district, or the possession of which is prohibited by any Act of Parliament, shall forthwith re-deposit the same without
injury as nearly as possible in the place from
which they were taken, and, in re-depositing
cockles in accordance with this Bye-law, shall
spread them thinly and evenly over the beds.

(3) Any person who shall commit a breach of any of
the foregoing Bye-laws shall be liable to a
penalty not exceeding for any one offence the
sum of 20*l*., and, in the case of a continuing
offence, the additional sum of 10*l*. for every day
during which the offence continues, and in any

case to forfeiture of any fishing instrument used or sea fish taken in contravention of or found in the possession of a person contravening such Bye-law.

MILFORD HAVEN SEA FISHERIES DISTRICT.

(Worms Head to Cemmaes Head.)

BYE-LAWS.

1. The following Bye-laws shall apply to the whole area of the Milford Haven Sea Fisheries District unless otherwise specified, and except in the cases to which the provisions of the 13th section of the Sea Fisheries Regulation Act, 1888, apply: Provided that nothing in these Bye-laws shall apply to any person fishing for Sea fish for scientific purposes or for stocking or breeding purposes under the written authority in that behalf of the local Fisheries Committee signed by their Clerk and in accordance with the conditions contained in that authority.

2. No person shall use in fishing for shrimps or prawns any net having a mesh through which a square gauge of three-eighths of an inch measured across each side of the square or one and a half inches measured round the four sides will not pass without pressure when the net is wet.

3. After the 30th day of April, 1897, no person shall use in fishing for mackerel or herrings :

    (a) Any seine, draft, drift, or stake net having a mesh through which a square gauge of one inch measured across each side of the square or four inches measured round the four sides will not pass without pressure when the net is wet ;

    (b) Any stake net except at the times and places at which and in the manner in which such nets have been heretofore commonly used for the capture of such fish respectively ;

Provided that this Bye-law shall not apply to that part of the District which lies above a line drawn across Milford Haven true south from the extremity of Milford Pier.

4. No person shall use in fishing for sea fish other than shrimps or prawns any trawl net having a mesh through which a square gauge of one inch and a half measured across

each side of the square or six inches measured round the four sides will not pass without pressure when the net is wet; provided that until the 1st day of May, 1897, this Bye-law shall not apply to any person using within a line drawn straight from the seaward extremity of Ragwen Point to the seaward extremity of Burry Holmes a trawl net with a beam not exceeding 18 feet in length measured between the trawl heads or irons and raising and clearing the net not less than once in every half hour and returning forthwith to the water with the least possible injury all undersized sea fish which may have been taken in the net.

5. No artifice or device shall be used so as practically to diminish the size of the mesh of any net.

6. No person shall use any net for taking sparling between the 1st day of March and the 31st day of August both inclusive in any year.

7. No person shall use in fishing for sea fish any stake net except in accordance with the following regulations :

(a) The site of the net shall be marked by poles, perches, or buoys, visible above the surface at high water of spring tides, and such poles, perches, or buoys shall be maintained so long as any of the stakes of the net continue in position ;

(b) No portion of the net shall be nearer the centre of any stream or channel than the edge of such stream or channel at low water of a tide the high water line of which registers 22 feet at Pembroke Dock Yard ;

(c) No portion of the net shall be nearer than fifty yards to any portion of another stake net.

8. No person shall fish for mussels except

(a) By hand ;
(b) With a dradge ; or
(c) With a rake not exceeding three feet in width, and used only from a boat when the mussel bed is covered with at least four feet of water.

9. No person shall use any rake for taking mussels during the months of May, June, July or August in any year.

10. No person shall use any kind of trawl net within those portions of the Milford Haven Sea Fisheries District

which lie to the landward side of the following lines respectively :

(a) A line drawn across Fishguard Bay straight from
the seaward extremity of Dinas Head to the seaward extremity of Penanglas ;

(b) A line drawn straight from the southern extremity
of Ramsey Island to the highest point of Black
Cliff near Nolton Haven ;

(c) A line drawn straight from the highest point of
Green Scar to the highest point of the Howney
Stone and thence straight to the highest point of
the Garland Stone off Skomer Island ;

(d) A line drawn straight from the seaward extremity
of Giltar Point to the seaward extremity of
Ragwen Point ;

(e) A line drawn straight from the seaward extremity
of Ragwen Point to the seaward extremity of
Burry Holmes ; Provided that this Bye-law shall
not apply to any person using within such last-
mentioned line a trawl net with a beam not
exceeding 18 feet in length measured between
the trawl heads or irons, and raising and clearing
the net not less than once in every half-hour,
and returning forthwith to the water with the
least possible injury all undersized Sea fish
which may have been taken in the net.

11. The deposit or discharge of any solid or liquid substance detrimental to Sea fish or Sea fishing is hereby
prohibited : Provided that this Bye-law shall not apply (1) to
the deposit by the Lords Commissioners of the Admiralty
within the area coloured pink on the chart marked S1526–
1896 in the possession of the Board of Trade of refuse
dredged or excavated in the course of any Admiralty works
within Milford Haven ; or (2) to the deposit by any other
person with the consent in writing of the Committee given
under the hand of their Clerk and confirmed by the Board of
Trade of any such solid or liquid substance on an area shewn
on a chart referred to in the consent, and in accordance with
the conditions laid down in that consent.

12. Any person who shall commit a breach of any of the
foregoing Bye-laws shall be liable to a penalty not exceeding
for any one offence the sum of Twenty Pounds, and in the

case of a continuing offence the additional sum of Ten Pounds for every day during which the offence continues and in any case to forfeiture of any fishing instrument used or sea fish taken in contravention of or found in the possession of a person contravening such Bye-law: Provided that, subject to the provisions of Bye-law 10 (d) and of any Bye-law pre-scribing a close season, in any case in which a prosecution is instituted for taking sea fish with a net or instrument the use of which for the capture of any particular kind of sea fish would constitute a breach of any of the foregoing Bye-laws a person shall not be deemed to have committed such a breach if he proves to the satisfaction of the court that he was *bona fide* fishing only for the particular kind of sea fish permitted to be captured with the net or instrument he was then using.

LANCASHIRE AND WESTERN SEA FISHERIES DISTRICT.

(*Cemmaes Head to Haverigg Point.*)

BYE-LAWS.

1. The following Bye-laws shall apply to the whole area of the Lancashire and Western Sea Fisheries District, unless otherwise specified, and except in the cases to which the pro-visions of the 13th Section of 'The Sea Fisheries Regulation Act, 1888,' apply. Provided that nothing in these Bye-laws shall apply to any person fishing for sea fish for scientific purposes, or for stocking or breeding purposes, or removing mussels during the close season for use as bait under the written authority in that behalf of the Local Fisheries Com-mittee, signed by their Clerk or Clerks, and in accordance with the conditions set out in that authority.

2. No artifice or device shall be used so as practically to diminish the size of the mesh of any net.

3. No person shall use in fishing for sea fish any net with any trap or pocket, provided that this Bye-law shall not apply to any person using a fish trawl net the mesh of which is in accordance with Bye-law 4.

4. No person shall use in fishing for sea fish, other than shrimps, prawns, mackerel, herring, sparling, or garfish, any net having a mesh through which a square gauge of one and three-quarter inches, measured across each side of the square,

or seven inches measured round the four sides, will not pass
without pressure when the net is wet, provided that between
the 1st day of June and the 15th day of November following,
both inclusive, it shall be lawful to use a trawl net having a
mesh through which a square gauge of one and a half inches,
measured across each side of the square, or six inches measured
round the four sides, will pass without pressure when the net
is wet, on the seaward side of lines drawn within the following
limits :—

   (a) A line drawn straight from the south-western
       extremity of Haverigg Point, in Cumberland, to
       the north-western extremity of Walney Island ;
   (b) A line drawn straight from Walney lighthouse to
       the Wyre lighthouse ;
   (c) A line drawn straight from the ' Star Inn,' South
       Shore, Blackpool, to the inner north-west sea
       mark on Formby Point ;
   (d) A line drawn straight from the lifeboat-house at
       Formby to the Crosby lightship, and then straight
       to the Leasowe lighthouse, in the County of
       Chester.

5. No person shall use in fishing for sea fish other than
shrimps or prawns, any trawl net except in accordance with
the following regulations : —

   (a) When the length of beam does not exceed eighteen
       feet between the trawl heads or irons, the cir-
       cumference of the net shall be not less than fifty
       meshes.
   (b) When the length of beam, measured as aforesaid,
       exceeds eighteen feet but does not exceed twenty-
       five feet, the circumference of the net shall not
       be less than sixty meshes.
   (c) When the length of beam, measured as aforesaid,
       exceeds twenty-five feet, the circumference of the
       net shall be not less than eighty meshes.

6. No person shall use in fishing for mackerel, herring,
sparling, or garfish, any seine, draft, drift, set, or stake net
having a mesh through which a square gauge of one inch,
measured across each side of the square, or four inches
measured round the four sides, will not pass without pressure
when the net is wet.

7. No person shall use in fishing for sea fish any drift net having a depth of more than 200 meshes.

8. No person shall use in fishing for sparling any net or instrument between the first day of April and the thirty-first day of October following, both inclusive.

9. No person shall use, in fishing for shrimps or prawns, any net having a mesh through which a square gauge of three-eighths of an inch measured across each side of the square, or one and a half inches measured round the four sides, will not pass without pressure when the net is wet.

10. No person shall use, in fishing for shrimps or prawns, any trawl net except in accordance with the following regulations :—

    (a) When the length of beam between the trawl heads or irons does not exceed twenty feet, the circumference of the net shall be not less than one hundred and twenty meshes.

    (b) When the length of beam, measured as aforesaid, exceeds twenty feet, the circumference of the net shall be not less than one hundred and forty meshes.

    (c) The length of beam, measured as aforesaid, shall not exceed twenty-five feet.

11. No person shall use, in fishing for shrimps or prawns, any shank or bow net having a less circumference than eighty meshes.

12. No person shall use, in fishing for shrimps or prawns, any hand or hose net having a less circumference than seventy meshes.

13. No person shall use, in fishing for sea fish from any vessel propelled otherwise than by sails or oars, any method or instrument of fishing except hooks and lines.

14. No person shall use, in fishing for sea fish, any stake net, except in accordance with the following regulations :

    (a) The site of the net shall be marked by poles, perches, or buoys, visible above the surface at high water of any tide, and such poles, perches, or buoys shall be maintained so long as the stakes of the net continue in position. All stake nets shall be marked with the owner's name, affixed to the end stakes, so long as the stakes continue in position.

(*b*) No portion of the net shall be nearer the centre of any stream or channel than the edge of such stream or channel at low water of a tide, the high water line of which stands sixteen feet above the level of the sill of the Old Dock at Liverpool.

(*c*) No portion of the net shall be nearer than one hundred and fifty yards to any portion of another stake net, not being a hose net.

(*d*) No mackerel baulk shall exceed 600 yards in length, no other stake net shall exceed 300 yards in length, and no stake net of the description known as a poke net shall exceed 150 yards in length.

15. No person shall use in fishing for mackerel, herring, garfish, sparling, shrimps, or prawns, any method or instrument of fishing, except at the times and places at which and in the manner in which such method or instrument may be reasonably calculated to take such fish respectively.

16. At the times and places at which, and in the manner in which it may be reasonably calculated to take eels or mullet only, an eel or mullet net may be used under the written authority in that behalf of the local Fisheries Committee, signed by their Clerks, Clerk or Superintendent, and in accordance with the conditions set out in that authority.

17. No person shall use, in fishing for sea fish, any seine, draft, trawl, bow, hand, hose, shank, stake, or otter net in that portion of the district which lies between a line drawn true west from the building known as 'Uncle Tom's Cabin,' on the coast, near and north of the Borough of Blackpool, and a line drawn true west from the building known as the 'Star Inn,' on the coast, within the said borough.

18. No person shall fish for cockles except—

(*a*) By hand or (*b*) with a craam, rake, or spade: Provided that between the first day of November and the last day of February following, both inclusive, it shall be lawful to use an instrument locally known as a Jumbo, not exceeding four feet six inches in length, fourteen inches in width, and one inch in thickness, provided that such instrument shall be constructed entirely of wood, and shall not be dragged across the cockle beds or artificially weighted.

19. No person shall remove from a fishery any cockle which will pass through a gauge having a square opening of thirteen-sixteenths of an inch, measured across each side of the square.

20. No person shall fish for mussels, except—

> By hand, or with a rake : Provided that on the West Hoyle Bank the rake must not exceed three feet in width, and may only be used from a boat and when the mussel bed is covered with at least four feet of water.

21. No person shall take mussels from the 1st of April to the 31st August following, both inclusive.

22. No person shall remove from a fishery any mussel less than two inches in length : Provided that no mussel shall be removed from the West Hoyle Bank measuring less than two and a quarter inches in length.

23. No person shall remove from a fishery any oyster which will pass through a circular ring of two and a half inches in internal diameter.

24. No person shall remove from a fishery any berried lobster or any berried edible crab.

25. No person shall remove from a fishery—

> (a) Any lobster measuring less than nine inches from the tip of the beak to the end of the tail when spread as far as possible flat.
>
> (b) Any edible crab measuring less than five inches across the broadest part of the back.

26. Any person who takes any shell fish, the removal of which from a fishery is prohibited by any of these Bye-laws, or the possession of which is prohibited by any Act of Parliament, shall forthwith redeposit the same as nearly as possible in the place from which they were taken, or, under the written authority of the Superintendent, on other suitable ground, and in re-depositing cockles in accordance with this Bye-law, shall spread them thinly and evenly over the beds.

27. No person shall use any method or instrument of fishing for sea fish other than the following—

> (a) A method or instrument permitted by these Bye-laws.
>
> (b) Hooks and lines.

M

 (c) A pot, hook, or basket, for taking eels, prawns, lobsters, crabs, or whelks.

 (d) A hedge baulk in use previous to the 9th of August, 1893, the catching parts whereof consist wholly of net having a mesh in conformity with Bye-law 4.

28. The deposit or discharge of any solid or liquid substance detrimental to sea fish or sea fishing is hereby prohibited, provided that this Bye-law shall not apply (1) to the deposit by the Mersey Docks and Harbour Board within the area coloured brown on the Chart marked S. 1568–1895, in the possession of the Board of Trade, of refuse or material dredged or excavated in the course of the execution under statutory power of any work by the said Docks and Harbour Board within the Port of Liverpool, or (2) to the deposit by any person, with the consent in writing of the Committee, given under the hand of their Clerk or Clerks, and confirmed by the Board of Trade, of any such solid or liquid substance on an area shown on a Chart referred to in the consent and in accordance with the conditions laid down in that consent.

29. Any person who shall commit a breach of any of the foregoing Bye-laws shall be liable to a Penalty not exceeding for any one offence the sum of Twenty Pounds, and in the case of a continuing offence the additional sum of Ten Pounds for every day during which the offence continues, and in any case to forfeiture of any fishing instrument used or sea fish taken in contravention of or found in possession of a person contravening such Bye-law: Provided that in any case in which a prosecution is instituted for taking sea fish with a net or instrument the use of which for the capture of any particular kind of sea fish would constitute a breach of any of the foregoing Bye-laws, not being a Bye-law prescribing a close season, a person shall not be deemed to have committed such breach if he proves to the satisfaction of the Court that he was *bonâ fide* fishing only for the particular kind of sea fish permitted to be captured with the net or instrument he was then using, and that he forthwith returned to the water with the least possible injury all soles, plaice, flukes, flounders, and dabs under 8 inches in length, and all turbot and brill under 10 inches in length, measured respectively from the tip of the snout to the end of the tail, if any such were taken by such net or instrument.

CUMBERLAND SEA FISHERIES DISTRICT.

(*Haverigg Point to Sarke Foot.*)

1. The following Byelaws shall apply to the whole area of the Cumberland Sea Fisheries District, unless otherwise specified and except in the cases to which the provisions of the 13th Section of 'The Sea Fisheries Regulation Act, 1888,' apply:—Provided that nothing in these Byelaws shall apply to any person fishing for sea fish for scientific purposes, or for stocking or breeding purposes, under the written authority in that behalf of the Local Fisheries Committee, signed by their Clerk, and in accordance with the conditions contained in that authority.

2. No person shall adopt any practice known as bunching or tying round the net, or use any artifice or devise so as practically to diminish the size of the mesh of any net, except the net or trawl used solely for the purpose of taking shrimps or prawns.

3. No person shall use, in fishing for sea fish, any net with any trap or pocket, unless the mesh of such net is in accordance with Byelaw 4.

4. No person shall use, in fishing for sea fish other than shrimps, prawns, mackerel, herring, eels, or sparling (otherwise known as 'smelts'), any net having a mesh through which a square gauge of one-and-three-quarter inches, measured across each side of the square, or seven inches measured round the four sides, will not pass without pressure when the net is wet. Provided that between the 1st day of July and the 15th day of October following, both inclusive, to the west and south of a line drawn from Bow House Point, near Caerlaverock, on the Scotch side of the Firth to Skinburness on the English side, it shall be lawful to use a trawl net having a mesh through which a square gauge of $1\frac{1}{2}$ inches measured across each side of the square, or six inches measured round the four sides, will pass without pressure when the net is wet.

5. Between the 1st day of January and the 30th day of June following, both inclusive, no person shall use in fishing for sea fish any trawl net having a beam of greater length than thirty feet between the trawl heads or irons, or any trawl net from any vessel exceeding 15 tons gross register.

6. No person shall use, in fishing for sea fish from any vessel propelled otherwise than by sails or oars, any method or instrument of fishing except hooks and lines.

7. No person shall use, in fishing for sea fish other than shrimps or prawns, any trawl net except in accordance with the following regulations :—

(a) When the length of beam does not exceed eighteen feet, measured between the trawl heads or irons, the circumference of the net shall be not less than fifty meshes.

(b) When the length of beam, measured as aforesaid, exceeds eighteen feet but does not exceed twenty-five feet, the circumference of the net shall not be less than sixty meshes.

(c) When the length of beam, measured as aforesaid, exceeds twenty-five feet, the circumference of the net shall not be less than eighty meshes.

8. No person shall use, in fishing for shrimps or prawns, any net having a mesh through which a square gauge of three-eighths of an inch, measured across each side of the square, or one-and-a-half inches measured round the four sides, will not pass without pressure when the net is wet.

9. No person shall use, in fishing for shrimps or prawns, any trawl net except in accordance with the following regulations :—

(a) When the length of beam, measured between the trawl heads or irons, does not exceed twenty feet, the circumference of the net shall be not less than one hundred and twenty meshes.

(b) When the length of beam, measured as aforesaid exceeds twenty feet, the circumference of the net shall not be less than one hundred and forty meshes.

(c) The length of beam, measured as aforesaid, shall not exceed twenty-five feet.

10. No person shall use in fishing for shrimps or prawns, any shank or bow net having a less circumference than eighty meshes.

11. No person shall use, in fishing for shrimps or prawns, any hand or hose net having a less circumference than seventy meshes.

12. No person shall use, in fishing for mackerel or herring :—

    (a) Any seine, draft, drift, or stake net having a mesh through which a square gauge of one inch, measured across each side of the square, or four inches measured round the four sides, will not pass without pressure when the net is wet ; or

    (b) Any stake net except at the time and places at which, and in the manner in which, such nets have been heretofore commonly used for the capture of such fish respectively.

13. No person shall use, in fishing for sparling (otherwise known as ' smelts '), any instrument between the first day of February and the first day of September following, both inclusive.

14. No person shall use, in fishing for sea fish, any stake net except in accordance with the following regulations :—

    (a) The site of the net shall be marked by poles, perches, or buoys, visible above the surface at high water of spring tides, and such poles, perches, or buoys shall be maintained so long as the stakes of the net continue in position.

    (b) No portion of the net shall be nearer the centre of any stream or channel than the edge of such stream or channel at low water of a tide, the high water line of which stands sixteen feet above the level of the sill of the Old Dock at Liverpool.

    (c) No portion of the net shall be nearer than one hundred and fifty yards to any portion of another stake net, not being a hose net.

15. No person shall fish for mussels except—

    (a) By hand, or

    (b) With a rake not exceeding three feet in width, and used only from a boat, and when the mussel bed is covered with at least four feet of water, provided that the use of a dredge shall be allowed when the mussel bed is covered with at least 20 feet of water.

16. No person shall take mussels during the months of May, June, July, or August in any year.

17. No person shall remove from a fishery any mussel less than two inches in length.

18. No person shall fish for cockles except—

(a) By hand, or

(b) With an instrument locally known as the ' craam,' having not more than three teeth :

Provided that between the first day of November and the last day of March following both inclusive, it shall be lawful to use an instrument locally known as the ' Jumbo,' not exceeding four feet six inches in length, fourteen inches in width, and one inch in thickness, constructed entirely of wood, and not dragged across the cockle beds or artificially weighted.

19. No person shall remove from a fishery any cockle which will pass through a gauge having an oblong opening of three-quarters of an inch in breadth and not less than two inches in length.

20. No person shall remove from a fishery any oyster which will pass through a circular ring of two-and-a-half inches in internal diameter.

21. No person shall remove from a fishery any berried lobster or any berried edible crab.

22. No person shall remove from a fishery—

(a) Any lobster measuring less than nine inches from the tip of the beak to the end of the tail when spread as far as possible flat.

(b) Any edible crab measuring less than four-and-a-quarter inches across the broadest part of the back.

23. Any person who takes any shell fish, the removal of which from a fishery is prohibited by any Byelaw in force in the District, or the possession of which is prohibited by any Act of Parliament, shall forthwith re-deposit the same without injury as nearly as possible in the place from which they were taken, and, in re-depositing cockles in accordance with this Byelaw, shall spread them thinly and evenly over the beds.

24. No person shall use any method or instrument of fishing for sea fish other than the following :—

(a) A method or instrument specified in and not otherwise prohibited by any of these Byelaws.

(b) A hook and line.

(c) A pot or basket for taking eels, prawns, shrimps, lobsters, crabs, or whelks.

(d) A hedge baulk in use previous to the 27th July, 1896, the catching parts whereof consist only of net having a mesh in conformity with Byelaw 4.

25. No person shall use in fishing for mackerel, herring, eels, sparling (otherwise known as 'smelts'), shrimps, or prawns any mode or instrument of fishing except at the times and places at which, and in the manner in which, such mode or instrument may be reasonably calculated to take such fish respectively.

26. The deposit or discharge of any solid or liquid substance detrimental to sea fish or sea fishing is hereby prohibited. Provided that nothing in this Byelaw shall apply to the deposit by any person with the consent in writing of the Committee given under the hand of their Clerk, and confirmed by the Board of Trade, of any such solid or liquid substance in an area shewn on a chart referred to in the consent, and in accordance with the conditions laid down in that consent.

27. Any person who shall commit a breach of any of the foregoing Byelaws shall be liable to a penalty not exceeding for any one offence the sum of twenty pounds, and in the case of a continuing offence the additional sum of ten pounds for every day during which the offence continues, and in any case to forfeiture of any fishing instrument used or sea fish taken in contravention of or found in the possession of a person contravening such Byelaw. Provided that in any case in which a prosecution is instituted for taking sea fish with a net or instrument, the use of which for the capture of any particular kind of sea fish would constitute a breach of any of the foregoing Byelaws, not being a Byelaw prescribing a close season, a person shall not be deemed to have committed such breach if he proves to the satisfaction of the court that he was *bonâ fide* fishing only for the particular kind of sea fish permitted to be captured with the net or instrument he was then using, and that he forthwith returned to the water with the least possible injury all soles and plaice under 8 inches in length and all turbot and brill under 10 inches in length if any such were taken by such net or instrument.

Of the other matters regulated by law throughout

British and neighbouring seas, four may here be considered. These are :—

1. The sale of intoxicating liquors in the North Sea.

2. The maintenance of the peace at sea.

3. The presence of fishing-boats in the territorial
waters of a foreign power.

4. The registration, numbering, and lettering of
fishing-boats.

1. The liquor traffic in the North Sea has long
been a serious problem, but was regulated with some
approach to finality by the Convention, signed in 1893.
This prohibits the sale of spirituous liquors on the
high seas, save by specially licensed persons or vessels,
and the latter are compelled to exhibit the recognised
mark, a black S on a white flag. The cruisers of
the High Contracting Powers have also clearly defined
rights of search and seizure.

2. With reference to keeping the peace on the high
seas, an Order in Council of 1889 fixes the maximum
penalty for every offence at £10, and makes special
provision for avoiding disturbance whenever a foreign
vessel is encountered in British waters.

3. As regards the treatment meted out to the
crews and masters of British fishing vessels in foreign
waters, much useful information of the various laws is
to be found in an interesting summary of ' Sea Fisheries
Legislation of Foreign Powers,' published as a Blue
Book in 1901. Not only is fishing within the territorial limits of continental countries strictly prohibited.
but some of the nations interpret the seeming inten-
tion to fish as a ground of prosecution. Holland, for
example, imposes high penalties, and provides for the
seizure and detention of foreign vessels until the fines
are paid. France issues strict rules respecting the

lettering and lighting of foreign vessels in French waters, as well as with regard to the compulsion to carry, and to show when required of them, their papers of nationality. Stringent regulations are also laid down with a view to preventing any obstruction of navigation. Belgium and Denmark impose similar restrictions, in addition to which they prohibit the landing of brill, turbot, plaice, sole, and some other fishes, under specified size limits. In Denmark heavier fines are exacted from trespassing steam-trawlers than from sailing smacks.

4. The strict lettering and numbering of fishing vessels, a public safeguard more recently extended to motor cars, is obviously important as an aid to detection in cases of collision, and all fishing-boats are required to register at one or other of the ports given in the following list, in which I have followed the same geographical order from Berwick round to Maryport. (See map.)

Port	Mark	Port	Mark	Port	Mark
Berwick-on-Tweed	B.K.	Dover	D.R.	Barnstaple	B.E.
Blyth	B.H.	Folkestone	F.E.	Bridgewater	B.R.
North Shields	N.	Rye	R.X.	Bristol	B.L.
Newcastle	N.E.	Newhaven	N.N.	Gloucester	G.R.
South Shields	S.S.S.	Shoreham	S.M.	Newport (Mon.)	N.T.
Sunderland	S.D.	Littlehampton	L.I.	Cardiff	C.F.
Hartlepool	H.L.	Portsmouth	P.	Swansea	S.A.
Stockton	S.T.	Cowes (I. of W.)	C.S.	Milford	M.
Middlesborough	M.H.	Southampton	S.U.	Cardigan	C.A.
Whitby	W.Y.	Poole	P.E.	Aberystwyth	A.B.
Scarborough	S.H.	Weymouth	W.H.	Carnarvon	C.O.
Hull	H.	Jersey	J.	Beaumaris	B.S.
Goole	G.E.	Guernsey	G.U.	Chester	C.H.
Grimsby	G.Y.	Exeter	E.	Runcorn	R.N.
Boston	B.N.	Teignmouth	T.H.	Liverpool	L.L.
Wisbeach	W.I.	Brixham	B.M.	Preston	P.N.
Lynn	L.N.	Dartmouth	D.H.	Fleetwood	F.D.
Great Yarmouth	Y.H.	Salcombe	S.E.	Lancaster	L.R.
Lowestoft	L.T.	Plymouth	P.H.	Barrow	B.W.
Ipswich	I.H.	Fowey	F.Y.	Castletown (I.	
Harwich	H.H.	Falmouth	F.H.	of M.)	C.T.
Colchester	C.K.	Truro	T.O.	Douglas	D.O.
Maldon	M.N.	Penzance	P.Z.	Ramsey	R.Y.
London	L.O.	Scilly Islands	S.C.	Peel	P.L.
Rochester	R.R.	St. Ives	S.S.	Whitehaven	W.A.
Faversham	F.	Padstow	P.W.	Workington	W.O.
Ramsgate	R.	Bideford	B.D.	Maryport	M.T.

By the Merchant Shipping Act, 1894, the name and portmark must be displayed in letters of not less than three inches. Two comments suggest themselves on the foregoing portmarks. The first is that the favourite selection of letters consists of the first and last letter of the name, and, in fact, more than two-thirds adopt that system. The departures from this rule include, besides several apparently capricious cases, seven which use only the single initial letter and one which uses three letters. The explanation is that the use of only the first and last letter might lead to confusion with some other port with a prior claim to the letters. Thus, the Scotch port of Campbelltown had a right to C.N. before Cardigan, Carnarvon, or Castletown. Even as it is, there are not letters enough to go round with a proper distinction between British and foreign ports, and there is, in the absence of any distinguishing flag or rig, some chance of confusion between vessels portmarked

R., which might stand for Ramsgate or Rouen.
H., „ „ „ „ Hull, Havre, or Helsingor.
B., „ „ „ „ Belfast or Boulogne.
B.K., „ „ „ „ Berwick or Basch Kapelle.
C., „ „ „ „ Cork or Caen.

These five examples could, if necessary, be increased to fifteen, but they suffice to illustrate one difficulty. Another is that foreign countries do not invariably adopt either the first or the last letter in their portmarks. Thus, the Dutch port of Terneuzen portmarks N.Z., while the German port of Teufelsbrück is indicated by the letters S.Y.

Another fact which must strike anyone examining the foregoing list is that the boats of some ports portmark as if they belonged to others. Thus, Hastings boats portmark as from Rye (R.X.), Mevagissey boats as from Fowey (F.Y.), and so on. The rule is for the vessels to portmark at the nearest Registration station.

Such existing laws as deal with the proper lighting of fishing vessels, or with the rule of the road at sea and right of way which certain classes of craft have over certain other classes, apply generally to merchant shipping, and have no special interest for the fishermen. For other and equally cogent reasons, I shall omit specific reference to such matters of purely local law as the right claimed by the fishermen of Yarmouth and Newquay to dry their nets respectively on the denes and Towan Headland, which severally adjoin their towns.

From the laws which have long been established I turn to those which are likely to occupy attention in the near future, and of these Lord Onslow's new Sea Fisheries Bill is undoubtedly the chief. Others will perhaps, as our scientific knowledge grows from more to more, include the establishment of a close time and protection of certain spawning grounds, but these are difficult of accomplishment as practical politics. When, for example, Lord Balfour of Burleigh was Secretary of State for Scotland, his countrymen pressed him to secure protection for the spawning grounds of the haddock; but it is by no means certain that these spawning grounds are accurately known. The fishes for which some have advocated the establishment of a close time are the herring and the mackerel, and this in spite of the fact that the quantities of both fish landed last year (1903) were in excess of the landings for many years previously. A proposal of the kind was brought before the urban council of Dungarvan as recently as September, 1903, but the Waterford fishermen very reasonably opposed it unanimously. Even had the shoals been spared on the coast of Waterford, they would have journeyed eastward or westward and been netted off either Wexford or Cork. Even assuming that a brief close time had attracted vast shoals, harried on other parts of the coast, into the asylum of undisturbed waters off Waterford, the moment the close season was at an end the nets would have been crammed to breaking point, and, after a passing glut in the market, conditions would have resumed their old level.

It is, however, less on behalf of the drift-nets and migratory fishes than in respect of the trawler and undersized flat fish that Lord Onslow is determined to secure suitable legislation. Certain facts in the life-history of the plaice were put before the reader in Chapter I., and if these be read side by side with the account of the trawl in Chapter II., there will be little difficulty in understanding the grounds on which the following four measures have from time to time been proposed as likely to restrict the trawler from wasteful fishing. They are :—

1. The closure of selected areas for either a yearly close time or for a period of years.

2. The further extension of the three-mile territorial limit.

3. A compulsory increase in the mesh of the trawl.

The first and third of these measures would have the effect of directly curtailing the catching power of the trawler. No. 2 may perhaps be regarded rather as a scheme of the foreigner to diminish British predominance in mercantile marine as well as fishing. The fourth and last aims rather at weakening the trawler's desire to do wrong.

4. The prohibition of the landing or sale of flat fish below certain specified size limits.

As a matter of fact, it is doubtful whether any of these proposed measures would answer in practice, with the exception of the last, which is, in fact, the substance of Lord Onslow's new Bill.

A brief examination of a few objections which will be found to lie against the first three must here suffice.

1. The objection to the proposed closure of areas is twofold : there is the difficulty of determining the right areas to close, and there is the cost of policing them when selected and generally of enforcing the law. If the areas are to be closed at all, it must be because they are known beyond all doubt to constitute nurseries for the young fishes. Although fishermen and biologists know tracts of the North Sea, Irish Sea, and English Channel which might fall under that head, the whole extent of these nurseries is as yet very imperfectly mapped out. Again, it has only hitherto been proposed to exclude the trawler ; but it is very doubtful whether any permanent good would be achieved, unless the hookers and smaller shrimpers also were kept out. Unless this were done, the banishment of the trawler would be the signal for fleets of hookers, hitherto excluded by fear of having their long-lines swept away by the trawl, to invade the protected areas. The newcomers would next strew the bed of the sea with thousands of baited hooks. Not alone would these catch many of the undersized flat fish saved from the trawlers, but, as was explained in Chapter II., there would be incredible waste when, in unfavourable conditions of wind and weather, the men were unable to haul their lines for days together, leaving the fish on the hooks to be devoured by crabs and dog-

fish. On some parts of the coast, indeed, as in Devonshire, a very decided objection to the exclusion of the
trawler comes from the hookers themselves. They
declare that the trawl does incalculable good by
ploughing up the submarine fallows, and they are of
opinion that, where it has long been kept out, mud
settles down on the sea-bed, smothering the fish and
hiding their natural supplies of food.

The most important case of an experimentally closed
area is that of the Moray Firth, a pet scheme of the
able scientific advisers to the Scotch Fishery Board, and
one with many results of which some of them appear to
have been satisfied, though others find no difficulty in
criticising the measure. In any case the full value of
such an experiment as an indication of what it is possible
to achieve by extension of the territorial limits is preju-
diced by the impossibility, under existing international
conditions, of also excluding the trawlers of other
countries; and to some it is a galling thought that
Danes and Dutchmen are left free to fish in British
waters closed to British fishing-boats. The Scotch line-
fishermen are, unlike their fellows in the Devon bays,
unanimously in favour of the exclusion of the trawler;
but this is class jealousy and has no scientific value.
So long, in fact, as only one class of fisherman is warned
off these protected areas there is no guarantee that
undersized fish may not be taken by other methods,
though spawning fishes may to some extent be naturally protected against the hooker by reason of their
habit of refusing baits when in that critical state. The
Moray Firth must cover an area not far short of 2,000
square miles, and, unless this is absolutely known to be
a flat fish nursery, the measure is clearly a very severe
one.

2. These objections apply with equal force to the proposed extension of the three-mile territorial limit, in addition to which there is the complication of international difficulties along an invisible frontier. If the signing of an international convention, or indeed, any international legislative reform in fishery matters, has to precede internal improvement, then I fear we have some time to wait. There is, for instance, little indication in the present attitude of Germany that she has yet abandoned her hostile attitude in respect of restricted fisheries legislation, which was clearly admitted in some letters from Dr. Heincke, which I put in as evidence before the Parliamentary Committee of 1893, and which were at the time reproduced in the Report. If, for the sake of argument, we assume that all difficulties in the way of a general extension of territorial limits were removed, every maritime nation of northern Europe being agreeable to the measure and pledged to respect it, we might, in the narrower seas, be confronted with the absurd position of two of the Powers practically dividing the sea between their respective coasts, like riparian owners on opposite banks of a river. As an outcome, for instance, of the new grouping of the Powers suggested by the recent Anglo-French Agreement, we might find Great Britain and France each extending its territorial limit to a distance of nine miles from the coast, with the result that no German, Dutch, or Belgian fishing vessel would be permitted to pass between Dover and Calais with her trawl down. Nor, in view of the difficulties already raised in attempting to enforce the law within the zone of three miles, could there be any hope of adequately policing the wider reserve. The hypothetical case here suggested is, of course, manifestly absurd; yet, in a

lesser degree, the complications in the narrow seas would be sure to prove most vexatious.

3. The most direct check on the mechanical catching power of the trawl yet proposed is the suggested compulsory increase in its mesh. At first sight, on paper, the remedy seems assured. By making the mesh of the net larger, it is not unreasonable to expect that it will become a sieve, letting the under-sized flat fish escape and retaining only those fit for the market. In practice, however, unless we are to increase the size of the mesh to such an extent as to render the trawl altogether inoperative, the remedy breaks down. A necessary accompaniment would be the reduction of the hauls to a very short period. For it is found that, under the strain of towing through the water, the wet mesh is so drawn together that the square assumes an oblong form, egress for the smaller fishes being rendered still more difficult by the pressure of the stones, weed, and general rubbish gathered by the trawl in its sweeping progress. It therefore appears that many of the small flat fish, which would pass easily through the dry mesh stretched to its full capacity, are imprisoned in these altered conditions, while it is by no means an established fact that, even if they escaped, they would retain sufficient vitality to survive so rough an experience.

It is not to be denied that scientific expeditions equipped for the purpose have made, by way of experiment, unpractically short hauls with equally unpractically large-meshed trawl nets, and that the results have, under these peculiarly favourable conditions, been not altogether discouraging. It must, however, be borne in mind that between fishing for scientific research and fishing for commercial results there is a wide gap; and a careful handling of the material, which would not be considered irksome on board a scientific vessel, could not fail to prove vexatious, if not indeed impracticable, on an ordinary trawler.

4. The foregoing methods of restriction apply directly to the catching power of the trawler ; the first two by curtailing the areas over which he fishes, the third by diminishing the efficiency of the engines of destruction. There remains another hope for the undersized flat fish, and one that commends itself to many who frankly recognise the impossibility, or at any rate the extreme difficulty, of preventing their capture. This plan, which is embodied in Lord Onslow's Sea Fisheries Bill, with which he so happily inaugurated his accession to office, is not indeed to prevent the trawler from catching these small fish, but to deprive his labour in so doing of all value by making their landing and sale at British ports a breach of the law. Here is a way out of the difficulty of the legislator which, while open to considerable criticism, looks on the face of it far less hopeless than the rest. Denmark and Belgium have already shown the way in this direction, and it seems time that Great Britain, with the largest fishing interest in neighbouring seas, should not lag behind.

The full amended text of Lord Onslow's Bill is given here, the purport of the amendment being shown in the italicised lines in Section 1 :—

A BILL (AS AMENDED BY THE SELECT COMMITTEE)

INTITULED

An Act to provide against the Destruction of Under- A.D. 1904.
sized Flat Fish.

Be it enacted by the King's most Excellent Majesty, by and with the advice and consent of the Lords Spiritual and Temporal, and Commons, in this present Parliament assembled, and by the authority of the same, as follows :—

1. (1) The Board of Agriculture and Fisheries may, if they think it expedient so to do for the purpose of preventing the destruction of undersized flat fish, make orders for prohibiting, either absolutely or subject to such exceptions and conditions as may be prescribed, the landing of any flat fish not exceeding the prescribed length : *Provided that before any order is so made a draft thereof shall be laid before each House of Parliament for a period of thirty days during the session of Parliament, and if either House before the expiration of that period presents an address to His Majesty against the draft, or any part thereof, no further proceedings shall be taken thereon, but without prejudice to the making of any new draft order.*

(2) If any person contravenes the provisions of any such order he shall be liable on conviction under the Summary Jurisdiction Acts to a fine not exceeding *one pound* for every package containing fish landed in contravention of the order, or where fish are not contained in packages to a fine not exceeding *twenty pounds*.

(3) Any officer of Customs or any officer appointed in that behalf by the Board of Agriculture and Fisheries, or by the Fishmongers' Company, or by the council of the county or borough in which any fish is landed, may seize as forfeited any fish landed in contravention of an order under this Act, and may dispose of those fish in manner directed by the authority by whom he was appointed, and may for the purposes of examination detain any package in which he has reason to believe that any fish landed

in contravention of an order under this Act are contained and may examine its contents ; and if any person impedes or obstructs the exercise of the powers conferred by this section he shall be liable on conviction under the Summary Jurisdiction Acts to a fine not exceeding *five pounds*.

(4) For the purposes of this section —

The expression ' prescribed ' means prescribed by order of the Board of Agriculture and Fisheries :

The expression ' flat fish ' means sole, plaice, turbot, and brill

The expression ' Fishmongers' Company ' shall mean the wardens and commonalty of the mystery of fishmongers of the City of London :

(5) The expenses of a council under this section shall, in the case of a county council, be defrayed out of the county fund, and in the case of a borough council be defrayed out of the borough fund or borough rate.

(6) In the application of this section to Scotland references to the Fishery Board for Scotland shall be substituted for references to the Board of Agriculture and Fisheries.

(7) This section shall apply to Ireland subject to the following modifications :—

(a) References to the Department of Agriculture and Technical Instruction for Ireland shall be substituted for references to the Board of Agriculture and Fisheries ;

(b) Every sum of money levied as a fine, in pursuance of this section, shall be paid and applied in manner directed by subsection (4) of section one of the Fisheries (Ireland) Act, 1901 ;

(c) This section may be cited with the Fisheries (Ireland) Acts, 1842 to 1901. 1 Edw. 7, c. 38.

Power to prohibit trawling in territorial waters. 51 & 52 Vict. c. 54.

2. (1) For the purpose of preventing the destruction of any undersized flat fish, the Board of Agriculture and Fisheries shall have the like powers as the committee of a fishery district under the Sea Fisheries Regulation Act, 1888, of making byelaws for restricting or prohibiting, either absolutely or subject to such regulations as may be provided by the byelaws, any method of fishing for sea fish or the use of any instrument of fishing for sea fish, and for determining the size of mesh, form. and dimensions of any instrument of fishing for sea fish, and for imposing penalties for breaches of any such byelaws ; and any byelaws so made may provide for the application of the byelaws, either to the whole or any part of that part of the sea adjoining the coast of England or Wales within which His Majesty's subjects have by international law the exclusive right of fishing, and the said Act shall apply as respects byelaws so made in like manner as it applies with respect to byelaws made under that Act.

(2) This section and the Sea Fisheries Regulation Acts, 1888 to 1894, may be cited together as the Sea Fisheries Regulation Acts, 1888 to 1904.

Short title and commencement.

3. This Act may be cited as the Sea Fisheries Act, 1904, and shall come into operation on the *first day of January, nineteen hundred and five.*

In passing some little necessary criticism on this Bill, I am anxious to view it in the same broad spirit as that in which, with some demand on our trust, the Government recently asked the nation to view the Anglo-French Agreement, a spirit which shall set general progress above the certainty of direct and immediate gain. The manner in which the Bill may fail is apparent. Since its object is to keep trawlers from fishing the grounds specially frequented by under-sized flat fish, its success assumes a more or less accurate knowledge of the bearings of these ' nurseries.' In this assumption the Select Committee, which recently took evidence on the subject, was in some measure justified, if only on the basis of evidence put in by Mr. Archer (of the Board of Agriculture and Fisheries) from the captains of Hull carriers. According to this evidence, it appears that undersized plaice form a large percentage of the catch on the grounds between Heligoland and the Horn Reef. Although, however, it is by no means certain that our fishermen have a very accurate know-ledge of all the ' nurseries ' in the portion of the North Sea over which they operate, Lord Onslow's Bill would at any rate save the small fish in our territorial waters, for there at least we know that small fish predominate. Again, the Bill gives no guarantee that our trawling skippers will not continue to fish the ' nurseries,' selling the larger fish in the home markets and disposing of the undersized residue in France or Holland. In short, apart from all question of leaving the uncontrolled foreigner a monopoly of the ' nursery,' if our men obey it in the letter, the new law would depend for its success upon a deeper knowledge and a better faith than is theirs. A good deal of opposition is, at the time of writing, promised to the passage of the Bill through the Commons, but Lord Onslow signified his readiness to accept a further amendment.

In its form, as given above, the Bill is, as will be seen, only experimental. It only provides for such restrictive power as the Minister of Agriculture and Fisheries may subsequently be asked, or see fit, to assume. There is at present no specified minimum size

for the flat fish which may be retained for sale. That
the fixture of this size so as to suit all requirements will
present no little difficulty is clear when we remember
that such leading authorities as Messrs. Cunningham,
Garstang, and Holt are agreed that a plaice becomes
mature in the neighbourhood of Plymouth at a smaller
size than in the North Sea. To impose the higher North
Sea limit at Plvmouth Barbican might exclude plaice
which had spawned on the grounds near the Eddystone
and which would consequently be fair merchandise for
the market. Somewhere, then, there would have to be
a dividing line. Without arguing this aspect quite to
the point of absurdity, let us put it at the accepted
boundary between the North Sea and English Channel.
What, in that case, would prevent the capture of undersized plaice (reckoned by the North Sea standard) being
trawled off the coast of Kent and sold on the beach at
Hastings ?

At the same time, it is infinitely satisfactory to all
who are genuinely interested in the welfare of that
great industry, which brings fish to so many points on
our 2,000 miles of coastline, that a Bill of some kind
should at length be given a fair trial. The second
clause, as will be seen, will, by giving the new Board
the same powers for making bye-laws as are now pos-
sessed by the Sea Fisheries Committees, tend to reduce
to some semblance of uniformity the extraordinary collection of bye-laws already given in this chapter. The
appointment of the new Minister, or rather the addition
of new interests to an old Department, was the anticipated outcome of the recommendations made in 1901
by the Committee on Ichthyological Research. Some
of the witnesses, it is true, advocated the formation of
one Central Department, in which should be merged not

alone the Scotch Fishery Board, with all its splendid record of independent work, but also the Fisheries Department of the Irish Board of Agriculture. Even had six members out of the eight appointed on that committee not been Scotsmen, there would have been ample ground for refusing to recommend the disappearance of the Scotch Fishery Board as a separate body. Among other witnesses, Mr. Garstang appears to have given strong evidence in favour of merging the fisheries interest in the Board of Agriculture. The evidence was logical, and the result is satisfactory; but it is amazing that Mr. Garstang should believe that a Minister of Fisheries pure and simple 'would have a rather limited field for his work.' If the protection and regulation of an industry which keeps the greater part of eight thousand vessels of various size busy throughout the year, carrying crews numbering in the aggregate thirty or forty thousand men and lads, an industry which attracts millions of invested capital, which provides cheap and wholesome food for the whole nation—if, I say, such an industry would offer 'a rather limited field' for the sole work of one Government Department, then Mr. Garstang must be a very favoured person, for clearly existing departments have revealed to him, and only to him, a superhuman capacity for hard work, for which it is to be feared an unappreciative generation gives them scant credit. This is only written by way of passing criticism of Mr. Garstang's otherwise clear and able evidence. It amazed me when I read it at the time, and not even my high regard for the useful work which he has been carrying out at Lowestoft has enabled me to get over the first feeling of surprise. Indeed, if anything, the admiration compelled by him in other ways has enhanced the disappointment at reading such evidence from one who, it might be thought, has some opportunities of appreciating the endless ramifications of the industry, the manifold side issues involved, the need of at any rate as much Ministerial attention as can be secured.   That Lord Onslow and his assistants will look after their new charge conscientiously and zealously no one doubts, and that the results will be more satisfactory than those of any previous administration of the fisheries by a member of the Government is the conviction of the great body of the industry.   The confidence felt in the new Minister was amply demonstrated by the support given to him at a dinner in his honour under the auspices of the Fishmongers' Company early in the present year.

The only Report so far issued by the newly constituted Board deals with the salmon fisheries.   If Messrs. Archer and Fryer devote the same attention to the sea-fisheries, the first Sea-Fisheries Report of Lord Onslow's Department may be awaited with confidence.

CHAPTER V

SCIENTIFIC INVESTIGATION

Greater Demand for Fish—Two Remedies for the Decreased Supply and Higher Price—Artificial Fish-culture—Legislation—Need for Greater Knowledge—The Marine Laboratory—Dr. Dohrn's Station at Naples—The Marine Biological Association—Its Laboratory—Other Laboratories—Work done by Professor Herdman and his Assistants—The Liverpool Laboratory Reports—Mr. Meek's Laboratory at Cullercoats—Conferences with Fishermen—The North Sea Investigations—The Stockholm Conference—Biological and Hydrographical Investigations distinguished—The Christiania Conference—The Copenhagen Meeting —The 'Huxley'—Mr. Garstang's First Report—Marked Plaice—System of Rewards examined—Deductions from Results—Information obtained from the Fishermen—The 'Huxley's' North Sea Work—Plankton Investigations in other British Seas—Criticisms of the Christiania Programme—Views of Professors McIntosh, Herdman, and Ray Lankester —Broader Reasons for this Country's Co-operation— Policy—Economic Gain.

WE have now taken some notice of how fish live in the sea, how they are caught in nets or on hooks, and how they are brought to market by rail or water. The varied engines devised by man for their capture, the complex machinery of their distribution inland have in turn engaged our attention, as well as the laws framed to check production when the fisherman's energy threatens to outrun nature's powers of supply. The present chapter aims at showing how scientific workers can help the law-makers.

Formerly there were more fish in the sea and fewer men on land either to catch or to eat them. There was

no fear that the fish of the sea might be seriously
diminished in number, much less exhausted. Steam-
trawlers were not busy ploughing every acre of sand in
the North Sea. Lobster-pots did not jostle one another
on every reef of rocks. Trains did not rush through
the night from all points of the compass to the capital,
groaning under their burden of fish. There were not
one-tenth the number of fishermen, not one-twentieth
the number of trains, not one-hundredth the number of
consumers that there are at the present day. In spite
of the small supply put on the market, prices ruled low,
for there was little demand. With every allowance for
the difference in the value of money, soles fetched as
little as the housewife of to-day must give for haddocks,
while haddocks were reckoned offal and, as such, flung
back in the sea. All this is changed by over-fishing, the
result of an increased demand. Soles are the luxury of
those who can afford them. Haddocks command their
price, and there is no more offal, save in the conservative language of the trade. That prices will rise yet
higher is the conviction of many with moderate views,
who refuse either to shrug their shoulders with the
optimists or to shake their heads with the pessimists.
Future operations, coupled with the unavoidable increase in the number of consumers, must tend to stiffen
prices. It is not necessary, in order to admit the force
of this argument, to regard the North Sea as either
inexhaustible on the one hand, or, on the other, as on
the verge of depletion.

For the situation thus in process of creation two
remedies suggest themselves. One of these, the legal
restraint of the fishermen, was considered in the last
chapter. The other is to replenish the sea by artificial
fish-culture. Both require the support of scientific

research before they can be projected with any hope of alleviating the evils of over-production.

In the arts of hatching sea-fish we have reached only the experimental stage. America claims to have achieved practical results with the shad, cod, and some other kinds of fish, and it is fortunately quite beside the mark to consider whether the claim has been justified or not. The fact remains that the United States Government has subsidised, and otherwise encouraged, experiment in a manner that reflects great credit on its intelligence, and compares very favourably with the apathetic attitude of some other governments. Not that attempts have not been made elsewhere. The Government of Sweden and Norway took up the question of hatching cod after Captain Dannevig had demonstrated its possibilities on his own account. The Scotch Fishery Board experimented in lobster-hatching at Brodick. The Government of Newfoundland has like-- wise devoted money to the same investigation. If, however, we are to farm the sea as we farm the land, if we are to sow as well as to reap, such operations must obviously be international. Where, as in agricultural land, there are personal ownership and stationary crops, private enterprise finds its due reward. Where, how- ever, as in the sea, there is no private ownership, and where the crops take the form of young fishes free to swim elsewhere, the Government must do the work of sowing. There could be no reason in the Hatchery at Piel spending Lancashire funds in turning out numbers of artificially reared sea-fish, in order that these might find their way into either the shrimp-trawls of Maryport or the holds of the Welsh trawlers in the Bristol Channel. Even carried out on an extensive scale with Government money, the artificial hatching of sea-fish might not bring any corresponding benefit. Nowhere else perhaps in her dominions is nature more 'careless of the single life' than in the sea. In all probability, not one egg in a hundred ever develops to a living fish; not one larval fish in a thousand ever reaches maturity; not one mature fish, of some species, in ten thousand is ever destined to be eaten by man. Possibly we might estimate the chances of the complete cycle, from egg to egg, as one in ten thousand; and, if this be a fair allowance, it is evident that, to be productive of any practical result, the re-stocking of the sea with artificially fertilised ova, as suggested by Mr. Fryer and Mr. Garstang (see Chapter I.), must be carried out on a stupendous scale. One eminent living biologist has declared that, even if not one single individual out of all the millions artificially hatched escaped the jaws of their natural enemies when turned loose in the sea, the fisheries would benefit. The explanation of this apparent paradox lies in the assumption that, thanks to this artificial supply of food for the hake, dogfish, and other predatory kinds, the more vigorous plaice and soles, hatched under natural conditions, would have a better chance of escape. Candidly, this argument seems to me to be better suited to the restricted area of the aquarium. In the enormous expanse of sea or ocean such intimate relations can hardly be established, besides which the predatory fish might permit their appetites to expand with the augmented supply and consume both the naturally and artificially hatched food.

Whether the salvation of our sea-fisheries lies, however, in the direction of artificial fish-culture or in that of restrictive legislation, a sound basis of accurate biological knowledge and of fuller statistics collected by more thorough and scientific methods is essential to success in either case. Further and fuller information as to the size, season, and place at which fish spawn, as well as accurate determination of the grounds frequented by the young fish as yet unfit for market, must be considered as of the first importance.

The marine biological work now being carried out in this country looks for its support to the Government, to the local Sea Fisheries Committees, or to the Marine Biological Association, of which some account will presently be given. The State finances the investigations in connection with the North Sea scheme. The Sea Fisheries District Committees encourage much useful biological work, and in some cases publish a considerable literature on the subject. Thus, Dr. Murie's Report on the Fisheries of the Thames Estuary was produced by order of the Kent and Essex Committee ; and the Lancashire and Western authorities, which recently made improvements in the laboratory at Piel, have published many valuable memoirs by Professor Herdman and his assistants.

The marine laboratory was practically a creation of the latter half of the nineteenth century. It has obvious advantages. Close to the sea, yet equipped with all the necessary microscopes, balances, and other instruments, besides reference works and general facilities, it enables the student to avoid the inaccuracies commonly associated with field work, while access to nature at first hand gives him a direct insight into those problems of the fisheries which must always be his first concern. He can take the evidence of the practical fishermen, while in some cases the vicinity of an important trawl-market places at his disposal an inexhaustible and varied store of material. The laboratory

founded, and still conducted, by Dr. Anton Dohrn at
Naples, is not only the pioneer of such institutions, but
remains a model for those of later inception. It is
subsidised by the German Government and has long
been in receipt of support from a number of scientific
bodies in other lands. Cambridge University, for
instance, owns one table, and the British Association
another; while, on the occasion of my last visit, I found
about forty students at work, including two American

THE MARINE LABORATORY, PLYMOUTH.

ladies and a biologist from Malabar. This cosmopolitan
character of its workers lends a varied interest to its
scientific publications, to which each contributes monographs or notes in his own language. The whole of
the living animals in the tanks on the ground floor are
furnished by the Bay of Naples, and I recollect Cavaliere
Salvatore Lo Bianco assuring me that to investigate
with any degree of thoroughness the fauna of that bay
alone would be the work of many years. This frank

admission on the part of the eminent Italian biologist has always since recurred to mind whenever I have heard of the time-limit prescribed for investigating the hundred and fifty and odd thousand square miles comprised in the North Sea.

The chief marine biological laboratory in England is that which stands on Citadel Hill, Plymouth. It is the property of the 'Marine Biological Association of the United Kingdom,' a scientific body which owes its existence to a meeting held for the purpose in the rooms of the Royal Society, March 31, 1884. Professor Huxley occupied the chair, and among those who addressed the meeting were the Duke of Argyll, Sir Lyon Playfair, Lord Dalhousie, Professor (afterwards Sir William) Flower, Sir Joseph Hooker, and Mr. Romanes. The actual formation of such an Association was proposed by Dr. W. B. Carpenter and seconded by Sir John Lubbock (Lord Avebury); and its first Honorary Secretary, subsequently President of the Council, was Professor Ray Lankester, to whom, with Dr. Günther, is credited the original architecture of the scheme. The object with which the Association was founded stands in the minutes as follows :—

> 'For the purpose of establishing and maintaining laboratories on the coast of the United Kingdom, where accurate researches may be carried on, leading to the improvement of zoological and botanical science, and to an increase of our knowledge as regards the food, life conditions, and habits of British food-fishes and molluscs.'

The laboratory was opened June 30, 1888, and stands about a hundred feet above the sea, commanding

a fine view of the Sound. In more respects than one
Plymouth furnishes an excellent headquarters. Only
Weymouth and Torbay on the South Coast could lay
claim to many of its advantages, while the collecting
grounds within reach of the more western port are
immeasurably richer in material. It has further the
advantage of them in the proximity of an active and
accessible fish-market, which is kept supplied with a
great variety of forms brought in by steam-trawlers,
smacks, drift-boats and hookers. The aquarium, or
tank-room, as it is called, is open to the public at a
small charge, and generally exhibits a variety of fishes
and other marine forms obtained from the Sound. It
has seventeen tanks, which range in length from about
30 feet to 6 feet and in depth from 5 feet down to
18 inches. Some are disposed along a central table, so
that the student can study the contents from above.
The rest stand against the walls. This arrangement,
while it has undoubted advantages in facilitating the
water-supply, has the drawback of compelling the
observer to watch the fishes from one side only. One
or two tanks should be placed, at any rate in every
aquarium designed for study, so that it may be
possible to watch the movements of the inmates from
below. The water in the Plymouth aquarium, aërated
by circulating on a simple yet ingenious principle,
proceeds in the first case from two large reservoirs
underneath, which, between them, can hold 100,000
gallons. Beneath the tank-room there are also
various cellars, while upstairs, on two floors, are
the working rooms and the private quarters of the
Director. The present Director and Secretary is Dr.
E. J. Allen, who contrives to acquit himself of very
varied tasks, scientific and administrative, with great
ability and enthusiasm.

The original minute, as to the objects with which the Association was founded, has not been lost sight of by those in charge of its destinies. Although matters of purely academic interest have not been wholly tabooed by those who have worked under its auspices, it cannot in fairness be complained that they have neglected the more practical problems connected with British food fishes and molluscs. A glance through the contents lists of the interesting Journal during the last fifteen years will show that, among other practical studies conducted at Plymouth, special attention has been given to the following:—

I. Notes by W. Heape on the fishing industry of Plymouth; by B. J. Ridge on the West of England mackerel fishery; and by W. Roach on the winter herring, long-line and pilchard fisheries.
II. Enquiries by J. T. Cunningham, W. L. Calderwood, and G. H. Fowler, into the occurrences of anchovies in British seas.
III. A series of notes by E. W. L. Holt and J. T. Cunningham on investigations carried out in the North Sea.
IV. Experiments by J. T. Cunningham in fish hatching and rearing.
V. Investigations by Messrs. Bateson and Hughes on the bait supply and experiments in the manufacture of artificial baits.
VI. A treatise by W. Garstang on the impoverishment of the sea, and a shorter note by the same biologist on the octopus plague.
VII. An important essay by E. W. L. Holt on the Grimsby trawl-fishery and the destruction of immature flat fish.

In addition to the chief laboratory at Plymouth, the Marine Biological Association has lately, with Government assistance, opened a branch establishment on the quay at Lowestoft, where Mr. Garstang superintends the work projected in connection with the Christiania programme. Before, however, giving some account of that international scheme of investigation, it will be convenient to enumerate the remaining marine laboratories in England and Wales. The next in importance to that at Plymouth are those at Piel and Port Erin, supported by the Lancashire and Western Committee and under the direction of Professor Herdman, with

Messrs. James Johnstone, Andrew Scott, and others to assist. The practical aspect of the culture of sea-fish appears to have engaged the workers under the Lancashire Committee to a greater extent than any others in this country. In addition to such matters, however, they have also studied and reported upon the food material of young fishes, and to this end they examined in one year alone the stomachs of nearly four thousand specimens. They have also worked on the size at which fishes reach maturity, the whereabouts of the chief spawning grounds in the Mersey district and Irish Sea generally, the percentage of flat fish likely to survive rough handling in the shrimp-nets, and the track followed by liberated drift-bottles. From time to time the laboratory has issued important memoirs on the fishes and fisheries of the Irish seas, one of the most interesting, dealing with a particular fish, being that on the plaice by Mr. F. J. Cole and Mr. James Johnstone. This monograph, which occupies upwards of 250 pages of the 1901 Report, with excellent plates, was perhaps worthy of a more widely distributed form of publication than the periodical report of a county laboratory. The Port Erin establishment was opened in 1893 and was preceded by an earlier workshop on Puffin Island, near Anglesey. The only remaining laboratory of the kind in South Britain, the small establishment used by Mr. Meek at Cullercoats, was recently destroyed by fire. It was situated on the beach in a most convenient position, and when I went over it last, Mr. Meek and his colleagues were making useful investigations in the shell-casting process in crabs and lobsters, as well as in the plankton of that coast and the fertilisation of waste ova. The laboratory had, I believe, been equipped mainly through the generosity of Mr. John Dent, of

Newcastle, and it is hoped that it may be restored, in order that the useful work may be continued, on a much larger scale. A Committee has, in fact, been formed for the purpose. One feature of the Northumberland District Committee's Reports always struck me as excellent and worthy of imitation at Plymouth and Liverpool, and that was the short accounts of conferences with fishermen along the coast, some of whom gave most valuable practical evidence.

We have so far considered the domestic investigation of marine life on our own coasts. Isolation, however, is not always permitted to great nations, nor, if it were, would it be an unqualified advantage; and it has been found desirable by His Majesty's Government, less, perhaps, in any hope of arriving at a millennium of biological knowledge than with the object of co-operating harmoniously with neighbours likewise interested in the fisheries of Northern Europe, to embark on its share of what is known as the Christiania Programme. A century ago, when fish enough to stock our then limited markets could be taken in small boats close to the beach, the investigation of even our own seas was, however absorbing from the purely scientific point of view, superfluous as an economic measure. Gradually, however, it became necessary to learn more of life in our bays and creeks. Indeed, there are eminent biologists to-day, among whom may be numbered Professor Herdman, who would rather see British money spent on the study of British seas, and who think that the 10,000 square miles of the Irish Sea, where our men fish comparatively free from foreign competition, might more profitably be studied than a vast area of fifteen or twenty times the extent, which is the common property of half Europe.

It is, however, as in the case of the recent Anglo-French Agreement, the broader grounds of a mutual understanding that have attracted the Government to this project, and the choice of the North Sea carries with it all the advantages, and also all the drawbacks, which belong to a divided control. Regarded as a purely scientific undertaking, it is too vast to hold out much hope of very definite results within the brief allotted time of three or four years. Considered politically, as tending to promote our interests in the most important sea shared by ourselves and other nations, it has much to recommend it. Briefly, the history of the scheme is as follows :—

Invitations to Stockholm to attend an International Conference of the maritime nations of northern Europe were issued for June 1899 by the Swedish Government. On that occasion Great Britain sent three delegates, Sir John Murray, Professor D'Arcy Thompson, and Mr. Archer; Germany sent four, Sweden six, Norway and Denmark three apiece, and Holland and Russia one each. Neither France nor Belgium took part in this preliminary conference, and, though the latter country was subsequently represented at Christiania, France has remained aloof throughout, her chief fishing interests being, no doubt, outside of the North Sea area. The Stockholm conference discussed and provisionally adopted a complicated scheme of biological and hydrographical investigations, and it will be convenient for the reader to distinguish between these two branches of research. The biological experiments and researches include everything pertaining to the food, development, distribution, spawning, and migration of the fishes, as well as to the effect of the various modes of fishing on the supply, the quantitative and qualitative analysis of plankton at different seasons of the year—in fact, all problems of fish life bearing, directly or otherwise, on the condition of the industry. To the hydrographical and meteorological investigations, on the other hand, are referred all records of temperature, readings of the barometer and hygrometer, and analysis of samples of sea-water, with a view to obtaining accurate records of its specific gravity, salinity, colour, and constituents.

It was recommended to the respective Governments represented at the Stockholm conference that the investigations should extend over a period of, at any rate, five years, and that they should be conducted over an area embracing the North Sea, the Northern Atlantic within certain stated boundaries, the Baltic 'and adjoining seas.' This scope predicates an extremely wide range of inquiry, and some attempt was at the outset made to define the nature of the investigations under each of the two aforenamed heads. Thus the biological researches were to consist in experimental trawling, the liberation of marked flat fish, the examination of specimens of plankton captured at different depths, and the collection and arrangement of statistics obtained from the fishermen or from the markets. On the other hand, the hydrographical portion of the programme was to concern itself with the vertical distribution of temperature, salinity, and drifts, and observations were with this object to be made once a quarter, in February, May, August and November, 'at definite points along the same determined lines,' the currents being further measured at the surface, at the bottom, and at certain intermediate depths. The importance of a complete knowledge of the currents is apparent when we remember the helpless condition of the floating spawn and drifting larval forms of our food fishes, of which something was said in the opening chapter. With the single exception of the herring, as has already been pointed out, the eggs of which anchor themselves securely to stones and weeds on the bed of the sea, all our important food fishes deposit floating eggs, while the same risk of dispersal by storms or currents attends the little growing fish in its earlier stages until it has either the instinct to lie buried in the sand, or the strength to breast the current. Before we can frame laws for the protection of threatened species it is evident, therefore, that we must know as much as possible of the force and direction of the tides and currents, which so irresistibly regulate their distribution in early life.

With the abnormal and fluctuating violence of storms exact science is powerless to reckon, but the precise direction and extent of the regular currents and drifts at different seasons of the year should, as the result of further investigation over a wide area, be accurately traced on the maps of the future. In order to acquire a fuller knowledge of their operation, it is essential that they should be measured at the surface and at the bottom, as well as in mid-water, by which is meant not the mathematical half of the total depth, but any level between the two. This may be studied in a variety of ways. It is desirable to note the effect of these currents on animate and inanimate objects, so that not only loaded bottles and other convenient objects are set free in the sea, but also marked flat fish. Both the drift-bottles and the fish are carefully marked, so that identification is easy. Of the former, some are recovered still floating, some find their way into the trawl, and others are thrown ashore by the waves. The flat fish bear small labels of bone or metal, buttons or discs, so attached as in no way to interfere with the breathing or movement of the fish. Dr. Wemyss Fulton, Secretary to the Scotch Fishery Board, has devoted one of the shorter ' Publications de Circonstance of the Central North Sea Committee to a strong plea in favour of using for this purpose a tab of pure white silk coated with paraffin. For the round fishes, at any rate, he regards this as perfect. In the case of flat fish, which have a habit of 'sanding' themselves—that is to say, of rubbing their bodies against the sand—he thinks that the silk tab might with advantage be enclosed in a quill or small glass tube. The marked plaice having been liberated, a system of rewards is widely advertised in the newspapers which circulate on the east coast, as well as in the ' Fish Trades Gazette' and other suitable channels likely to attract the notice of the fishermen. With every regard for Mr. Garstang's work, the system of rewards seems to me to be open to much criticism. He offers, for example, in addition to the market price of the fish thus surrendered, a sum of two shillings for the fish and label complete, with information as to place and date of capture. For the label alone, with the same information, the reward is a shilling; and for the bare label, with neither fish nor information, sixpence. The interest of the tab alone is as a guide to the ' intensity' of fishing and the chances that released fish have of escaping the lines or nets. But it is to be feared that there will be few applicants for the sixpence when the addition of a little information, accurate or otherwise, doubles its value. Indeed, if the method of fixing the labels is common knowledge in the neighbourhood, a fish might be forthcoming as well. I should have thought that a slightly higher reward for the whole thing—fish, label, and information—of, say, half-a-crown, and no descending scale, would have met the difficulty. There would be less inducement to practise deception if it became known that the inspectors could tell by reference to their books whether this was the actual fish or not, and any-one with the fish would as soon give the true facts as to the date and place of capture (if he knew them) as falsify these returns. Hundreds of plaice have been liberated in this way, and I believe that more than 10 per cent. have found their way back into the hands of Mr. Garstang and his staff. Without definitely com-mitting himself on the strength of such meagre material to conclusions of permanent value, he was already in his first Report able to suggest one indication of the results obtained, and that was that some of these plaice must have travelled within a couple of months a dis-tance of not less than 160 miles. He was further enabled to infer that the supply of flat fish in the southern areas of the North Sea, down to the Thames estuary, is kept up by migrations of flat fish from the ' nurseries' on the Dutch coast. With few exceptions, the plaice liberated in the North Sea were recovered at North Sea ports; but one found its way into the English Channel. It was liberated on the Leman Ground, in the North Sea, during December 1903, and was recovered off Winchelsea, 200 miles distant, early in April 1904.

The recommendations made by the Stockholm Con-ference of 1899 have been given above. Certain modi-fications were introduced into the programme by the second conference, held at Christiania in May 1901, on which occasion the British delegates numbered four— Sir Colin Scott Moncrieff, Professor D'Arcy Thompson, Mr. Garstang, and Dr. Mill. Germany now sent five delegates, Sweden six (as before), Denmark three, Norway, Russia, and Belgium each two, and Finland one. The North Sea, North Atlantic, Arctic Sea, and Baltic were carefully mapped out for purposes of investigation, and sections were allotted to the special enterprise of one or other of the contracting parties. The Dogger Bank was made a converging point of their various activities, Great Britain operating from $2°$ E. westward to the British coast, as well as north of $58°$ N. to the Faroes, or about $62°$ N. The Danes take the area between the Cattegat and Horn Reef, and the Germans are occupied with the waters between the Horn Reef, Borkum, and the Dogger. These and other limits are not, however, laid down with the object of drawing any hard and fast lines, for friendly collaboration, not international rivalry, is the very essence of the scheme. A third meeting was held at Copenhagen in July 1902. It differed slightly in character from those which preceded it, and the British delegates for the occasion were Sir Colin Scott Moncrieff and Professor D'Arcy Thompson, with Mr. Garstang and Dr. Mill as scientific expert advisers. It is not easy to compare the precise financial share of the burden borne by the different parties to the arrangement, for they have given their assistance in various ways. His Majesty's Government for instance, is pledged to the extent of at least £42,000, of which sum £4,000 went in the equipment of steamers, with an annual subsidy of £12,700 for at least three years for the working expenses, the salaries of the naturalists employed, and the necessary contribution towards the expenses of the Central Bureau and Commissioners. Germany spent £16,500 on a new steamer for the purpose and contributes £7,500 per annum. Russia spent £16,000 on her steamer, and gives £12,800 a year. Denmark contributed £9,600 down and spends a further £5,500 a year.   Finland spent £6,000 on a steamer and laboratory and subscribes £2,849 a year. Sweden and Norway spent between them about £10,000 in the first instance, and still contribute rather less than £10,000 a year, but they are pledged to contribute for a period of five years, while the rest commit themselves to three only by way of experiment.   The figures given here are not offered as an exact statement of the finan-

THE ' HUXLEY.

cial responsibility undertaken by each Government, and are quoted only for the purpose of showing that, considering its paramount stake in the North Sea fisheries, this country has not committed itself excessively.

The 'Huxley,' the vessel specially commissioned to carry out our share of the investigations, was originally a Grimsby steam-trawler, and a number of alterations, both on deck and below, have rendered her suitable to the work. Dr. Allen was good enough to take me over her when she lay on one occasion at Plymouth, and she seemed to me comfortably appointed, though an opinion on that question would, I am aware, come more properly from one of the staff. She has been hired in the first instance for three years, and is fitted with a beam-trawl on the starboard side, and an otter-trawl on the port. This affords opportunities of comparing the relative catching power of the two patterns, the beam-trawl being used on the grounds frequented by the Ramsgate and Lowestoft smacks, while the otter-trawl comes into operation when the 'Huxley' is steaming over those fished by the steam-trawlers of Hull or Scarborough.

Mention has already been made of the small branch laboratory opened at Lowestoft by Mr. Garstang, the naturalist entrusted with the North Sea investigations. The 'Huxley' started her experimental voyages in the month of November 1902, and by the middle of June following she had completed twelve voyages, these having embraced the coasts of Holland and Heligoland, as well as various grounds in the vicinity of the Dogger. As a result of these voyages upwards of 34,000 fishes, the majority of them flat fish, were measured, while the food contents of some 3,000 were carefully analysed and noted. As evidence of the amicable spirit which has throughout inspired these international investigations, it may be mentioned that more than one of the foreign experts were on board the 'Huxley' during these trips.

Another important part of the international programme is the collection of statistics from the fishermen themselves. It has been too much the fashion to sneer at the views of the toilers of the deep as either

deliberate falsehood or ignorant superstition, but, whatever preference those who fish for amusement may
traditionally have for perverting the truth, fishing for
a livelihood on the great waters is a serious calling, and
in the course of more than an average familiarity with
all classes of fishermen, I have never found them habi-
tually given to misstatements. Now and again, it is
true, they are goaded by the official inquisitorial manner

DECK OF THE 'HUXLEY' (SHOWING THE BEAM-TRAWL.)

(which they abhor and suspect of ulterior motives)
to give a deliberately wrong account, but, properly
approached, they are often intelligent and generally
willing to impart of their knowledge.

The determination of the staff engaged on this North
Sea inquiry to take all possible advantage of the empiric
knowledge of the fishermen is yet another proof of its
intelligence. The Marine Biological Association has
issued books of forms with room for entries at the rate

of two hauls a day. The form supplied for the southern portion of the North Sea, that is to say, south of the Wash and Dogger, is given below. That for the more northern surveys would substitute entries for wolf-fish, witches, megrims, and such northern types.

MARINE BIOLOGICAL ASSOCIATION OF THE UNITED KINGDOM
SURVEY OF TRAWLING GROUNDS.

Date .... Vessel .... of ....

Name of Ground...

Position or Bearings.................................Depth..... . . ..

Nature of Bottom................................Hour when shot. ....

How long towed ....Hours.......................

Fish		Number of	Fish		Number of
Plaice	Large	... Fish	Cod	Large	... Fish
	Medium	... Trunks		Medium	Trunks
	Small	... Trunks		Codling	Trunks
Flounders		... Trunks	Gurnard		. Trunks
Dabs		... Trunks	Latchets (Tubs).		—
Lemons		—	Ling		—
Turbot	Large	... Fish	Haddock	Large	... Trunks
	Small	Fish		Small	... Trunks
Brill		... Fish	Whiting		... Trunks
Soles	Large	... Pairs	Skate		—
	Medium	... Pairs	Roker		—
	Slips	... Pairs			

REFUSE AND SUNDRIES.

Kind	Quantity	Kind	Quantity
Dog-fish	...	Squid	
Star-fish	...	Whelks	

SPAWNING FISH.

Plaice Cod	Turbot Whiting	Sole Haddock

Signed ....Master. Date ....

Dr. Wemyss Fulton, whose labours in the interests of the sea-fisheries would have occupied considerable space if the scope of this book had embraced Scotch fisheries and the work of the Scotch Fishery Board, draws my attention to the Board's Twentieth Annual Report, wherein is set forth an improved basis now adopted for such statistics. The chief departure is in the direction of getting at first hand, from skippers of selected Aberdeen steam-trawlers, information as precise as possible as to the exact grounds on which the various fish are caught. A series of such returns alone. can help us to an accurate estimate of the impoverishment of important grounds. Five heads are suggested in the report, under which, to be of permanent use, such information should be classed. These are :—

1. The quantities of the various kinds of fish landed.
2. The method of fishing by which the fish are caught.
3. The places where the fish are taken.
4. The duration of the fishing operations.
5. The season of fishing.

It is interesting to compare with the above the six heads under which, in Mr. Garstang's Report, the North Sea work of the 'Huxley' falls.

1. The nature of the bottom.
2. The nature and abundance of animal life living on the bottom and serving as food for the fish or otherwise.
3. The size and weight of the fishes caught.
4. The food of the more important fishes.
5. The condition of the fishes as regards sex, maturity, or spawning.
6. The temperature of the sea at the surface and bottom.

Apart from this North Sea work, the British naturalists are responsible to the Central Council for hydrographic and plankton investigations at twenty carefully selected stations, extending from the Bristol Channel and Mounts Bay to the Isle of Wight. Very accurate records have been taken of the temperature (to one-tenth of a degree Centigrade) at ten different depths, ranging from 5 metres (roughly, $16\frac{1}{2}$ feet) to 125 metres (roughly, 67 fathoms); and eight hauls are made of plankton with nets, some of which have a mesh of $\frac{1}{150}$ inch, at depths of 10 metres, mid-water, and the bottom.

The foregoing is the merest outline of the Christiania programme. The whole scheme has been criticised from more than one standpoint, and such eminent authorities as Professor McIntosh and Professor Herdman have reprinted their objections in pamphlet form. Professor McIntosh maintains that the Council should have left the hydrographical portion of the programme to other bodies, letting the naturalists confine their attention to the distribution of the food fishes and the history of the salmon during its stay in salt water. The criticisms offered by Professor Herdman, himself a member of the Committee on Ichthyological Research, are still more severe. He declares that 'there is not even a reasonable probability that the work will lead to any conclusions of economic importance.' Among other biologists hostile to the scheme in their evidence before the Committee were Dr. Wemyss Fulton, of the Scotch Fishery Board, and Mr. E. W. L. Holt, naturalist to the Fisheries Department of the Irish Board of Agriculture. Even Professor Ray Lankester, who always favours purely scientific investigation, confessed that he would rather have seen the money devoted to the study of British seas.

Looking at the matter broadly from the scientific point of view, it certainly seems as if the joint efforts of half a dozen nations bordering on the hundred and sixty thousand square miles of North Sea can be but a drop in the ocean.   Only the fringe of the area specified in the programme can be worked by that strange friendly fleet of many flags, the ' Huxley,' ' Michael Sars,' ' Poseidon,' and ' Wodan.'   Speaking generally, the contents of a trawl do not afford the vaguest clue to the contents of a second trawl towed a few hours later over the same track, so that any effectual investigation of the vast bed of the North Sea is out of the question.

However faulty the programme may be when analysed on a purely economic basis, it would never have been correct for the country with the greatest stake of all in the North Sea fisheries to have declined the invitation of the Swedish Government.   Even France, with her paramount fishing interests in more southern latitudes, was hardly able to remain aloof without exciting comment, and Great Britain is differently placed.   As was shown above, she has not taken up more than her proper share of the financial burden, and, in the interests alike of scientific progress and international good will, His Majesty's Government did wisely in associating itself with those of other countries in the work.   Had it done otherwise, a blow would have been struck at the hope of international legislation in fishery matters, which, though not yet accomplished, need not be abandoned.   As a piece of scientific work on an elaborate scale, the North Sea scheme is not unworthy of a century which opened with the discovery of radium and the N-rays.   As a measure of high politics, it is at least equal to the Anglo-French Agreement, of which so much more has been heard.

CHAPTER VI

THE FISHERY PORTS: THE TWEED TO THE THAMES

Paramount Importance of the East Coast—North Sea Fisheries—Migration of Trawling from Devon—Recent Development of the West Coast— Four Sea-fisheries Districts on the East Side—Coastline under no District—Berwick-on-Tweed—Wolf-fish—Other Stations in Northumberland—Evidence of Mr. Dent as to Depletion on that Coast—Mussel Bait—'Brat-nets'—Line-fishing—Typical Craft at Cullercoats—Crabpots—Proposed new Marine Laboratory—Work of Mr. Alexander Meek —North Shields—Its Qualifications as a Fishing Port—Local Associations and their Objects—Superiority of Hull and Grimsby—Sunderland and Hartlepool—The Yorkshire Coast—Tidal Harbours—Disabilities of Whitby Harbour—Scarborough: the Trade and the Corporation—Scarborough as a Herring and Trawling Station—Brixham Men on the Yorkshire Coast—Scarborough Market—Meaning of 'Offal'—Hull Fleets—Water Carriage to Billingsgate—Details of Catches—Railway Rates—Grimsby and the Great Central Railway—The Great Strike of 1901—Cod-chests—Boston—Trawling and Shell-fisheries—Yarmouth deserted by Trawlers—Sale of the 'Short Blue' Fleet—The Shrimptrawler—Steam-drifters—Lowestoft and the Great Eastern Railway Company—The Thames Estuary—Dr. Murie's Report—Leigh—Pollution and Shell-fish—Berried Lobsters at Harwich—Stow-nets for Whitebait—Sprat Fishermen and the Conservancy—Medical Evidence and Southend Oysters.

THE East Coast of this country has long held a paramount position in our sea-fisheries, though it is no part of my present task to trace its supremacy further back than the rise of Scarborough, Hull, and Grimsby. That the two Humber ports receive between them as much fish in the course of the year as all the remaining ports of England and Wales put together, is a fact borne out by

reference to available statistics. To this premier posi
tion in steam-trawling may be added the enormous
landings of winter herrings at Yarmouth and Lowestoft,
and the harvest of the smacks fishing out of Lowestoft
and Ramsgate ; and we then form some idea of how the
East Coast stands in respect of other coasts and the
North Sea in respect of other fishing grounds. True,
the herring fishery off the shores of Norfolk and Suffolk

A MAY MORNING, SCARBOROUGH.

is not entirely carried on by boats belonging to the
locality, for fleets converge in those waters from far
northern ports in Scotland and from far western ports
in Cornwall ; but against this we may set the activity
of the Yarmouth and Lowestoft boats, when their turn
comes, in the bays of the west country and in the sea
lochs of the North. The North Sea is the meeting
ground of fishing fleets under many flags, and Germany

alone sends a hundred and fifty steam-trawlers, each of them well provisioned and carrying a crew of ten hands. Twenty-five of these, last season, belonged to Hamburg, and many of the rest to Bremen. The vessels shoot their trawls when they clear the Cattegat, and their voyage lasts on an average rather more than a week.

It has been calculated that this country draws fish from the North Sea amounting in annual value to over £5,000,000, while Scotland takes £1,500,000, and all the other nations put together £3,000,000. Adding these together, and calculating quite roughly on the average price of fish, we find that this amounts to not far short of 800,000 tons weight extracted from that wonderful sea every year. Surprise has often been expressed that Devon men should have migrated from Brixham to develop the trawl fisheries of the east coast, but what is more remarkable is that those already on the spot should not have kept the industry in their own hands. The agricultural interest was, however, in those days paramount in that region, so that the men of the west, having first exploited the rich grounds of the east, had little difficulty in getting matters into their own hands ; and, after working them for some years from so distant a base as Brixham, they finally transferred their families to the bleak foreshore of Norfolk and Lincoln and are now masters of the trade. The familiar Devon accent is heard on all sides at Hull and Grimsby, while still further north, at Scarborough, families of west country extraction are far from uncommon.

It is not quite easy to understand the geographical reasons for the superiority of the North Sea fisheries, though the East Coast of Scotland and Ireland are also, on the whole, more important in this aspect than the west, and to this result the calmer seas and less broken coast, together with the greater remoteness from land of the deeper water, in which the fish escape the operations of both nets and lines, no doubt contribute. The west coast of England and Wales, however, occupies a considerably more important position in the industry to-day than when, thirty years ago, Holdsworth correctly referred to Tenby as the only fishing station of importance on the coast of Wales. Two important developments, the remarkable fostering of Milford by the Great Western Railway Company and the simultaneous advance made further north by Fleetwood, have completely revolutionised the conditions of the west coast fisheries.

The Sea Fisheries Districts having authority on the east coast are four in number (see map). The Northumberland District rules north of the Tyne; the North-Eastern has jurisdiction from south of the Tyne to the mouth of the Humber; and the Eastern embraces the coast round Boston, Lynn, and some other ports on the Wash. The fourth is the Kent and Essex, which administers the bye-laws between Dovercourt and Dungeness; and it will not escape notice that a considerable stretch of coast, on which stand two such important fishing ports as Yarmouth and Lowestoft, is under the jurisdiction of no Fisheries District Committee whatever. This absence of control, which rests on the organised opposition of the shrimp-trawlers and line-fishermen, is an anomaly which the Board of Trade, and, in its turn, the Board of Agriculture and Fisheries, attempted more than once to rectify. The arguments against either the extension of an existing district or the creation of a new one to cover these ports are weak, for if, as alleged, no harm is done by the fishermen to undersized flat fish, then the officers of a District would not be called upon to introduce vexatious legislation. A petition came before the Board of Trade during 1903 to include Yarmouth and Lowestoft within the Eastern District, and Mr. Fryer, as was stated in an earlier chapter, heard *ex parte* evidence at more than one centre, but the trade opposed a firm front to the proposed extension of the District and the matter was still under discussion in the early part of the present year.

This and the next two chapters have been written to give the impressions gathered on a rapid tour from Berwick-on-Tweed round to Maryport, and embracing the principal fishing centres on the coast of England and Wales.

At Berwick itself, the chief fishing takes the form of salmon-netting and raking for cockles, neither of which fall within the scope of the present volume, since this is concerned only with trawling, drift-fishing, hook-and-line fishing, and kindred methods of taking sea-fish proper. The Berwick fishermen do, however, carry on a little line-fishing between October and May ; and when the lines fail to take remunerative quantities of cod, haddock, and whiting, the men catch what they can in their crab-pots. The cod and haddock fishery of Berwick and Spittal is steadily declining. January is perhaps the best month, and the returns made by the Northumberland Sea Fisheries Committee for the year 1903 show, for that month, 1,252 cwt. of cod, value £857, and 180 cwt. of haddock, value £202. Fifteen or twenty cobles were fishing from the Tweed at the time of my visit, all of them stiff craft, built at

Tweedmouth, and either sailed or rowed by four hands. A typical catch, which I saw brought ashore at the quay one morning in May, consisted of four small barrels of young crabs, mostly females, three large cod, and a few small whiting. Earlier in the year the men had been catching plaice as near home as Goswick, but the halibut, for which those inshore waters were once famous, seem to have completely dis-

HAULING THE SALMON NETS, BERWICK.

appeared. The wolf-fish or cat-fish (*Anarrhicas lupus*), though practically unknown at the Channel ports, is familiar on the north-east coast, and at Berwick is mostly bought on the quay for threepence apiece by fishwives and by them filleted and hawked round the town. Between the Tweed and Tyne a number of small hamlets engage in herring-fishing, crabbing, and line-fishing. Thirteen stations may be enumerated, which between them furnish probably some six or seven hundred fishermen, and these are Holy Island, North Sunderland, Beadnell, Newton, Craster, Boulmer, Alnmouth, Amble, Hauxley, Creswell, Newbiggin, Blyth, and Cullercoats. There can be little reason to doubt that the inshore grounds on the coast of Northumberland have been depleted by trawling. Mr. Dent, still Chairman of the District, told me that he could remember how in the sixties and early seventies of last century immense catches of fish were made on inshore grounds, which the fishermen would not dream of visiting at the present day. The fishing at Holy Island is practically limited to herring and crabs, and the dwindling quantity of fish (haddock, ling, and halibut) still taken on the lines about seven miles off Emmanuel Head on the forty-fathom ground is used as bait for the pots. The most important hook-bait on that part of the coast is the mussel, and the fishermen pay a yearly toll of one shilling to Lord Tankerville for leave to remove mussels from the Fenham Flats.

At Beadnel there is a little long-line fishing, in order to catch bait for the pots, which are used for crabs and lobsters, and a little drift-net fishing for herring. The trawlers have depleted the grounds of all else. Newton, which has one of the best small natural harbours on that coast, maintains only its herring fishery, many of the men fishing in summer only and finding occupation for the winter months ashore. At Craster, also, a number have abandoned the fishing and taken up more regular employment on land. It is hereabouts that the turbot, known locally as ' brat,' is taken in the curious ' brat-net,' which is worked as a kind of anchored drift-net—this is a contradiction in terms, but approximately describes the engine—on the spawning grounds of the herring.   It has an immense mesh, seven inches along the side of the square, in which the turbot strangle themselves, and it is seven meshes deep and a hundred and twenty fathoms long.   Long-lines for haddocks are also shot close to the land.   Craster has no harbour, the cobles being either hauled up on the beach, or in bad weather taken to Boulmer or Newton.

Boulmer is perhaps the most successful line-fishing station on the coast of Northumberland, and cod, ling, and haddock are its principal fish.   Turbot are also caught in 'brat-nets,' and there is some crabbing, though the fishermen of the locality declare that the French visitors to those waters rob and even destroy their pots.   The line-fishing of Alnmouth, once in a flourishing condition, has fallen off of late years, while the salmon-nets, on the other hand, have given better results both there and at Newbiggin.   So precarious, however, is the fishing, except at the height of the season, that many Newbiggin men find employment in the coal-pits.

At Cresswell, as at other stations on that coast, line-fishing is carried on only with the object of providing bait for the crab-pots, the haddock being too scarce to pay for bringing to market.   The latest report to hand for the District (1903) shows a considerable improvement in the number of soles at Cambois Bay and some other stations.

With Cullercoats I reached what may be termed the Tyne district proper, and, after North Shields, this is perhaps the most interesting fishing station on the coast of Northumberland.   The local boats, of a type very familiar on that open coast, are admirably suited to launching and beaching in all but the worst weather. Cullercoats depends on salmon-netting in the sea, as

well as on its crab-pots and line-fishing, though the
last-named has fallen away to such an extent that only
half a dozen boats now regularly engage in it, bringing
ashore haddock from the twenty-fathom ground during
the first two months of the year.   Inshore trawling has,
however, practically destroyed the hooking on all the
nearer grounds.   The crab-fishing occupies Cullercoats
in early spring, and early in May I found the women

TYPE OF BOATS USED AT CULLERCOATS.

taking their last creels of crabs to the train, after which
the cobles would engage in the salmon-fishing.   The crab-
pot in local use is strongly made, on a model not unlike
that used by the Breton crabbers, whom I afterwards
encountered in the Scilly Islands.   I also visited Mr.
Alexander Meek and his small marine laboratory, which,
as mentioned in the previous chapter, was burnt down
in the early part of the present year, but which is, I

understand, to be replaced by something more worthy to represent the county's interest in marine biological work.

The chief port of the district is, of course, North Shields, which indeed ranks among the first dozen trawling ports of England and Wales. Newcastle itself does no fishing. At one time, it is true, the county town aspired to a monopoly of the local fish trade, and the progressive Corporation went to the expense of erecting a spacious fish-market with what were then all the newest improvements. It was, however, soon made plain that this was mistaken policy and that the market was not needed, so the authorities promptly and wisely converted it into a cold store for meat. The history of the fishing industry would, if its chronicles were diligently searched with that object, reveal many similar examples of the futility of attempting to oust a firmly established market. The buyers made themselves comfortable at North Shields long ago, and there they have remained. Even South Shields, just across the mouth of the River Tyne, was unable to attract any of the trade, though it made strenuous endeavours to do so, and it has consoled itself with such profits as can be made out of shipbuilding and oil-stores. Newcastle gets its fish so quickly and so cheaply by rail from North Shields that a second market in the neighbourhood was clearly superfluous.

The line-fishing of North Shields has declined like that of neighbouring ports, the smaller fishermen taking to crabbing or drift-net fishing, with which trawling is less likely to clash. It is, however, as the northernmost trawling centre on the East Coast of England that North Shields is now notable, though, since the first steam-trawler fished out of the Tyne on November 1 1877, its history as a trawling station is little more than a quarter of a century old.   Its steam-trawlers number to-day not far short of a hundred, with as many steam and sailing drifters and smaller craft engaged in line-fishing.   As some indication of the remarkable difference which the new method made in the landings at the port, it may be mentioned that in the year ending March 1877, just before the introduction of steam-trawling, only 406 tons of fish were landed, while in 1900 the amount landed was 16,000 tons.

THE FISH-MARKET, NORTH SHIELDS.

In some respects North Shields is an almost ideal fishing port.   The railway facilities at the fish-market were perhaps its most noticeable weakness, but the matter has since, I believe, been taken in hand by the Town Council.   The quay has a river frontage of 2,350 feet, with abundance of deep water, and the fishing boats are able to berth just inside the mouth of the Tyne without any of the risks of river navigation in the fogs which prevail there at some seasons of the year. Ice, coal, and salt are available in quantity, and there are curing-houses and smoking-sheds in close proximity to the market. At the time of my visit, a printed notice was prominently displayed in many windows conveying a prohibition of presents of fish. Such a veto on liberality would have been superfluous in most towns, but I was informed by Mr. Stephenson, Secretary of the Fishing Boat Owners' Association, that out of the comparatively harmless practice of giving a ling or a pair of lemon soles to anyone paying a visit to a trawler there had grown the abuse of giving fish wholesale to loafers on the quay, who then disposed of it and shared the proceeds with the donor. The detection of such secret commissions is always difficult and often impossible, but the leakage in profits was thoroughly appreciated after the custom had been put a stop to, and it then became apparent how much had been robbed in this way. Thefts by 'market rangers,' as such pilferers are called, have always been a recognised evil at every fishing centre, but this ingenious system of presents long baffled the owners. As to the Fishing Boat Owners' Association, I was assured by its then Chairman, the late Mr. W. H. Storey, that, though originally formed for offensive and defensive purposes, a long time had elapsed since there had been any difficulty with the men. The present duties of the executive are practically limited to watching all Parliamentary Bills and all county or municipal proposals for reform. An Association was formed in that district early in 1903 on the side of the men, and entitled the 'Inshore Fishermen's Protection Association,' and, in a communication which I received at the time of its inception, the Chairman pointed out the vital necessity of keeping a hardy fishing population in those coast villages as a source of supply for the Naval Reserve and for volunteers for the lifeboat and rocket apparatus. The ostensible aims of the Association are to impose restrictions on the steam-trawler, on the salmon conservancies, and on riparian owners. It has its work cut out.

South of the Tyne, we enter the domain of the North-Eastern District, which extends to Donna Nook Beacon, off the Humber, and includes a score of centres, of which two, Hull and Grimsby, come before all others in the Kingdom, while the remaining eighteen are, with the exception of Whitby and Scarborough, comparatively unimportant. It will be seen that these ports stretch along the coasts of Durham and Yorkshire, and their names are: Whitburn, Sunderland, Seaham, Hartlepool, Seaton, Middlesbrough, Redcar, Saltburn, Staithes, Whitby, Robin Hood's Bay, Scarborough, Filey, Flamborough, Bridlington, Hornsea, Withernsea, and Paull.

Nearly 75,000 tons of fish are now landed at Hull in the course of the year, to say nothing of the considerable amount of Hull fish carried direct by water to Billingsgate, and not far short of 150,000 tons are annually landed at Grimsby. These figures mean that Hull and Grimsby between them do as much trade as the other hundred and fifty fishing centres of England and Wales put together, a wonderful record for two ports of such recent antecedents. It is, however, necessary to bear in mind that, in comparing the landings at Hull with those at ports like Ramsgate or Plymouth, the latter gather much of their harvest almost in sight of home, whereas the Hull market is supplied in great measure from the distant waters of Iceland or far out in the North Sea, and rarely are Hull nets shot within sight of the British coast.

Sunderland has fallen off in its fisheries of late years. Its trawling history dates from the late sixties, when, during a long spell of summer calm, a small local tug used to tow the sailing trawlers of those days over the fishing grounds as an experiment. In course of time the tugs were themselves fitted out with trawls, and made excellent catches for some years, by the end of which they had exhausted the inshore grounds. They were paddle-steamers, but they boldly ventured out to the deeper grounds of the North Sea, where they were presently joined, and finally supplanted, by newer screw vessels. The combined activities of these craft soon made trawling on even those grounds unprofitable, whereupon some of the owners, with an enterprise that rose to every occasion, fitted them with lines and sent them long voyages after halibut. The old-time coble-fishing of Sunderland is practically extinct, though a few of these stout little boats, measuring thirty or forty feet over all, still engage in winter line-fishing and summer crabbing. There is still a herring season, but the boats employed in it come from either Scotland or the West country. Even the indigenous trawling-fleet has dwindled sadly from its prime, and Sunderland maintains no more than a dozen smacks and half a dozen steam trawlers, which land cod, ling, haddock, and flat fish.

Of somewhat greater importance is Hartlepool, and for this superiority the proprietary railway company is probably in great measure responsible, or so much at any rate we may assume in the absence of any geographical or other advantage to account for it. The port is for some reason or other popular with fishing-fleets from elsewhere, and the Scotch trawlers in particular appear to give it the preference over every other port on the north-east coast of England. Scarborough men, with an eye for cheap coal perhaps, rather than for landscape, put in here to fill their bunkers and land their fish. The quays and basins are the property of the North-Eastern Railway Company. Excellent as they may have been ten years ago, when the industry was in its infancy, the accommodation is now palpably inadequate, and, if one may judge from a

SCOTCH HERRING-BOATS AT HARTLEPOOL.

flying impression, the authorities are either reluctant or powerless to cope with the growing demands of the industry. At the time of my visit I found the shipping huddled together in too small a space and was given to understand that the railway company had repeatedly promised better things, even to the extent of shifting the quays to a more convenient site, but that they had not hitherto gone beyond the stage of promise.

Without claiming that picturesqueness is a condition of success in a fishing centre, it must be remarked that the winding path which leads from the Hartlepool quays over the bridge to the railway station was, on a wet day, the most disagreeable walk on the whole tour

Photo, W. Brown.

LOW TIDE, WHITBY.

of the coast. The combination of rain, coal, and reeling seamen in a path only a few feet wide refuses to be eradicated from a memory anxious to condone. Mr. Pugh, then responsible for the Board of Trade returns, pointed out the Scotch herring-boats lying at their berths, and told me of the interesting and remunerative manner in which their crews combine netting and hook-fishing, hauling the herring in the nets on one quarter, and paying them out as bait on the lines on the other.

Redcar brings us to the Yorkshire coast, and there is a strong contrast to Durham in the bold rocky fore-shore, the tidal harbours of which are in many cases useful only at high water. All round our coast, and nowhere more than in Yorkshire and Cornwall, the tidal harbours have suffered a decline in their trade from the modern tendency to build fishing craft of larger size and deeper draught, which is part of the inevitable policy of syndicates controlling large capital doing everything on a lavish scale. Another consideration, which also commends the larger fishing-boats, is the growing need to exploit more distant grounds as those near the land are in turn exhausted. Heavy smacks of the description now in vogue are better afloat than on the mud, with the result that harbours like Whitby on the north-east and St. Ives on the south-west command a dwindling measure of patronage.

Whitby owes its present prosperity to its popularity as a watering-place. The money spent in the town by summer visitors has done a good deal to rob the fishermen of their independence and ruin the fishing industry. At less fashionable centres like Staithes, where the population must either work or starve, and where a man does not receive gratuities equal to a week's keep simply because he is a picturesque subject for the hand-camera, the fishing is taken more seriously, and, in proportion to the size of the port, the landings are larger. To the unbiased eye, however, the state of Whitby harbour at low tide looks quite sufficient reason for the decay of the fishing, without imputing any of the blame to promiscuous charity. Seen at the lowest ebb of a

spring low tide, with a stinging north-easterly gale
blowing outside the pier-heads, and with mud flats
extending almost to the surf, conditions under which no
boat could get either in or out, the decline of Whitby's
fisheries does not seem surprising. Those with fish
outside the bar take their catch to the more sheltered
market at Scarborough. Those within the river perforce
keep their cobles and mules and ploshers, as they call
the three local classes of craft, inside until the weather
moderates. A glance at a map of the Yorkshire coast,
on even so small a scale as fifteen miles to the inch,
will show how Scarborough is protected by its Castle
Hill from the full violence of the dreaded N.E. gales,
whereas at Whitby the sheltering hill, crowned by the
famous ruins, is on the south side of the town, where it
affords no protection from the wind which Yorkshire
fishermen have most cause to fear. Apart from the
exposed position of its entrance, Whitby harbour was in
a dreadful state within. The Harbour Trust seemed at
the time to be financially unable to keep it in repair,
for the only dredger belonging to the port was away
elsewhere on hire! All the labour and capital of the
locality seem to have been attracted to the shipyards, and
it looks as if the fish trade would follow the jet industry
into oblivion. The hope is from time to time expressed
by local Micawbers that the North-Eastern Railway Company may take over the harbour and develop the natural
resources of the Esk estuary as a haven for fishing
craft. It is not unusual to invoke the aid of a neighbouring railway company, and then, when it has done what
is required, to accuse it of abusing its monopoly ; but
in this case the Company seems in no hurry to take over
the responsibilities of resuscitating Whitby's stagnant
energies. Nor is the reason for this attitude far to seek.

As the Company owns the fish quays at Hartlepool, to the north, and as it also controls all the inland traffic out of Scarborough, Whitby's rival to the south, it has no object in helping Whitby itself out of its muddle. The summer herring-fishery still brings grist to the mill,

[*Photo, W. Brown.*

VARIOUS FISHING CRAFT, WHITBY.

and the salmon-fishing is likewise profitable, the Esk Board, to which Mr. W. Brown, of the Saw Mills, is Clerk, having plenty to occupy its attention. The line-fishing, however, may be regarded as extinct, though pathetic evidence of its former importance may be found in an old local directory, in which three women described as ' line-baiters ' are given as dwelling in the same house. The names of the three local classes of fishing-boats have already been given, the mules being the largest, the ploshers coming next, and being engaged in the herring-fishing, and the cobles, smallest of all, being employed in line-fishing.

Scarborough is altogether a more flourishing port. Among the many reasons given for its increasing supe- riority over Whitby, the most absurd is that it offers more amusement of an evening after the day's work is done, on which account it is supposed to attract the buyers, the final arbiters of where the trade shall esta- blish itself. The buyers, however, are hard-headed men of business, and have other things to think of than how they shall spend their evenings. As one of my informants in Scarborough said to me, in criticism of this theory : ' Many of them are Scotchmen ; and did you ever know *them* go anywhere for pleasure or foolery of that sort ? '

Scarborough combines in a unique degree the quali- fications of a thriving fishing centre and a fashionable watering-place. Folkestone, Hastings, Brighton, and Plymouth suggest themselves in the same category, but, with the exception of the last-named, they are not im- portant fishing ports, and Plymouth, on the other hand, is not in the front rank of South Coast watering-places. At Scarborough, indeed, the dual cult of the visitor and the trade has more than once brought the Corpo- ration and the fish-buyers into serious collision ; and early in 1903 the situation was so acute that the diffi- culties seemed impossible of adjustment. The Corpo- ration, for fear of driving fastidious visitors to rival resorts, actually contemplated prohibiting the daily carriage of herrings from the quay to the railway station by way of the main street. Had this measure been carried through, the Scotch fleet would undoubtedly have deserted the port for either Whitby or Bridlington, where it would have found a more accessible railway station, and where also it would have been hampered by no ridiculous injunction to cart away its fish by night only. If such a restriction had been imposed at Scarborough, it is difficult to imagine that the fish, kept on the quay until nightfall, could have reached London until it had first reached a state of decomposition. So much deference to the visitor, at the expense of the trade, would have been a fatal mistake. It is not uncommon—though I know nothing specifically of the Scarborough Corporation—for those who take a leading part in the conduct of municipal affairs to have their own reasons for attracting as many visitors as possible. To the unbiased mind, however, it is clear that Scarborough can never, with all its natural beauty and fine climate, become a second Brighton. It does not, in the first place, lie within fifty miles of the first city in the Empire, the teeming millions of which find in the Sussex resort a convenient change of sea and air. It is not, in the second place, equally suited to the requirements of winter residents. Moreover, England is narrower north of the Humber than south of the Thames ; and those who seek change from the great Yorkshire business centres have the choice of other watering-places on the west side. It thus happens that, for all its undoubted charm, Scarborough has its ' season' for visitors, whereas the fishing is (if we include the trawling) perennial. The prosperity based on a solid industry, such as fishing, must be sounder than the fleeting gains which hotel syndicates and the proprietors of lodging-houses make out of summer visitors. To have discouraged the fishing merely because those who catered for the visitors complained that the herring carts were a source óf annoyance to their customers, who, they feared, might thereby be driven to patronise Filey instead, would have been the height of folly. Fortunately for all parties concerned, the exercise of some tact and patience enabled them to arrive at a compromise. A position which at one time threatened to become acute was averted by the undertaking on both sides to use sand more liberally, in order to lessen the offensiveness of the dripping carts. The fish-sales-men undertook to keep plenty of sand in their carts, while the Corporation similarly pledged itself to sprinkle it in greater quantity in the hilly streets. Thanks to this arrangement, the picturesque herring-fleet pursues its summer labours undeterred; and that it is still a source of pleasure and interest to the visitors them-selves may be gathered from the number who, equipped with sketch book or camera, daily haunt the quays, watching the unloading of the boats and the work of the busy Scotch girls engaged in cleaning the herrings for transport by rail.

As it is, Scarborough has sacrificed much to the cultivation of the visitor, for the shipyards are for the most part closed, in order, it is said, that local capital may be invested in embellishing the town and adding to its many natural attractions.

It is a pity, however, that some of the local funds could not have been employed in improving an in-different harbour, which, with all the protection afforded by the Castle Hill, leaves very much to be desired. The port needs only a little encouragement to rise to con-siderable importance in the fish-trade. As regards the herring-fishery, in which its own boats take little part, it lies geographically almost mid-way between the herring centres of Cornwall and Scotland. Nor is its trawling industry, even now, inconsiderable, and, although far behind them in commercial importance, it takes historic precedence of both the Humber ports.

It was in order to supply Scarborough visitors with fresh fish at high retail prices that, in the early eighteen-hundred-and-forties, the Brixham trawlers regularly repaired to that neighbourhood in the summer months. It was while they were engaged in this traffic that the historic storm dispersed the fleet and led, as already related, to the discovery of the Silver Pit, in its day the most remarkable fishing ground in the North Sea. Thus, by a curious cycle of history, the visitor, who was nearly made responsible for the annihilation of the Scarborough fish-trade, was wholly responsible for its establishment, and, further, for the development of the industry at Hull and Grimsby.

The harbour, though roomy and protected from north-east gales, is practically useless at low water. As a rule, the steam-trawlers lie outside the piers and discharge their catch into small boats. In fine weather, however, they are able to drop anchor so close to the beach as almost to unload direct into the carts waiting in attendance to convey the fish to the market. The photograph shows the exact position of affairs. The; cart once filled, the horse is driven at a smart pace over the hard sand, and within very few minutes the varied catch is laid out in rows, according to the different classes of fish, for the inspection of the buyers. The kinds of fish brought ashore depend on the grounds fished, and also, in some degree, on the season of the year. Thus, in the month of May, I counted in one catch fifty-two 'woof,' or wolf-fish, and sixty-eight cod. The rest of the catch comprised eighteen ling and four boxes of fine haddocks. A boat that had been line-fishing brought ashore on the same morning a large catch of coal-fish, some of great size. There is no accounting for tastes. Personally, I regard both the coal-fish and ' woof' as good eating only when either is Hobson's choice, and in any case I never found much

LOW TIDE AT SCARBOROUGH.

to choose between them. Yet it is a fact that in some of the Yorkshire manufacturing towns the larger coal-fish sell well under the name of 'woof,' the deception being aided by skinning and filleting the fish.

Scarborough market presents an animated scene in the forenoon, as there are probably five-and-twenty or thirty buyers at all seasons and twice the number when the herring are in, so that when the bell rings, and they crowd round Messrs. Sellars & Harrison, the auctioneers, business is often brisk. Most of the fish goes to Billingsgate by the afternoon train, reaching the Central Market early next morning, so that the fish sold in the West End of London on Thursday was caught on the Monday or Tuesday, sold in the market at Scarborough on the Wednesday and despatched that afternoon to town. It would be easy to give the actual prices realised in the market that morning by both prime fish and offal, for I happened to jot them down, but this seems to me unnecessary. Anyone wishing for a general idea of the market price of fish at any particular time of year cannot do better than consult the ' Fish Trades Gazette,' to the columns of which, during the past ten years, I have been indebted for endless information. The term ' offal,' by the way, is used above only in its trade significance. The word is, in fact, an anachronism in its application to all kinds of fish other than sole, turbot, and brill. In the days when trawling had not yet emptied the inshore waters of the North Sea of their best fish, only such ' prime ' kinds as soles, brill, and turbot, were retained for sale, the rest, including plaice, dabs, ling, and hake, being thrown overboard again as valueless, for the reason that railways were not established. What with over-fishing, however, and a growing demand for fresh fish, all this is changed, and, while there are still residents of Hull who remember when ten or twelve stone of fresh soles fetched no more than 7s. 6d., plaice, regarded in those happy days as ' offal,' now make 10s. or 12s. a stone.

Although line-fishing for soles is still carried on in the local wykes or bays, there has been a marked falling-off in the inshore hooking in the neighbourhood during the last twenty years, in great measure due, no doubt, to the operations of the steam-trawler. One of the witnesses who gave evidence before. the Select Committee of 1893, stated that he and his father would catch on lines, many years ago, as many haddock in a single trip as all the Scarborough fishermen put together now catch for the whole winter. Whether this astounding contrast is to be read *au pied de la lettre* or not, it is evident that this class of fishing is ruined. It has been urged that the comparatively shallow water on that part of the Yorkshire coast, of which, roughly speaking, Scarborough stands at the centre, would furnish an ideal nursery for young immature fish, if the trawler could be effectually excluded. The mere enacting of a law which keeps him outside of the three-mile limit is apparently a dead letter in the absence of an adequate police. The immature flat fish cannot be regarded as menaced by the line-fishermen, for these fish at night only for soles, and, as a general rule, the smaller fish are not on the move in the dark hours.

As regards the railway station at Scarborough, of which something was said in an earlier chapter, it cannot be described as conveniently situated in respect of the fish-quay. The hill which leads from the sea to the terminus is almost as steep as that at Brixham, with the added drawback that at the Yorkshire port the carts have to traverse fashionable thoroughfares.

Long-line fishing is the chief method practised on the forty miles of coast between Bridlington and the Spurn Head, and of this fishery perhaps Withernsea may be described as the most important centre. The long-lining is now chiefly for haddock and cod, though formerly there were large catches of halibut as well. It is conducted from small boats, each manned by three men. These would use approximately a mile of line carrying sixteen hundred hooks in eight 'packs' of two hundred apiece. These line-fishermen are very bitter in their complaints of the manner in which the herring-drifters, fishing out of Yarmouth and Grimsby, shoot their nets on the inshore grounds and carry away their lines. The trawlers no longer annoy them by actually fishing in the same waters, though they adhere to the probably correct opinion that they have swept the inshore grounds bare of halibut and other fish. The crabbers are not so bitter against the trawlers, but this is merely because their pots are laid on rocky ground, where the trawl-net dare not venture for fear of being torn.

And now we have arrived at the Humber, and of the enormous bulk of trade done at Hull and Grimsby much has incidentally been said.

The distinctive features of the Hull fishing are two: the long-distance voyages to grounds as remote as Iceland and the Faroes, and the 'fleeting' system of water-carriage to Billingsgate already described in a former chapter dealing with the particular subject of distribution. By this system the 'Red Cross,' 'Great Northern,' and 'Gamecock' fleets send their catch direct to London by fast steam-carriers known as 'cutters,' a relic, perhaps, of the days in which one famous owner used actually to send fish to Billingsgate in sailing cutters. Another example which occurs to mind of similar confusion in the names of vessels and their different rigs is that of the trawlers going by the name of 'fishing vessels' in the days when they had one boom.

Each of the three Hull fleets numbers about fifty vessels, and each fleet sends one carrier every day to Billingsgate, as a rule. Some years ago the 'Great Northern' fleet alone sent, during one week of April, no fewer than 14,500 boxes of small plaice, which fetched only 4s. 3d. per box instead of the 30s. or 40s. that would have been paid for the larger plaice of other days. An average weekly landing at Hull would be about 1,600 tons, fetching £5 or £6 a ton.

While I was engaged in conversation with one of the leading members of the fishing industry at this port, a clerk brought in particulars of the catches lately made by seventeen of the company's vessels off Iceland and in the North Sea, and as these were interesting, I asked, and obtained, leave to publish them. They were as follows :—

FROM THE NORTH SEA.		FROM ICELAND.	
Name of Vessel.	Kits.	Name of Vessel.	Kits.
Springfield	225	Rome	1,576
Iolanthe	243	Plutarch	1,503
Argonaut	222	Torbay	740
Sabrina	209	Othello	1,142
Honoria	208	Titania	792
Portia	235	Norman	1,026
Spartan	198		
Broxholm	212		
Imperial Queen	157		
Valkyrie	170		
Cornelia	191		

The 'kit' weighs, roughly, $1\frac{1}{11}$ cwt.

In four cases, as will be seen, the catch from Iceland was so enormously in excess of the catches from the North Sea that it might at first sight seem remarkable that the fleets do not confine their activities solely to the more remote ground. It must, however, be remembered that the cost of the Iceland trip is far in excess of the equipment of that for home waters, as the vessels have to be specially manned and fitted out to fish grounds nearly a thousand miles distant.

Hull men are unanimous in their condemnation of the existing railway rates as excessive, and their resentment finds some expression in the attention which, as has been seen, they give to the despatch of fish by water. If, they say, the Danes can send fish from Esbjerg to Parkestone (for Billingsgate) for less than it would cost to send it to the same market by rail from the Humber, it is time that the railway rates were lowered. At the same time, it must be borne in mind that, stimulating as such competition may be on patriotic lines, particularly in view of Mr. Chamberlain's pro-

HULL TRAWLERS.

gramme for the confusion of the foreign producer, it is no business of the railway companies to compete with the necessarily cheaper water carriage. The consumer in this country often loses the British-caught fish altogether, as masters of trawlers have been known to steam away to Rotterdam, there to realise higher prices, rather than send the fish to London merely, as they put it, to benefit the railway company. Whosesoever the

fault, it is a matter for regret that, in view of the
immense quantities of fish that we import oversea
from both British possessions and other nations, any
British-caught fish should be diverted to foreign markets. These imports of fish are considerable. Counting herrings and other fresh fish, sardines and other
cured fish, with shell-fish imported for either food or
breeding purposes, as in the case of oysters, their value
amounted in the year 1901 to £3,637,284, or, excluding
the oysters imported for laying down, a total weight of
upwards of 115,000 tons. Considering that more than
430,000 tons were caught and landed that year on the
coasts of England and Wales by British vessels, such
imports look very large.

It is not uncommon for the looker-on to think that
he sees more of the game than those who play it. I do
not personally believe that his vision is really longer
than theirs ; but such impressions will not be removed.
Thus, it struck me as remarkable that the great fish-
dealers at Hull had not, at any rate when I was there,
appointed zealous agents in the Yorkshire centres, as
well as in Manchester and Birmingham, like those they
have long since appointed at Billingsgate. It seemed
to me, and it still seems, that some such organised
arrangement would give them advantages out of all proportion to the expense entailed in supplying direct the
teeming population of three great industrial counties.
Again, one might have expected some equivalent of the
Cornish 'jowder.' (see Chapter VIII.) to hawk fresh fish in
the country districts. Possibly the northern populations
may be less addicted to a fish diet; possibly, again, the
more complicated system of railways, in a degree impossible in hilly Cornwall, might rob the 'jowder' of
his *raison d'être*. Yet, when we hear of quantities of

fish being wasted because it does not pay to send it to London by rail, some such solution of the difficulty by an improvement of the facilities for local distribution suggests itself. Nor is one's surprise at such apathy lessened by learning that a Scotch dealer takes van-loads of cheap cod, partly cured, split, and salted, by water to Scotland, and thence re-exports it to Devonshire. At such large inland centres as Preston, Bolton, Wigan, and Warrington, all within comparatively easy reach of Hull, and still nearer the trawling quays of Fleetwood, the fishmongers' shops were very poorly supplied with variety, even for May. It would therefore look as if the existing system of distribution must be open to improvement, unless, indeed, there is little demand for fresh fish in those industrial districts. I made vain efforts to obtain some reliable statistics on this subject, thinking that they might throw valuable light on the primitive system of distribution with which the trade seems satisfied in the north.

The history of the Hull fishing industry, as we see it to-day, may be referred to the developments of the last fifty years. Looking at its busy quays and thriving ice-factories and general prosperity to-day, so short a life seems well-nigh incredible ; but, as a matter of history, if we go back to the late 1840's, we find Hull owning only a few sailing trawlers, most of them old Brixham boats. If we now take the census in 1872, their number had increased to 313. In 1893, it is true, the smacks had fallen to 300; but the new era had dawned, for the port now had in addition 150 steam-trawlers, a number which in those days exceeded that of the fleet of Grimsby. At the present day the sailing vessels are few and work only in and about the Humber, but the steam-trawlers number between four and five hundred.

The curing of fish does not appear to exercise the port as much as formerly, and this branch of the trade is more cultivated at Grimsby.

The journey to the latter port is agreeably accomplished, by steam ferry and train, under the auspices of the Great Central Railway Company, which has made Grimsby what it is, transforming a borough of great historic associations, but somewhat quiescent energy, into the premier fishing port of Europe. Anyone standing on the summit of the tower, the 300 feet of which are comfortably ascended in a hydraulic lift, is able to get on moderately clear days a comprehensive bird's-eye view of the two fish-docks with their joint area of nearly thirty acres, as well as of the graving and general docks. On very clear days this view is said to extend to Cleethorpes in one direction, and to the chimney-stacks of Hull in the other; but, as often as not, the observer encounters a fog, through which he cannot see even the Humber at his feet.

The port is somewhat unnecessarily known as Great Grimsby, without even, as in the case of Great Yarmouth, the excuse of a puny rival from which to differentiate itself. Of its greatness, in fact, there could be no doubt, even were the prefix omitted from its official designation. Besides ranking as the metropolis of the fishing industry, Grimsby has an extensive trade in shipbuilding and a brisk Continental traffic with the steam-packets of the Great Central Company and other lines. The Great Central is practically the ground landlord of a large part of the town, and on its property stand the busy stores owned by Messrs. Alward, Carter, and others. Nowhere else on our coasts could we see such a spectacle as that of Grimsby on a busy afternoon, with four trains abreast loading up with fish from a score of steam-trawlers, ice from the factory or from abroad, salt from Cheshire—every known device by which the precious freight may reach its destination on the morrow as fresh as possible. Thus, some of the trucks are so constructed as to carry the fish wet; in others it drains off during the journey; while some which I saw carry both wet fish and dry on different levels.

GRIMSBY DOCK.

The Grimsby fleet numbers upwards of 500 vessels and these, at the time of my visit, were thus classified :—

424 steam-trawlers,	50 steam-liners,
29 sailing trawlers,	18 sailing liners.

As may be imagined, this immense fleet employs a vast number of hands, amounting in fact to not fewer than 4,773. The steam-trawlers carry about nine hands each, and a similar crew is required for each sailing liner. The steam-liners, however, carry as their full

R

complement thirteen hands, while the sailing trawlers ship only five, including men and boys.

The history of Grimsby's fisheries is, as has already been shown, still more recent than that of Hull. Two steam-trawlers of very primitive type fished out of the port in 1882. Ten years later there were 113 of these vessels. Sailing trawlers, on the other hand, have declined in numbers from 820 in 1886 to 686 in 1892,

[*By permission of the Great Central Railway Company.*

THE QUAYS, GRIMSBY.

and 29 in 1902. These figures may be relied on as absolutely accurate, for they are taken from the evidence given by Mr. G. L. Alward before the Select Committee of 1893.

If we now contrast the Grimsby of to-day with the Grimsby of fifty years ago on the basis of the quantities of fish landed at these periods, we shall find an even more remarkable picture of progress. In 1854, for instance, the total landings at the port amounted to

453 tons, a weight commonly exceeded of late years in a single day. In 1902 the total had gone up to 165,510 tons. Every day of the year the railway company despatches between two and three hundred waggon-loads of fish. Perhaps the record was reached in Easter week 1903, for the corresponding week of the present year showed considerably less traffic. On the Wednesday before Good Friday 1903, the company despatched the enormous total of 1,153 tons in 372 waggon-loads, carrying 19,672 large and 4,651 small packages. Obviously the traffic of that week is abnormal, but it may be of interest to set down the actual quantities with which Captain Barwick, Port Master at Grimsby, and his assistants had to deal.

EASTER WEEK 1903.

	Waggons	Tons
Monday	284	827
Tuesday	260	763
Wednesday	372	1,153
Thursday	182	464
Friday	94	205
Saturday	93	207

Were it not for the vast increase in the catching power, as regards both the numerical strength of the fishing-fleet and the individual efficiency of the unit, there would be something consoling in this despatch of between three and four thousand tons of fresh fish in six consecutive days from a single port. It would seem to furnish a retort to those who lament the impending exhaustion of the sea. As a matter of fact, our satisfaction in contemplating such figures cannot but be moderated in face of the increasingly longer voyages, the increasingly larger trawls, the increasingly greater fleets despatched to all points of the compass to sweep the nation's food off wide areas of the bed of the sea. At the same time, we are probably a long way from exhaustion yet, and, in face of such continued plenty, there are many who will elect to follow Professor McIntosh when he regards the sea as inexhaustible.

Though a few old ' Cleethorpers,' as the small sailing-boats are called, may still be seen alongside the quays, practically all of Grimsby's fish is landed from the steam-trawlers. When Grimsby took up the grander style of fishing, these practically obsolete sailing craft were eagerly bought up by Cleethorpes men, many of whom have never navigated a hundred miles away from the Humber, and their opportunity came during the great strike of 1901, during which four hundred of the larger vessels were laid up for three months of idleness, when the ' Cleethorpers ' were able to take their fish direct to Billingsgate and realise excellent prices.

In good times Grimsby presents an epitome of the fishing industry of to-day, with its busy smoking-houses and ice-factories, which shoot the ice direct on board the trawlers, and its tens of thousands of empty packages stored in lofty rows over a great acreage of otherwise waste space.

Its prosperity, however, though phenomenally rapid, has not been without its checks, and of these the gravest was the strike of three years ago. The men went out on strike, the boats lay idle, the women and children starved or lived on charity and the town was paralysed. The history of the strike has been written, but it is here necessary to give the barest outline of the events which led up to it, the course which it ran, and the award of the arbiter appointed to settle the matters in dispute.

If we reduce the Grimsby strike to its lowest terms,

we shall find as its first cause not the greed of the employer, not the discontent of the employed, but that dangerous talent for over-production which has so often brought ruin on the Anglo-Saxon. Grimsby had a proud place to maintain in the trade, and every nerve was strained to break its own record. The fleets had been worked regardless of expense, and the dwindling catches no longer warranted such outlay of capital. The 'bonus' system, by which owners completed their crews at the last moment by bidding high for the services of loafers on the quays, had been productive of all the abuses of which it was capable. It became necessary for the capitalists to curtail their risks. If they saw this sooner than the men, the reason is obvious. They considered various proposals for a readjustment of the wages tariff, and the most reasonable seemed the payment of a lower fixed wage, together with a royalty, or poundage, on results. From the employer's point of view this arrangement has two advantages : it gives the men a direct interest in making as good a catch as possible, and it lessens the expenses of a bad voyage. It was even demonstrated by some simple figures, which will presently be given, that it need not, in moderately favourable circumstances, be hostile to the interests of the men themselves.

After long and careful deliberation, the 'Federated Owners' Protecting Society' published, early in July 1901, the new conditions for the signing on of crews. It is necessary to examine these conditions somewhat carefully. The men would in all probability have submitted, albeit perhaps with a bad grace, to the clauses fixing the maximum crew of a short-voyage trawler at nine, of trawlers working the Iceland grounds at ten, and of vessels engaged in ' salt-fishing' at eleven hands.

Nor, indeed, would they have seriously opposed the stipulations touching the conditions under which, during the voyage, the rest of the crew should, for an agreed bonus payment, render assistance to the engineers. The real trouble lay in the new rate of wages and poundage, and the following figures show the exact measure of the proposed alteration :—

Old System	New System
Chief Engineer, 40s. a week	30s. plus 4d. in the £ sterling.
Second Engineer, 36s. a week	24s. plus 3d. in the £ sterling.

Similar modifications were proposed in the pay of the third hand, deck hands, and cook, but these examples are sufficient to illustrate the spirit in which the owners endeavoured to face the difficulties brought on by over-production and extravagance. Although, as will be seen, Sir Edward Fry's subsequent arbitration conspicuously favoured the men, it is not easy to criticise these proposals as unfair.

In the hope of convincing the men that, with average luck in the catch, they would benefit by the new regulations as well as their employers, some figures were prepared comparing, on the basis of recent average voyages, the earnings which each member of the crew would get under both systems. How far the voyages were fairly described as ' average ' I have no authority for saying, but if such a description was accurate, it is clear that the men would have benefited rather than otherwise by the new system. The figures were based on a settling bill of an eight weeks' voyage that had terminated just previous to the lock-out, the nett profit on which, deducting £186 12s. 5d. for expenses, was £517 6s. 11d.

Under the old system the first and second engineers would have received for this voyage :—

First Engineer, 8 weeks at 46s., £18 8s.
Second Engineer, 8 weeks at 36s., £14 8s.

Under the new system :—

First Engineer, 8 weeks at 30s. plus 4d. in the £ on £517
i.e. £20 12s. 4d.
Second Engineer, 8 weeks at 24s. plus 3d. in the £ on £517
i.e. £16 1s. 3d.

From these figures, so far as they go, the First Engineer would, under the proposed change, have been the gainer to the extent of over £2 4s., the Second Engineer to the extent of over £1 13s. The men, however, had no stomach for either figures or argument. A firm front was opposed to the owners by two important labour organisations, the 'Port of Grimsby Share Fishermen's Protective Society' and the 'Joint Disputes Committee.' Through their representatives the men declined even to take the vessels to sea experimentally on the owners' terms until a settlement was reached. For many weeks the chances of a compromise seemed remote. Mr. Doughty (now Sir W. Doughty), the borough Member, offered to mediate, but the men resented the interference of one who was himself an influential owner and took a prominent part in the deliberations of the Federation, which they regarded as opposed to their interests. The struggle lasted through the summer and into the autumn. The landings of fish at Grimsby in the year 1901 fell 8,000 tons below those of the preceding year, according to the return made by the Board of Trade inspectors, though, from statistics issued by the Great Central Railway, the difference would seem to have been only 5,000 tons. Grimsby was paralysed; the trade throughout the country was affected. The only parties to gain by this prolonged dispute were one or two rival ports and the aforementioned Cleethorpes fishermen, who, for the time, found their obsolete boats in request to supply a slack market. During the earlier weeks of the lock-out the men behaved with exemplary moderation, which gained for them general sympathy and bore witness to the proper influence of the professional orators employed for the occasion by the central committee. Suddenly, however, as a prelude to the end of the struggle, violence and disorder took the place of sullen resistance, and looting and wrecking were rife.

[*By permission of the Great Central Railway Company.*

BUSY TIMES, GRIMSBY.

The rioters broke into the offices of the Federation and set them on fire. The Secretary and certain of the owners escaped only with the greatest luck from the infuriated mob. The Riot Act was read in the streets. The police force was increased. There was even some talk of calling out the military. It seems, however, that the constabulary broke the heads of the more turbulent with such address that the riot subsided as

suddenly as it had started. Soon came the silver lining
to the cloud, for Lord Yarborough intervened successfully and persuaded the men to accept arbitration. The
lock-out was at an end. The vessels, long idle, got up
steam and sailed away down the Humber, and with their
departure that labour dispute ended more picturesquely
than most. Both parties knew that, so far as arbitration can ever be very hopefully regarded in that light,
a complete understanding was only a matter of time.
Work therefore had been resumed for many weeks
before the publication on December 16, 1901, of the
full text of Sir Edward Fry's award. Of this document,
which runs into fifteen pages, the briefest summary must
here suffice. After a preamble, dealing with the causes
which led up to the dispute, it stipulates that henceforth
the skipper shall make his own contract with the men,
and that the crews shall then sign on only at the Board
of Trade Offices at Grimsby. This was one of the
matters, to which, for reasons of their own, the men
attached great importance. The re-arrangement of the
wages and poundage now fixed by the arbitrator is a
happy compromise between the old scale and the new,
providing as follows :—

> Chief Engineer, 34*s.* a week and 3½*d.* in the £.
> Second Engineer, 27*s.* a week and 2½*d.* in the £.

These are the payments for the full settling, but if the
engineers signed off before the end of the full settling,
the poundage was not paid. In its place the Chief
Engineer got 5*s.*, and the Second 4*s.*, more a week.
Payment was assessed in proportion for the other hands.

The remainder of the Award need not be discussed
here, as it is purely technical and has little or no
bearing upon such causes of the strike as have been

considered, dealing only with the commissions, charges, and expenses which are to be deducted from the total amount of sales before reckoning the men's poundage, as well as with the duties of every member of the crew, whether the vessel is at sea or in dock.

That the Award was an able one, there is little room for doubt, but that, favourable though it is to the men, it furnishes any lasting guarantee of peace at Grimsby it would take a sanguine man indeed to assert. For the present, however, it has established harmony, and Grimsby, though still suffering from the aftermath of that conflict, is rapidly regaining the prosperity which was hers before the trouble, at which time it was said that a capital of two and a half millions sterling was more or less profitably sunk in the industry.

The purer water of the Humber, in such close proximity to the sea, gave Grimsby an advantage over Hull in the use of chests, measuring 7 feet by 4 feet by 2 feet, in which to store live cod, and these were at one time in very general use there, though of late years they have been less in favour. Eighty or a hundred of them, however, may still be seen floating in the docks in the season between October and January. Chests of somewhat similar construction are used by the fishermen of Mecklenburgh in the Baltic, for keeping flat fish alive until required for the market. These I brought to the notice of the Parliamentary Committee of 1893 in connection with the immature flat fish question, one of the chief subjects on which it took evidence.

The next fishing port of importance is Boston, which lies on the low sandbanks of the Wash, within the jurisdiction of the Eastern Sea Fisheries Committee, of which Mr. Herbert Donnison is the energetic inspector. It is provided with a slipway for steam-trawlers and

has abundance of ice, a good depth of water at most
stages of the tide, and an excellent railway service by
the Great Northern.   Little wonder, then, that the trawling at this port, chiefly in the hands of the 'Boston
Deep Sea Fishing and Ice Company, Limited,' has
rapidly developed.   This company has a fleet of thirty-
six powerful steam-trawlers, which operate over most
of the North Sea grounds, and even as far as Iceland

[*Photo lent by Mr. H. Donnison.*

ON THE SHORES OF THE WASH.

and the Faroes.   In the year 1902 the fleet lauded fish
to the value of £112,000.   Besides this deep-sea fishing
on a large scale, there is in the neighbourhood an extensive fishery for sprats, soles, mussels, whelks, cockles,
crabs, lobsters, and shrimps.   This district is second to
none in England for its shell-fish, the backwater of the
Wash being admirably suited to their conditions of life.
From one bed in the course of a single season there

have been taken 5,000 tons of mussels, while the Wash
has yielded 10,000 tons of cockles in a year, and more
whelks are probably landed at Sheringham than at any
other port in the kingdom. A considerable and varied
fishing is also carried on from King's Lynn. Men in
those parts sow as well as reap; and mussel culture is
extensively carried on at Wells, Blakeney, Brancaster,
and other Norfolk harbour towns, at least a thousand
tons of brood mussels being required every year to keep
the beds going. The Eastern Sea Fisheries Committee
also leases foreshore allotments for the cultivation of
oysters, mussels, and cockles on the west side of the
Wash.

Both brown and pink shrimps, the latter, as on so
many parts of the coast, being known as 'prawns,' and
indeed having some affinity to the prawn family, are
trawled in immense quantities in and near the Wash,
and the beachmen of the Lindsey foreshore use a peculiar
trawl drawn by horses for the capture of brown shrimps.
Were it not for the roughness of much of the ground,
which tears their nets, the trawlers would probably
catch still more than they do, so that the unevenness of
the sea-bed is a kind of protection imposed by Nature.

So plentiful indeed are whelks on this part of the
coast that large numbers are often thrown up after the
heavy winter storms, and these also find their way to
the market. The crab and lobster fisheries of Cromer
and Sheringham are also of first importance, and it is
satisfactory to note that the yield on the Norfolk coast
appears to be in no way falling off, though let us hope
that this larger output is not in reality a sign of
threatened exhaustion. Whereas in the year 1897 the
total catch in the district amounted to 688,000 crabs
and 23,200 lobsters, the numbers in 1901 had risen

to 1,320,000 crabs and 34,000 lobsters. A number of French vessels frequent the banks near the mouth of the Wash for thornback and rays, while steam-trawlers from the northern ports are often busy on the nurseries for soles and brill situate between the Wash and the Humber. The territorial waters are protected by bye-laws, and seven trawlers were in one season caught close to land by the cruiser belonging to the Committee.

The only other fishing in the neighbourhood of Boston consists of a little line-fishing for cod, soles, and plaice, and there are one or two nets in local use, of which the ' trim-net,' which is set for eels, flounders, and smelts in the mouth of the rivers Nene and Ouse, is perhaps the most interesting. Such small operations, however, while they interest anyone making a special study of the locality, and ought not therefore to be wholly omitted, scarcely merit serious consideration on a footing with the larger fisheries of the present day.

It has already more than once been pointed out in these pages that the important ports of Great Yarmouth and Lowestoft have hitherto succeeded in remaining outside the jurisdiction of any Sea Fisheries District. The Eastern District extends only to Happisburgh, and from here to Dovercourt, where the control of the Kent and Essex has its northern boundary, there is no local legislation whatever.

Although easily distinguished from its insignificant, though certainly more picturesque, rival in the Isle of Wight, Great Yarmouth no longer retains its old greatness among fishing ports. The manner in which of late years Lowestoft has contrived to supersede it can only be explained by the greater initiative of the Great Eastern Railway Company at the latter port (the affairs of Yarmouth being controlled by the Corporation), the want of a proper trawl-market, and the apathy of Yarmouth crews, who, receiving a fixed wage, without any poundage on the catch, are said, with how much truth I know not, to have been slack in the performance of their duties. Be the cause what it may, the trawling glory of Yarmouth is ancient history, and it is sad to think that the vessels composing the once famous 'Short Blue Fleet' of Messrs. Hewett—the 'Euphrates,' 'Lady Love,' 'Hewett,' 'Bridesmaid,' and 'Lord Alfred Paget' —were put up to auction in August 1903, but failed to find a single buyer.

The present prosperity of Yarmouth as a fishing centre rests on its herring-fishery, though there is also a considerable activity in shrimp-trawling. This latter is a very simple commercial venture. The picturesque little shrimping-boats, which are a familiar sight moving in and out of the river, are worked by their owners, who catch, boil, and sell their produce, running little risk and being in all probability better off in their unsophisticated way than many of those whose interests are vested in bigger ventures.

The herring-fishing is, however, Yarmouth's present business, and the steam drifter has entirely replaced the trawler and almost superseded the sailing drifter as well.

Unlike the plaice and sole, the herring and mackerel are wandering fishes, and the caprice with which they suddenly crowd and as suddenly desert certain bays, compels the pursuing fleets to move with similar abruptness, one result of which is continual disturbances between the wandering fleets and the native fishermen of the ports which they visit. For the Newlyn Riots, some account of which will be given in the next chapter, the mackerel was alone responsible, but the herring has also caused trouble in more than one northern port.

The catches of herring which have of late years been landed at Yarmouth run into figures that stagger the ordinary imagination. Thus, during the season of 1902 between five and six hundred millions of herrings were brought ashore at the port, and in each of the years 1900 and 1901 the total, though less enormous,

A SHRIMP-TRAWLER, YARMOUTH.

also reached two-thirds of this amount. These aggregates are easily arrived at by reckoning the official return of 44,005 'lasts' (1902) at 13,200 of fish per 'last.' It must be remembered that at Yarmouth a 'long' hundred of fish means in reality 132, or four to the warp, and thirty warps to the long-tale hundred. In parts of Cornwall, again, a 'hundred' of pilchards means 120. At Whitby the herring, and at Yarmouth the mackerel, count 124 to the trade 'hundred.' At

Plymouth the 'hundred' of mackerel is really 126. These peculiarities of provincial terms are endless. Even in ordinary conversation we speak of a 'hundredweight' when we mean 112 lb. Such anomalies are not therefore in any way confined to the fish trade, but they are very puzzling at times, and, on a heavy turnover, the difference works out at a considerable figure. In Scotland, I believe, without exception, herrings are sold by

COMING ALONGSIDE.

the 'cran,' which is approximately $3\frac{1}{2}$ cwt. of fresh fish, and, for practical purposes, we may reckon ten crans to the English 'last.' The 'last' is usually packed in a peculiar type of basket known in Yarmouth and neighbourhood as a 'swill,' and of these it should fill twenty.

Whatever may be said of the trawling industry, the herring-fishing at Yarmouth is in a flourishing state. Anyone visiting it to-day, without having known the place ten years ago, would be struck by the signs of prosperity. The immense acreage of nets drying on the denes, the crowds along the river bank, the hustling in the narrow 'Rows,' all point to brisk trade. Although the summer herring-fishing of 1903 was among the worst on record, there is no need to write 'Ichabod' across the strangely dimidiated lions with the tails of herrings which adorn Yarmouth's escutcheon.

The actual state of affairs is that one industry has survived the vicissitudes of centuries, and is now as brisk as ever; the other, which had no respectable antiquity behind it, has migrated to a neighbouring port.

The neighbouring port, Lowestoft, owes its prosperity as a trawling port to its admirable fish-market and to the arrangements made by the Great Eastern Railway Company. The rise and development of Lowestoft trawling may be said to date from the early 1860's, so that the industry at that port is little more than forty years old. In the year 1860 there were no more than twenty trawlers, and none of these were over thirty tons burthen. Their chief harvest consisted of soles trawled on the flats near home.

A little later, Brixham men, seeking new fields for their enterprise, as is their wont, found the place to their liking, established trawling on a larger scale, introduced ice, and brought the remoter North Sea grounds within the sphere of activity of the Lowestoft fleet. By 1870 there were three times the number of vessels, and the average tonnage had gone up two-thirds. By 1880 there were perhaps 120 trawlers; by 1890, roughly, 300. At that time the tonnage had reached its highest, an average of eighty tons. Since that time there has been here, as at Plymouth, a

tendency to return to smaller vessels of thirty or forty
tons. To-day Lowestoft has over 300 deep-sea trawlers
and as many drifters, besides other boats engaged in
shrimp-trawling and line-fishing.

It is a curious fact, and one which has some bearing
on the immature flat fish question, that the Lowestoft
boats, which work on comparatively near grounds under
sail, catch a small plaice measuring only ten or twelve

THE TRAWL-MARKET, LOWESTOFT.

inches in length in the neighbourhood of the Mask
Lightship. As long as the present generation of fishermen can remember, these have been captured on that
ground, and they are locally regarded as a distinct race.

When we hear that the geographical position of
Lowestoft adapts it particularly to the requirements of
sailing trawlers, and indifferently to those of steam-
trawlers, we must take this to mean that it lies close to
productive fishing grounds, as compared at any rate

with the vast distance which separates Hull from Iceland. Under normal meteorological conditions, it also has its share of fair winds to and from the grounds. As at Ramsgate and Brixham, a spell of summer calm keeps the sailing trawlers in port and provides a rough and ready close time for the fish.

A comparison between the facilities at Yarmouth and those at Lowestoft tells wholly in favour of the southern port. Instead of the fish-quays being situated a mile or more from the open sea, with the railway station still further away, as at Yarmouth, the trucks can be brought at Lowestoft within a hundred yards or so of the harbour mouth. The trawlers are thus enabled to discharge in the main harbour, while the herring-boats have a separate basin of their own, just inside the north pier.

The trawl-fish which, in June, I found most abundant at Lowestoft were plaice, soles, and red gurnard of large size. The haddock and coal-fish, so conspicuous at Scarborough nearly a month earlier, were wanting, while the 'stocker' (see page 294) consisted almost entirely of the Greater Weever.

The quantities of trawl-fish landed at Lowestoft have increased considerably during the past ten years, though there has been an absence of the almost sensational progress of Hull, Grimsby, and some other steam-trawling centres. Thus in 1892 the total was 31,379 tons; in 1902, 77,329 tons, or an increase of nearly 250 per cent.

The establishment of Mr. Garstang's laboratory, referred to in the preceding chapter, now invests Lowestoft with an interest for the industry distinct from its commercial aspect.

Between Lowestoft and the kindred sailing port of

Ramsgate, which is within the jurisdiction of the Kent and Essex Committee, there are several second rank fishing stations, including the whole of the Thames estuary, on the fisheries of which Dr. Murie, sometime Prosector to the Zoological Society, has lately published an interesting report under the auspices of the Committee. The chief fishing activity in this district consists in inshore trawling for small soles and dabs, with a little irregular herring-fishing and line-fishing, a few lobster-pots and kettle-nets, and a considerable amount of raking and dredging for whelks and cockles.

At Leigh there is the famous stow-net fishery for Thames whitebait or sprats, according to the season of the year, a fairly productive shrimp-fishery, and a cockle-fishery which has known better days.

All these smaller operations appeal rather to the artist or antiquary than to the student of a great modern industry, but the proximity of these ports to London invests their fisheries with some interest. Eliminating such adventitious appeals, however, it is a fact that the aggregate output of a dozen of these Essex hamlets for the year is far below that of Hull or Grimsby in a month.

In some of these villages the fisheries have fallen on bad days. Anyone standing beside the heaps of cockle-shells at Leigh and looking forth upon the fishing-boats that lie idle on the mud banks, may easily realise the ruin brought on once flourishing communities by the inexorable mandates of modern hygiene. With the accuracy and justice of the medical evidence on the subject of Thames shell-fish I have no desire or qualification to quarrel, but it is impossible not to feel deep sympathy with those who, their occupation gone, patrol the otherwise deserted quays and silent streets.

On the open coast between Lowestoft and the Nore the fishing is here and there in a comparatively flourishing condition. Before we come to the northern boundary of the Kent and Essex district, the estuary between Felixstowe and Dovercourt, there are Southwold, Thorpe, and Aldeburgh, all of which support, on a modest scale their share of trawling, line-fishing, and drifting. The Felixstowe grounds are worked by boats out of Harwich, where I must have seen, either moored or under sail, a hundred or a hundred and fifty small and handy craft, mostly engaged in inshore trawling or in setting hoop-nets for lobsters. This was in June; and I noticed with regret that a number of the captured female lobsters carried spawn. These should, by rights, have been returned to the sea to reproduce the species.

Other small and unimportant stations on the coast of Essex, most of which lie a short way up one or other of the many estuaries with which that coast is so freely indented, are Wyvenhoe, chiefly engaged in shrimp-trawling; Brightlingsea, with considerable dredging for shell-fish; Mersey, with netting for eels; Tollesbury and Maldon, also employed in dredging and shrimp-trawling; Burnham, with oyster-dredging, trawling, line-fishing, and stop-nets, all on a small scale; and lastly, Southend and Leigh. At these latter, particularly since the condemnation of the shell-fish, the shrimp- and whitebait-fisheries are of first importance.

During the winter and early spring, as set forth in an earlier chapter, the whitebait are caught in stow-nets; during the summer months they are taken in small-meshed seines. From August 1 to October 30 has been set apart as a close time for whitebait, but I understand that the fishermen do not keep the law, and complaints of its breach are numerous. There is also a good deal of illegal fishing for whitebait in the River Medway, and in both rivers it is said that the dealers are to blame, not merely tempting the fishermen to break the law, but actually binding them by contract to do so. How far this grave charge can be substantiated by fact I am not prepared to say, and it is here mentioned only as an opinion current in the locality.

The sprat-fishery is responsible for another trouble. Ordinarily, the Thames Conservancy prohibits the use of the stow-net in the lower Thames during the winter. Moved by the representations of the fishermen, a deputation of the Kent and Essex Committee waited upon the Conservancy, with the result that the prohibition was experimentally withdrawn between November 1 1899, and February 14, 1900. The result seems, however, to have been unsatisfactory to all parties concerned. Not only did the Leigh men catch very few fish during that period, but the Conservancy evidently found no good reason for qualifying its veto on the winter netting. The prohibition has therefore once more been enforced, on the ground that the practice threatened the immature fish.

With my visit to Leigh, just as the last of the stow-nets were being laid up and the seines brought out in their place, ended the first section of my coast tour. It had included the greatest, as well as the smallest, ports on the East Coast. As regards the latter end of it, it could hardly be expected that the fisheries of an estuary lying only a few miles below the metropolis of the Empire, and receiving much of its impurities, could even maintain their old position, much less rise to one of first importance. In spite of some recent signs of a return to cleaner conditions under the *régime* of the London County Council, the impure state of the lowest reaches of London's river is too obvious to need the support of evidence, but the fact that the Dutch eel-boats have long ceased to bring their fish alive in their wells to Billingsgate speaks for itself. Some importance was not long since attached by enthusiasts to the capture of a salmon at Leigh, though the interest investing so rare a wanderer to the Thames chiefly bears upon the praiseworthy efforts of the Thames Salmon Association

THE EBB TIDE, LEIGH.

to restock the river artificially with a splendid fish which, left to its natural impulses, has long ceased to seek its indifferent hospitality.

The gravest aspect of pollution and chemical poisoning in the Thames estuary is the ruin which they have brought upon once thriving fisheries. The report of Dr. Bulstrode, which was made some years ago by direction of the Local Government Board, seems to have condemned the oysters and cockles of the Leigh and Southend beds in terms which admitted of only one construction. More recently, in the summer of 1903, Dr. Nash, Medical Officer of Health for Southend, published some figures which showed the undoubted danger of typhoid from these contaminated shell-fish. His results demonstrated that, whereas the typhoid patients among those who ate no shell-fish were only three in every thousand, among shell-fish eaters they were as high as fifty-one per thousand. These show that it is hopeless, until we discover some more satisfactory method of disposing of the sewage, to attempt anything for the fisheries of the Thames estuary.

If things remain much as they were, it is not for want of admonition or effort. It would seem that the only remedy would be to bring the estuary of the Thames under the Rivers Pollution Act, and to this there may, for all I know, be technical objections.

The shell-fish of Southend, Wyvenhoe, and Brightlingsea were all condemned in Dr. Bulstrode's report. Southend lies so close to the sea that oysters bedded to the east of the long pier are regarded as far freer from contamination than those laid on the other side. Moreover, Messrs. Baxter, the chief proprietors, wisely closed their beds at Southend, so long as certain important drainage operations were in course of completion, and removed their oysters to other beds in the Medway.

Wyvenhoe, which is on the Colne, was still more severely condemned than Southend, and a local oyster-merchant found himself compelled to take up sites on the opposite side of the river.

The most important oyster centre in Essex is Brightlingsea, which lies on the joint estuary of the Colne and Blackwater, with other creeks discharging in the vicinity. Dr. Bulstrode found that many of the storage pits were too close to sewage outfalls. I understand, however, that extensive drainage schemes are contemplated, which will put all these beds above fear or reproach. The chief sanitary objection to Leigh cockles, the somewhat disgusting habit of washing them in the creek after boiling, is also said to be removed, as they are now rinsed in clean water.

What we must, however, clearly grasp, is the fact

DREDGERS AT WORK.

that, apart from any question of impurity, the lower waters of the Thames can never be the centre of a great fishing industry. In his report on the Leigh fisheries, Dr. Murie attributes their decline to the accretion of mud in the already shallow channel of the creek, a modification of the shore which has been variously attributed to the influence of Southend Pier and the cultivation of mussels.

London has, however, more serious work for its river, and even the water carriage of fish to Billingsgate is hardly capable of that extreme development which has been held as a sword of Damocles over the railway companies whenever they were thought to be charging excessive rates. Billingsgate itself, which, by virtue of this water-borne fish, figures in the returns as a 'Port or Village,' is chiefly important as the Central Market for fish conveyed by rail, and in this aspect it has been previously described.

CHAPTER VII

THE FISHERY PORTS: THE THAMES TO PLYMOUTH

General Review of the Ports—Whitstable and Emsworth Oysters—Unimportance of Hampshire and Dorset—The Solent—Bournemouth—Isle of Wight—The South Side of the Thames Estuary—Ramsgate—Share of Profits taken by Steam Gear—Fishing Grounds—Profit-sharing—The Harbour—French Visitors—Decline of the Herring-fishery—Dover and Folkestone—The Dungeness Fisheries—Kettle-nets—The Sussex District—Dengemarsh and Galloway—Hastings—Rye Bay and other Grounds—A Harbour for Hastings—Brighton—Former Trade with France—Selsey—Cost of Bait—Undersized Lobsters—Decline of Poole Fishing—Swanage and Lulworth—Dorset and East Devon—A Plea for Inshore Trawling—Decline of Exmouth Herrings—'Sprats' and 'London Sprats' at Teignmouth—Fixed Nets at Babbacombe—Landings at Torquay—Importance of Brixham—Pioneering Work by Brixham Fishermen—Stocker Bait—Mumblebees—Plymouth Barbican—The Bait Difficulty—Plymouth and Government Yards—Careless Gun Practice.

In disregard of obvious affinities between two strongholds of smack-fishing like Lowestoft and Ramsgate, it is convenient to make a dividing line of the Thames estuary, on the south shore of which we now start on the second stage of our tour. This will embrace the stations on the coast line of three important counties, Kent, Sussex, and Devon. It will also, of course, take us along the foreshore of two other counties, Hampshire and Dorset, but both of these display an apathy in fishery matters which can only be attributed to the paucity of fish in their inshore waters, as well perhaps as to the paramount agricultural interest and the desire to cultivate the summer visitor. The Solent is increasingly given up to yachting and steamer traffic, while a popular resort like Bournemouth, with a growing population of both residents and visitors, possesses not one single fishing-boat. During the sixteen years in which I have known Bournemouth there is just one man who, more or less regularly, worked pots for crabs and prawns, while practically all the fresh fish consumed in its hotels and boarding-houses comes from either Grimsby or Devonshire—most of it from the more regular supply of the northern port, but the mackerel, dory, red mullet, and a few soles from Brixham and Plymouth. Cowes procures all the fish for its summer invasion of yachting folk from Grimsby. This fact is not, of course, unduly thrust upon such visitors as may prefer to persist in the belief that their dinner sole was burrowing in some sandy bay near the Needles that morning. Nevertheless, the only fishery with which I am acquainted in that part of the Isle of Wight is the oyster-fishery belonging to Paskins at Newtown. A few little boats are, it is true, engaged in desultory hooking out of Portsmouth and Southampton, but their aggregate catching power is so small as to be negligible. The narrow seas between the mainland and the Wight are not congenial to fishes, nor indeed is there any fishery port of first importance between Folkestone and Brixham, the whole of Dorset and East Devon being unimportant.

The interest of the section of coast under notice centres in Ramsgate, Hastings, Brixham, and Plymouth, though Folkestone has of late years acquired added importance from the decline of Dover. Brighton, though not as prosperous as it was, has not yet fallen out of the fishing world, and Selsey is the principal centre of the shell-fish industry on the eastern half of the south coast.

Gravesend, Queenborough, Sheerness, Faversham, Graveney, Whitstable, Herne Bay, Birchington, and Westgate all contribute towards the output of the Thames estuary, of which something has already been said. Oysters, shrimps, and whitebait are their chief products, though Herne Bay, Hythe, and Whitstable, which lie nearer the open sea, have crab- and lobster-fisheries of some importance. The cockle-beds of Graveney and the shrimps of Pegwell Bay—the latter is beyond the Thames estuary—may also be mentioned, while it is only necessary to allude with similar brevity to the shrimp-trawling of Gravesend, the whitebait fishery at Sheerness and Queenborough, and, at Faversham, the method of taking whelks on 'trot' lines baited with worms. At Graveney they use a peculiar fixed net, regarded by some as especially destructive to undersized flat fish. Whitstable, which we associate chiefly with 'native' oysters, also does a little small-boat trawling in summer for flat fish, while a good many whelk-pots are set in the neighbourhood. At Herne Bay there is hand-lining for small dabs and whiting, dredging for oysters, and seine-fishing for grey mullet. Birchington has fewer fishing craft than Herne Bay, being chiefly busy with push-nets for shrimps and lobster-pots. A precarious winter herring-fishery survives at Westgate, but, considered after that of Yarmouth and Lowestoft, it can hardly be taken seriously. Margate, formerly a fishing station of importance, is now reduced to shrimp-trawling, which engages ten or a dozen boats, in addition to a little drift-net fishing for mackerel in summer and for sprats and herring in winter. The winter herring-fishing extends to Broadstairs, which also has lobster-pots in summer, and a little hook-and-line fishing for whiting in the autumn.

It is at Ramsgate that we come to the first important fishing port of the English coast between the Thames and Plymouth, and much that was said of Lowestoft would apply to this sister station of sailing trawlers. The Ramsgate vessels are sailing trawlers, with steam-gear to haul the nets (the escaping steam is plainly seen in the frontispiece to this book), and the fleet numbers approximately two hundred, employed on

TRAWLERS IN RAMSGATE HARBOUR.

board of which are not fewer than eight hundred men and lads. As far as the style of fishing goes—the contentment with the older methods, the aversion for the steam-trawler—Ramsgate has, as we shall presently find, much analogy with Brixham. The chief difference between them is in respect of their geographical relation to the fishing grounds. The Ramsgate vessels catch their fish comparatively near home and land it at their own port, unless, that is, bad weather makes them run for Lowestoft; but the Brixham men, imbued with a spirit of adventure that has not its equal in the men of any other port, rove away to the Bristol Channel and during more than half the year land the bulk of their catch at Milford.

At Ramsgate, then, the sailing trawler persists, and the steam-trawler stays away. Ramsgate owners congratulate themselves indeed on the fact that their harbour and the neighbouring sea are alike too narrow to attract the steamers of Hull and Grimsby, for which they have very little affection. The smaller craft of thirty or forty tons, which would be considered ridiculous at the more busy centres of the industry, are good enough for Ramsgate, and the interest taken in steam by its fishermen does not go beyond its use in hauling the heavy trawl-net. A somewhat sarcastic epithet, 'little big toshers,' which the visitor may sometimes hear bestowed on the smaller trawlers belonging to the port, has reference to the increasing room taken up by the steam-gear and the consequent reduction in tonnage. Apart from its mechanical aspect, this steam-gear on board smacks has its economic interest, for it takes as its share 5 per cent. of the profits of each voyage. For this reason it is jealously excluded from many of the trawlers down in Devon, a county in which labour-saving machinery is not viewed in a friendly spirit. A similar arrangement is, however, tolerated on the Brighton boats, where the steam-winch takes one share.

The fishing grounds of the Ramsgate trawlers extend over a considerable area of the home portion of the North Sea, mostly within a hundred miles of port, and not, as a rule, north of a line drawn from Lowestoft Ness to the Texel. The smaller boats, indeed, reap their harvest still nearer Ramsgate, on the grounds behind the Goodwin Sands and East and North of the Foreland, where they catch soles, plaice, skate, brill, and turbot.

The men work on a satisfactory system of profit-sharing, by which, of the seven shares in which the

WHISTLING FOR THE WIND.

catch is divided, the skipper gets $1\frac{1}{4}$; the deck hands get 1 each, and their share of the 'stocker';[1] the apprentice gets spending money, and such stocker as is

[1] For an explanation of this word see later in the chapter, under Brixham.

left. Each trawler carries five hands. There is the skipper, and there are, in addition, either two men and two boys, or one man and three boys.

In spite of continual dredging and supervision, Ramsgate harbour runs nearly dry at spring low tides. A reference to the Admiralty chart will reveal the shallowness of the sea hereabouts, for, given a favourable wind, it would be possible at spring low tide to sail from Ramsgate across to Deal without ever having more than six fathoms of water under the keel.

French hookers often visit Ramsgate for herring bait, having got which they return to their fishing grounds, which lie only just outside our three-mile limit, and there catch skate for their own market. The Entente recently promulgated in high circles hardly extends its pacification to the fishermen, for collisions are not rare, though adjustment of differences is usually accomplished swiftly and effectually by a kind of informal tribunal, under the auspices of the Ramsgate Fishing Vessel Mutual Society, and the Commander of the French gunboat sent to hold inquiry into the circumstances of the case. When, as sometimes happens, English fishermen are brought before the authorities in foreign ports, there are those who, when asked how H.B.M. Consuls and Vice-consuls serve their countrymen in such circumstances, compare them with the fifth wheel of a cart. They declare—with what accuracy I have not sought evidence to show—that, whereas in like cases French or Danish consuls at English ports would leave no stone unturned to get their clients off with nominal penalties, British officials are as likely as not to side with the foreign authorities against their fellow-countrymen.

The fishing of Ramsgate to-day is practically confined to trawling. Twenty years ago the port had an important drift-net fishery for herrings, but these capricious fish have deserted the neighbourhood, just as they deserted Exmouth. Temporary failure and sudden revival are common episodes in all manner of fisheries. The herring, for instance, has returned to many Swedish fjords after an absence of sixty years, while, after a failure of twenty years, Selsey oysters are once more plentiful.

The Pegwell Bay shrimping grounds belong to Ramsgate. Deal, though its sturdy luggers and punts do a little winter lining for cod and whiting and a little drift-net fishing for sprats, is celebrated rather in the annals of those who fish for sport. Dover has been taken over, lock, stock, and barrel, by the War Office, and its once active trawling-fleet, which I have many a time seen return from the Varne grounds laden with fine turbot and soles, is dispersed. The only trawl working in the district when I was there in June 1903, was kept on a private yacht.

Folkestone is the next fishing port of any moment. It has over fifty sailing trawlers, in addition to drift-net fishing for mackerel in summer and for herring in winter. On its busy quays may be seen hoop-nets for prawns and long-lines for conger—more long-lines, as a rule, than at any other port in England and Wales. Dog-fish and skate are the fish most in evidence in the summer months, and form, indeed, no small proportion of the returns of the year. The mackerel-fishery is, however, very considerable in some years. Something like a record was established in the September of 1903, when a single vessel landed 20,000 mackerel, while three others followed in her wake with nearly 50,000 between them, and another six with an average of 10,000 apiece.

The market value of such an aggregate catch, with mackerel fetching 5s. or 6s. per hundred, is very considerable.

As will be seen from one of my photographs, Folkestone Harbour runs very shallow at low tide. Still, in spite of such natural drawbacks, the fishing industry is firmly established. Contrasted with Dover, which is merely a Government dockyard, the port owes its fishing prosperity to the absence of too much coast defence.

FOLKESTONE HARBOUR.

Folkestone is practically the last station in the Kent and Essex district, for there remains only Dymchurch, with a stretch of coast east of Dungeness, on which may be seen a peculiar kettle-net worked inshore for mackerel and herring.

The Sussex district begins west of Dungeness, and in the vicinity of that landmark mention must be made of the Dengemarsh and Galloway seines and the Camber kettle-nets. As regards Rye, it is chiefly useful as the port of Hastings, and in this capacity it will, I imagine, continue to serve pending the somewhat uncertain completion of the Hastings harbour works. Time was when Rye had prosperous fisheries of its own, but to-day it owns only a single steam-trawler and a few smacks, which land their fish as a rule on Hastings beach.

Hastings itself is an historic and interesting fishing centre. Considered solely on the basis of the quantities of fish landed on its sloping beach—the harbour is not yet utilised for such purposes—it must be content with a very humble position in the list of fishing ports. It has, however, its interest, not merely because, with the exception, perhaps, of Brighton, it is the chief centre on the Sussex coast, but because it probably does more trade than any other without a harbour. The fish is landed in small boats. I have often stood by the fish-market and seen these bring ashore their freight in an appalling ground-swell and surf, though the fine break-waters erected at the east end of the town, and latterly the unfinished harbour pier, afford a good deal of protection from the south-easterly gales. As regards their landings of fish, Hastings and Brighton are much on a level. In 1901 Hastings had (including shell-fish) fish to the value of £20,509 and Brighton £21,157. Folkestone in that year was credited with £27,651, and Dover with £4,611.

During the summer months the Hastings trawlers often catch their fish within three or four miles of home. Rye Bay would seem to be all but inexhaustible, though the quality of the fish has sadly deteriorated, and tiny soles and plaice that, when I was a lad at school there, in the early 1880's, would never have been seen, now find eager buyers on the beach. In the winter the fleet fishes twenty or thirty miles away, on totally different grounds. There is also some hook-and-line fishing for dog-fish, cod, and whiting, the small reefs of rocks, which at low tide may be seen in parallel lines mostly running from N.W. to S.E., furnishing abundance of food for inshore fish.

Hastings smacks, which portmark RX (Rye) are from forty to forty-eight feet long. I measured several

A FISH AUCTION ON HASTINGS BEACH.

on the beach during my visit, in a rough and ready way, and found some under forty and others over forty-eight, but these are average figures. The smaller punts I found to measure from twenty-eight to thirty feet. It is only at a very few stations like Hastings that it is possible to measure the fishing craft drawn up high and dry.

All the Hastings fishing is, I believe, done on the

share system, the mode of division differing somewhat in trawling and drift-net fishing, as follows.

On trawlers, the catch makes 5¾ shares, divided thus :

> The vessel takes 3 shares
> ,, skipper takes 1¼ share
> ,, 2nd hand takes 1 share
> ,, boy takes ½ plus a share of the stocker.

The drift-net boats ship a larger crew, and the shares number 9, of which

> The vessel and gear take 5 shares
> The skipper takes 1½ share
> Two men take 1 share each
> The boy takes ½ share.

Moreover, the men and boys are found in food, the owner advancing 10s. a week to each man, of which he risks the loss, should the season be so bad as to leave insufficient to cover the advance.

The question of the advisability of a harbour for Hastings is one which concerns those who reside in the place rather than the wider public to which this book is addressed. Though opposed to a policy of stagnation, and friendly to any scheme which promises usefully to employ labour, I look back with pleasure to the many years of fishing prosperity in which I knew the place without its harbour, and feel some misgiving over so great an expenditure with so little prospect of industrial expansion to warrant it. Moreover, it is impossible to be sure that the erection of a roomy harbour may not attract the grimy steam-trawler, and much as I admire its activity at Hull and Grimsby, I should regret its being brought into competition with the hardy Sussex fishermen who have so long been immune from its rivalry.

Between Hastings and Brighton there are only
Eastbourne and Newhaven, the former a flourishing
watering-place and health-resort, the latter the headquarters of a Continental packet traffic. Eastbourne,
it is true, does a little unimportant inshore trawling,
and yachting men know that there are a good many
crab- and lobster-pots on the rough ground off Beachy
Head, but Eastbourne has no existence as a serious fishing

SMACKS OFF HASTINGS.

centre. Newhaven has the added dignity of a couple
of steam-trawlers and a score of small smacks, and its
fishermen engage in a little winter hooking for whiting
and dredging for shell-fish. It is not, however, necessary to halt until we reach Brighton.

Brighton has, as has been indicated, some points
of resemblance to Hastings, notably the absence of a
harbour, a defect which there seems to be neither the

need nor the ambition to rectify, probably because the place is flanked on either side by Newhaven and Shoreham. More important as a fishing station even to-day than is commonly understood, there can be no doubt that the fisheries of Brighton are on the decline, and it seems probable to those who know the local conditions that in five years' time there may not be a single owner ashcre. Not only are the landings dwindling, but two influences have combined to put a stop to the long-established packing of fish for the French market, consignments being formerly sent daily by the Newhaven boat. These are, in the first place, taxation by the French Government for the encouragement of the home industry, and, in the second, the apparent impossibility of getting the fish to Paris in good condition. The fault of this, however, lay not with the packers, but with the slowness of the ' Grande Vitesse ' service, which was allowed three days for the journey.

The fishmarket of Brighton is down on the beach among the arches, and long before the visitors in the large hotels have lounged out of the breakfast-room the day's work is over and the hose is playing on the débris. A crowd of humbler residents may usually be seen loafing against the railings on the parade and watching the buyers as they press round Mr. Gunn, the salesman. As at Hastings, the trawlers anchor off the beach and send the fish ashore in small boats, two men carrying the heavy baskets between them up the steep shingle. This may be a primitive style of trading, but few who have watched both would deny that it is more picturesque than the steam-cranes and railway trucks of Grimsby and Fleetwood. Now and again the solitary Rye steam-trawler lands a cargo of plaice and soles here, but what interested me more were some boxes of mackerel from Mevagissey, a Cornish port that I knew well, bearing the familiar stamp of Messrs. Pawlyn Bros. This had come by rail all the way from Cornwall to compete (and, as I soon saw, to compete successfully) with the larger mackerel landed from the boats that morning. Having during the last few weeks listened to so many complaints against the railway companies for charging such iniquitous rates for the carriage of fresh

ON BRIGHTON BEACH.

fish, I was at a loss to understand how it could pay to send these few fish by land through half a dozen counties to sell against water-borne fish of the species. No very intelligible explanation of the mystery was to be had at Brighton, but, curiously enough, when I got out of the train at St. Austell, the G.W.R. station for Mevagissey, four or five weeks later, I found Mr. Pawlyn, whom I had known there for years, sending off thirty

more boxes, each containing sixty mackerel, for the
Brighton market. He explained to me that he sent
such consignments only on receipt of a wire from his
Brighton agent. The hotels, it seems, prefer these small
Cornish spring mackerel to the coarser Irish fish, not
only on account of their size, but also because they
actually reach the Sussex resort in a fresher state than
those brought by sea from far-off grounds. They would
in all probability realise 10s. or 15s. more per thousand
on Brighton beach than if sold at Mevagissey, so that
even the payment of the railway charges left a small
profit. The fish are packed neatly in flat boxes, over them
a layer of pounded ice, then a sheet of newspaper, and,
on the top of all, the lid loosely nailed on.

Shoreham and Worthing may be compared to Newhaven and Eastbourne, the one a harbour, the other
a seaside-resort. They do a little trawling, drift-net
fishing, lining, and crabbing, but they cannot be regarded
as of any importance in the fishing industry.

Of still less industrial importance are Littlehampton
and Bognor, though their prosperity as watering-places
increases every year.

Selsey is the most important centre of the crab-,
lobster- and prawn-fisheries on that part of the coast.
Selsey Beach, which is dotted with lobster-pots and
tarred huts, lies about a mile from Selsey village and
just east of the Bill. I always regard the Bill, which
separates the shingle of Sussex from the sand of Hampshire, as the geographical, though not of course the
recognised, boundary between the two counties. Selsey
is connected by a light railway with the system of the
L.B. & S.C.R. at Chichester, to which, however, much of
the shell-fish is still sent by road. The only other fishing
at Selsey is a little drift-net fishing for herring, though

when it is added that in 1901 the value of the herrings amounted to £277 as against the £4,678 of shell-fish, it will be seen that the one method of fishing has practically the monopoly.

There is no harbour, the men carrying their boats up the beach, generally by interlacing the oars. The Bill, however, affords lea water, on one side or the other, in all winds. Of larger boats there are about nineteen or twenty. They are stiff, cutter-rigged craft of five tons,

SELSEY BEACH.

and take a crew of two. Of prawn-punts, which are smaller, but also take two men, there would be about the same number. The bait for the pots is brought all the way from Grimsby, and costs each boat about 10s. per week.

Those who write freely of the earnings of fishermen on different parts of our coast rarely make sufficient allowance for the cost of bait, which is often a very considerable item. It has been computed, for instance, that bait costs even the small hookers at Plymouth not less than £100 a year. The price of bait varies, like the price of everything else, with the relations for the time being between demand and supply, and pilchards may cost per thousand as little as 5s. or as much as 50s. A thousand pilchards are soon used up in baiting a long-line of 1,500 hooks.

Selsey fishermen are busy one way or another all the year round, and the seasons for their different fisheries are approximately as follows :

February to December	Crabs and lobsters on the rough ground six miles out near the Owers Light.
March to October	Prawns on the near ground a mile off.
September to April	Oyster-dredging, which has latterly revived after a cessation of twenty seasons.

The lobsters fetch about 9d. per pound, and the crabs about 4½d., on the beach.

It is no part of my task to give in these pages evidence against the fishermen or dealers round the coast, without whose cordial co-operation I could never have attempted to write this book, but I speak in the interests of Selsey itself if I suggest that Lord Onslow might do worse than make it the headquarters of his study of the undersized lobster question, which will soon be scarcely less acute than the one so well provided for in his Sea Fisheries Bill. Few marine animals of equal value are more easily exhausted by man than the lobster, and the waste that is going on unchecked on the Sussex coast is terrible. Whether the Sussex District has in contemplation any bye-law to supersede the ' Oyster, Crab and Lobster Act' of 1877 I do not know. The Southern District, which, since its jurisdiction reaches to the west of Hayling, comes very near the grounds of the Selsey men (and, as a matter of fact, includes some of the nearer ones), has raised the limit for lobsters by 1 inch. As it is, however, the Act here cited declares that it is illegal ' to take, have in possession, sell, expose for sale, consign for sale, or buy for sale . . . any lobster which measures less than eight inches from the tip of the beak to the end of the tail when spread as far as possible flat.' This law is rarely respected at Selsey, and indeed it is not easy to suggest offhand any means by which its observance could be ensured. The present method of inspection is totally inadequate. Yet in many cases the fishermen would welcome protection against their own greed. It is not many years since some of the fishermen on the east coast unsuccessfully petitioned for a size-limit for flat fish, and I believe that the men of Selsey would, if properly consulted, show similar good sense.

From Selsey Bill to Berry Head must be a distance by coast of over 125 miles, and it may safely be asserted that no other stretch of coastline of such length in this country is so unproductive of fish. There is, in fact, no single fishing station of importance between Selsey and Brixham. It is, however, desirable, for the sake of completeness, to glance at the coast between these points.

The reasons for the insignificance of the Solent fisheries have already been outlined. There has lately been a proposal to make Bournemouth contribute its share of expense to the Southern District, even though it owns not a single fishing-smack, but the interesting point in the ethics of taxation raised by the case cannot be discussed here.

Portsmouth does, as already stated, a little trawling, and there are oyster-beds at Emsworth and Hamble.

Poole, the first station in Dorsetshire, has thirty or forty small trawlers, which work in the shallows in Bournemouth Bay, chiefly at night, but also during the day. I have watched them scores of times from Bournemouth Pier, and unless that pier is about four miles long, they certainly fish well within the three-mile limit. In the eighteenth century Poole used to send fresh fish to Devizes, and from there it was sent on Oxford. The once productive oyster-beds, which Hutchins (in the ' History of Dorset ') regards as second only to those of Essex and Kent, do not nowadays repay the trouble of dredging, to such an extent has the oyster scare cut down the demand. There is a small fish-market on the quay, but the landings are very small. Thus, during the six months ending March 31, 1903, the total was rather over £1,150.

Swanage and Lulworth, with one or two other villages on the coast between St. Alban's Head and Portland Bill, do a little fishing for crabs and lobsters. Lulworth, however, which lies in one of the most beautiful coves to be seen anywhere on our coast, did not strike me as so prosperous as Selsey. Some of its failure may perhaps be attributed to the even greater difficulty of communication with the main line (L. & S.W.R.) at Wool. I believe that the Southern District last year withdrew experimentally some of the restrictions which had hitherto closed Weymouth Bay to trawlers, but I have not been successful in ascertaining with what results. Weymouth is no longer a fishing centre of any account, but fifty years ago it was not unimportant, and in the county history quoted above we read of it that   . ' the markets are also very much improved of late years . . . and are well supplied with the choicest fish from the West every day that the wind will permit . . .'—a quaint reflection on the old days of smacks.

The whole of the coast of Dorset and East Devon, as far as Torbay, is of very little moment. Portland, Wyke, Abbotsbury, Burton, and Lyme do a little seine- and drift-net fishing for mackerel in summer and herrings in winter, in addition to which Lyme has pots for crabs and lobsters.

Seaton, Beer, and Sidmouth—we are over the border of Devon now—do more with the lobster-pots, though Beer also has fifteen or twenty small trawlers, which work on the home grounds, where they catch rays and plaice. All these villages in East Devon lack harbour accommodation, which is not found until we come to the estuary of the Exe at Exmouth. As at Selsey, the small fishing-boats of Seaton, Sidmouth, and Budleigh Salterton have to be hauled up on the sloping shingle, while even the pleasure steamers that ply up and down the coast in summer have to run ashore and land their passengers by swing gangways. At all these watering-places a small stream enters the sea, but in no case is it wide or deep enough at the mouth to be navigable. It is a curious fact, and one that in a measure qualifies the advantages claimed for the suppression of inshore trawling, that all these protected bays of Devon are said to have become of late years so silted up with débris that neither the hookers nor the seine-fishermen make the catches which used to reward their efforts in the days when trawlers came close inshore, sweeping the sea-bed clean and stirring up the food.

Important salmon-fisheries and cockle-raking are the chief activities of Exmouth and Teignmouth fishermen, while off both ports the outside fishing is insignificant.

As already mentioned, the Exmouth herring-fishery, so profitable twenty years ago that the London and South Western Railway Company would carry away as much as forty tons of herrings to Billingsgate on many days in the months of February and March, is an industry of the past. The capricious wanderer has deserted Exmouth in the same way as its cousin, the 'sardine,' or pilchard, has more recently deserted Brittany. The Exmouth fishermen, never a very prosperous class, could not afford to sink capital in their nets while waiting for the herring to return, so they sold their gear; and the shoals might visit that estuary to-day with impunity, since there would not be nets enough to catch them.

Here, as at Teignmouth, there is a regular seine-fishery for sand-eels, sold in the neighbourhood for food or bait. The sand-eels are known at Teignmouth as 'sprats,' the true sprats, which are sometimes netted in great quantity in the winter, being distinguished by the name of 'London sprats.'

There are a few fishermen at Exmouth, Dawlish, and Teignmouth, who carry on a little hooking for whiting and other ground-fish in the autumn and winter months, and a few lobster-pots are also set in the neighbourhood, while mackerel-seines work in August and September in the bays. The chief inshore fishery at Babbacombe is the setting of fixed nets for peal, the local name for sea-trout.

Both Torquay and Paignton have a few small fishing-boats, but their proximity to so important a trawling station as Brixham robs their fishing of what interest it might have with a less unfavourable contrast. Torquay indeed has always figured higher in the official returns than its own activity warrants, owing to the fact that, when the wind blows from the north-east, many of the Brixham boats land their fish there. This is not the only leakage in Brixham's credit in the statistics, for its smacks land immense quantities of fish at Milford and other ports in South Wales. These discrepancies are mentioned not in any spirit of deprecation of the official figures, which give all the information claimed by their compilers, but merely to indicate the danger of drawing deductions on such a basis

WAITING FOR THE BREEZE, BRIXHAM.

without a clear knowledge of the facts. Torbay is the easternmost point in the English Channel at which the pilchard figures officially, and, seeing how uncertain the pilchard-fishery is everywhere west of Plymouth, it might as well have been omitted.

Some historians have pretended to trace the origin of trawling to Barking, in Essex, but the consensus of opinion assigns this honour to Brixham, which thus acquires an historic interest out of all proportion to its

U

present prosperity.   At the same time, Brixham is still, comparatively speaking, a flourishing centre of the industry, and, notwithstanding the fact of large quantities of fish caught by its smacks being landed on the shores of the Bristol Channel, the port itself received 2,858 tons in 1901 and 2,389 tons in 1902, exclusive in each case of shell-fish.   Including the latter, the total value of fish landed at Brixham in 1901 amounted to £67,778, and for 1902 to £57,610.

To the adventurous spirit of the men of Brixham a tribute has already been paid, but it would take the skilled pen of a romancer to relate, as the story deserves, how the sleepy little Devon port, which nestles under Berry Head, sent forth its sons three-quarters of a century ago to open up the North Sea fishing grounds and to found on those low shores the greatest fishing settlements of modern times.   Long after some of its families had permanently made their homes at Hull and Grimsby, Brixham continued to send forth crews to the North Sea, where, year after year, they fished in company with Lowestoft boats until their pioneering spirit led them to discover new grounds in the Bristol Channel, whither eventually the Lowestoft boats have followed them.   This restless pioneering instinct seems to have been almost peculiar to Brixham.   Plymouth, in the same county, knows it not.   It was the Brixham men who, long before the advent of the railways, used to land fresh fish daily on the beach at Tenby and the quays at Liverpool.

It is this roaming spirit in the men which has enabled Brixham to hold up her head in defiance of the competition of newer ports that move more with the times.   The exploiting of more distant grounds is the secret of this continued well-being.   The Brixham fleet catches more fish than ever, but it catches them in the Bristol Channel, and, instead of, as formerly, landing their fish two or three times a week at Brixham itself, the smacks put into Milford Haven every five or six days. From January until August the fleet of large trawlers is absent in the West. About the time of the regatta, in August, this portion of the fleet returns home, remaining there, as a rule, for the rest of the year, and fishing the grounds between Portland and the Lizard, between twelve and thirty miles from land, while a few return to the Bristol Channel almost at once.

This arrangement means that Brixham gets practically no fish during the first eight months of the year, except what is landed by the small trawlers, known in the locality as 'mumble-bees.' To the owners and fishermen this does not matter, for the fleet is earning dividends in distant markets, but this change of port takes trade away from the salesmen in the town, as well as from resident tradesmen who live by supplying the requirements of the fleet when at home. This is why anyone making inquiries on the spot about the present prosperity of the place is apt to hear conflicting opinions, according to the point of view.

The steam-trawler keeps aloof from Brixham. A single Grimsby trawler did, as a matter of fact, experimentally land its fish during the summer of 1902, but this enterprise did not meet with such success as to encourage either a repetition of the venture in subsequent years or emulation by other vessels. The conditions of the port would often render it necessary to land the fish in small boats, and this perhaps entails too much labour and delay with the large catches made by steam-trawlers, though a similar method is, as we have seen, adopted at Scarborough. The obstacles in the way of introducing steam, or even of indefinite development of smack-fishing, are Brixham's lack of harbour accommodation, its remoteness from the best fishing grounds down Channel, and its exposure to the north-easterly gales, one of which strewed the foot of Berry Head with wreckage one fateful night in 1866 and filled the little churchyard with the dead. The inacces-

A SLACK TIME AT BRIXHAM

sibility of the railway station, which stands on the summit of a high hill, is another drawback. Plymouth Barbican not only offers far better accommodation, but is also several hours' sail nearer the deep-water fishing grounds.

Its defects, however, notwithstanding, Brixham is likely to maintain its position for some time to come. The elements of complete effacement, such as we saw in Dover, or even of gradual decline, as at Brighton, are sought in vain here. Some kinds of fish, it is true, show a fluctuation. Hake, for example, are less plentiful than they were in the years when this part of the coast was more regularly visited by shoals of pilchards. Red mullet, too, which the trawler catches only when sailing at great speed, have been scarce of late years. Other fish, however, cannot be said to have shown a corresponding falling off, though the once famous Torbay dabs are now little more than a name.

Brixham possesses the largest *indigenous* fishing-fleet on the South coast. There are one hundred and fifty, more or less, of the large class of trawlers, smart craft of 30 to 40 tons; there are about half as many of the 'mumble-bees,' smaller boats of 15 to 25 tons; and there are twenty or so still smaller hookers.

Whether in the Bristol Channel or on the home grounds, soles are the chief harvest of the Brixham boats. The 'mumble-bees' do most of their trawling on the home grounds at night, not because the water is shallow, like that of Bournemouth Bay in which the Poole boats fish, but because soles are caught better at night. Plymouth trawlers, on the other hand, find their best market for the rougher kinds of fish, and therefore trawl for choice by day. Moreover, some of the grounds worked by the Plymouth boats lie in the track of the big liners, and fishing by night might be attended with considerable danger.

The number of men and boys employed at Brixham on the boats themselves must amount to close on a thousand. The apprentice, an obsolete institution at many larger centres, is still a feature of the industry at both Brixham and Plymouth. It is easy to understand the reasons that have prompted the great fishing syndicates of Hull and Grimsby to abolish a personal servant like the apprentice, who is in many cases a son or nephew of the skipper or of one of the crew. Not that Brixham is self-supporting in the matter of apprentices, for there is increasing difficulty in finding recruits, such distant institutions as Plymouth workhouse and Dr. Barnardo's homes being laid under contribution, with excellent results. The spread of education, with its by-product of discontent, as well as the extra induce ments held out of late years to join H.M. Navy, has not lessened the difficulty.

The mention of apprentices suggests an explanation of the term ' stocker,' or ' stocker bait,' already used in connection with Ramsgate, and sometimes written ' stock-a-bait.' Formerly, stocker, which consists of either useless kinds of fish or the undersized or bruised specimens of marketable species, was a perquisite of the apprentice in consideration of his cleaning up the smack when, on arrival in port, the master and mate had gone ashore. Gradually, however, the apprentice has lost his monopoly of the stocker, which has been apportioned among various members of the crew. Another change has come over it. The increased value of many rougher kinds of fish, which once were rejected as unmarketable offal, but now sell readily at a price, has led to even the owners claiming a share. Thus, dog-fish were once regarded as stocker, for they sold only at a nominal figure as bait for the crab-pots, and the entire proceeds went to the crew. To-day, however, there is a brisk winter market for dog-fish, and this not, as might perhaps be expected, solely for the poorer quarters of large inland towns. Further than mentioning its ultimate destination I do not propose to follow the dog-fish, which is usually filleted for retailing purposes, on its travels.

What here concerns us is that this altered view of stocker bait led to a strike at Brixham as long ago as in the 1880's, and the present arrangement is that any stocker over and above the value of £1 goes into the vessel's earnings, while the boy's share is restricted to 2s. 6d. a week. A broad and inadequate definition of stocker bait has already been given, but it is desirable to understand some distinctions. At Lowestoft, for instance, I was shown heaps of weevers under this denomination. In the Plymouth district the men on board the trawlers get the thick-back soles, scallops, lobsters, and he-crabs, while the she-crabs and squid are the perquisite of the boys. The livers have always been regarded as stocker. They are stored in casks, each of which when full fetches 10s., and the men have a trick of adulterating the contents of the casks with anemones. On the drift-boats the stocker consists of the small or bruised mackerel, as well as of such hake and dog-fish as get entangled in the nets. On the hookers, the stocker consists of ling, pollack, or conger, whichever happens to be in least demand locally.

The stocker is sold, whether as bait for crab-pots or for treatment in fried-fish shops, on landing, and the men get their share of the ready money after each sale, instead of having to wait for the weekly account sales and cheque.

At Brixham, as at some other ports, the salesman now takes the risk of bad debts, formerly borne by the catcher. This risk seems but poorly covered by a commission of only 5 per cent., which, on large amounts, is further subject to a discount to the buyer of $2\frac{1}{2}$ per cent., but the system seems to work satisfactorily. Speaking critically, any arrangement is preferable to the loss falling on those who, while they readily risk their lives and forfeit their comfort at sea, are but indifferent business men when it comes to striking a bargain on land.

The Brixham trawlers make eight shares of the profits on the voyage, of which

> The owner gets 4¾ shares and finds a boy
> The skipper and men divide the rest.

The smaller ' mumble-bees ' trawl close in under the Devon shore, their territorial limits being reckoned across the headlands. During a residence of several autumns on that part of the coast I have known them sail through the small boats that anchor for whiting on the Babbacombe ground, perhaps taking intentional advantage of the ground-baiting thus provided by the forty or fifty boats assembled there in September and October.

Dartmouth, Torcross, and Yealm have only second-rate fishing interests, and Plymouth is the next fishing station of importance, and the last on this section of our coast tour.

At Plymouth we reach the western limit of jurisdiction of the Devon district on the South coast, though we shall later find ourselves in its northern section on leaving Cornwall at Welcombe.

In many respects, without being quite perfect, Plymouth Barbican is a most admirable fish-market. With ample accommodation for both smacks and steam-trawlers, situated far enough down Channel for vessels that have to bring their catch all the way from the Bay of Biscay, protected from every wind and all weathers, it is a busy fishing centre all the year, and it accommodates a large mixed fleet of steam and sail, some belonging to the place itself, others hailing from as far distant as Lowestoft and Boulogne, and all discharging fish throughout the week.

When a stiff breeze blows from the Breakwater to the Hoe, I have known the smacks win the race to the Barbican, getting the first of the market before the heavier steam-trawlers can get alongside. A more usual condition, however, particularly in summer, is a dead calm, in which the whole of the catch landed by

THE BARBICAN, PLYMOUTH.

the steamers is sold and packed for despatch by rail before the foremost of the smacks comes creeping towards the quay, unless indeed it has been found possible to engage the services of a convenient tug.

The fleet of smacks has dwindled in numbers during the last fifteen or twenty years, but previous to that period not a single steam-trawler was ever seen at the Barbican. Conditions are indeed changed, and I have seen the steamers of half a dozen East Coast and West

Country ports landing their fish side by side on a July morning. Some of them hail from as far away as Aberdeen; and I recently, in fact, watched the ' Ben Venue (A 83) ' unloading scores of boxes of hake and conger; then, when this rougher stuff was all out, came a few fine turbot and plaice, the result, in all probability, of a week's fishing in the Bay of Biscay, a couple of hundred miles south of Scilly.

An immense quantity of fish is landed at Plymouth in the course of the year; and, besides sending away six or seven thousand tons by rail, the Three Towns consume between them nearly half the fish brought ashore. As regards the weight of fish landed, the trawling is as prosperous as ever it was, but the indigenous fleet has fallen away in numbers and is much inferior to that of Brixham. I can remember the days when close on a hundred smacks were said to be doing well, and to-day probably no more than half that number of Plymouth craft are fitted out for the fishing. Where fifty dozen whiting were formerly taken in a tide by the hookers just outside the Sound, ten dozen is an exceptional catch at the present time. The mackerel trade is also on the downward grade, Falmouth having supplanted the place to such an extent that nineteen-twentieths of the mackerel despatched to-day from the Cornish port would formerly have gone from Plymouth. What a serious falling off this means for the latter port may be measured by a single year's increase in the Falmouth returns, the landings at that port having gone up from 538 tons in 1900 to 886 in 1901. Much of the present prosperity of Falmouth may probably be traced to the deflection of traffic consequent on the Newlyn riots. Though—since the conditions may have been abnormal —the returns of a single week are often misleading, it is perhaps interesting to take the landings at Plymouth during a week of August 1903. For the week ending August 15 of that year there were landed at the Barbican :

Trawl and hook fish	. 126 tons.
Mackerel	. 7 tons.
Shell-fish	. 2 tons 7 cwt.

The Plymouth trawlers are, like those belonging to Brixham, from forty to fifty tons, and the greater number are built in the neighbourhood, though a few are bought from Brixham or Galmpton. The drift-boats, on the other hand, are mostly built in the yards of Penzance or St. Ives.

The trawlers are cutter- or dandy-rigged, and their crew includes the skipper, three men, and a boy. There are, besides, forty or fifty dandy-rigged boats of smaller size engaged in hooking. These also, however, when the pilchard shoals come close enough to the land, lay aside their long-lines and use drift-nets for the surface fish. Their long-lining is done in the deep water, forty or fifty miles outside the Eddystone. Other favourite grounds for the hook-fishing on a large scale are situated twenty miles off the Start, as well as off Bolt Head and Prawle, while hooking on a smaller scale is carried on on the ground known as Hand Deeps and elsewhere on the rough ground inshore, wherever smacks are unable to use their trawls. When the hookers can get squid for bait, they give it the preference ; otherwise, they use pilchard, and in times of great scarcity I have even heard of skate and dog-fish being used not altogether unsuccessfully. The bait question is one of the problems kept in view by the experts at the laboratory of the Marine Biological Association on Citadel Hill. As some compensation, it must be remembered that the very fact of squid or pilchard being abnormally scarce in the district means that the fishes themselves are on short rations, hence, no doubt, the temporary success of skate or dog-fish baits.

The smaller Plymouth trawlers fish comparatively close to the three-mile limit, which is reckoned by headlands. When anchored in my small lugger a mile

THE FISH-MARKET AT PLYMOUTH.

or two south of the Deadman, or Dodman, Head, just west of Gorran Haven, I have often seen them busy inshore of a line drawn from our bow to the Rame.

The oyster-beds of Plymouth are not what they were, and one hears no more of the former famous layings in the Cattewater ; while even those of the Tamar, off Saltash, seem no longer flourishing. Indeed, I believe that most of the oysters consumed in Plymouth at the present time come from near Falmouth, which thus seems to have rivalled the Devon port in more branches than one of the fishing industry.

Like Dover, Plymouth owes some of the decline of its fisheries to the activity of the War Office. That there is another side to this complaint is obvious, for the barracks and dockyards afford work and wage for many who, in the altered conditions, would find a difficulty in earning a living wage on board of the trawlers. I am, however, concerned with the subject only from the fisherman's standpoint, and there can be little doubt that the Government works are responsible for much of the deterioration on the inshore grounds. The mudhoppers deposit their rubbish on what were once prolific fishing grounds, covering the natural food of the fish and suffocating the small fry. Moreover, the forts and batteries are a source of fear, if not, indeed, of danger, to the fishing smacks, as the following extract from the 'Western Morning News' (June 1903) will illustrate :—

PLYMOUTH FISHING-BOAT STRUCK BY A SHELL.

The smack 'Test,' of Plymouth (Mr. W. H. Pease, captain and owner), was making for the fishing grounds off the Eddystone on Friday morning, and when between Penlee Point and the Breakwater she was struck by a shot from the Picklecombe Fort. The missile (now in the possession of the owner) dropped on the deck, striking a large iron ring belonging to the fishing gear. The smack was travelling at the rate of two knots an hour ; the sea was almost a dead calm, and the weather fine. The shot measured 2½ inches in length and an inch in diameter ; it weighed ten ounces and was grooved.

The smack was about half a mile from the fort. It seemed as if the shot came from a quick-firing gun.

This is heinous. That the War Office and Admiralty should do all they can to keep the coast defences up to

the mark no one will deny. No agreements nor junket-
ings under the auspices of the 'Entente Cordiale,' no
interchange of royal visits nor any diplomatic amenities
can warrant a moment's relaxation of vigilance; and
it is a trite but true maxim that by being ready for
war we shall best ensure peace. At the same time, it
exceeds the bounds of expediency to make targets of
British fishing-smacks. I do not, of course, seriously
suggest that the 'Test' was the victim of anything but
an accident; nor, in the absence of more detailed evidence than I was able to lay my hand on, though I
went over to Plymouth at the time for the purpose, am
I in a position to say that none of the blame should
have fallen on the skipper or the crew. Such risks,
however, ought to be made impossible. Nor do these
accidents occur only at Plymouth. Seventeen years
ago, when I was at Shoeburyness, I recollect a very
similar narrow escape on the Maplin Sands; while even
in the Solent I have heard of a spent torpedo striking
a fishing-boat with such force that all hands had first
to man the pumps and then to run the craft ashore.
Seeing how very few boats fish in the Solent at all
nowadays, all the more blame fastens on the authorities
for torpedoing that almost solitary example.

Not always are casualties reported. Not always,
indeed—seeing that neither does the gunner realise what
he has done nor does the victim, if alone in a small
boat, survive to tell the tale—is official notification
practicable. Now and again a crabber, with her crew
of two, has been missing on the Devonshire coast, and
it is invariably assumed that the little open boat
foundered in a squall. The men can rarely swim, and,
even if they could, their sea-boots and heavy mackintosh
aprons would sink them. Sometimes there is a squall

to justify the assumption; sometimes there is not, and the assumption then rests on a charitable desire to give the benefit of the doubt. Surely other practice grounds might be chosen. Throughout April and May in the present year, H.M.S. 'Narcissus' was constantly practising just outside Bournemouth Bay, and not a fishing-boat was ever the worse. The reason will be gathered from what was said above.

DRYING THE TRAWL-NETS.

There is another way in which the Admiralty interferes with the fishermen, and that is by holding the speed trials of large warships over the track of the fishing-vessels. On that very water which I have already mentioned, between the Deadman and the Rame, it is not uncommon to see cruisers and destroyers dashing to and fro with a despatch that would elicit more spontaneous admiration but for the constant fear of being swamped by their wash. Polperro recently made formal protest against this practice, and a question was asked in the House of Commons, but no satisfactory promise was given of any other arrangement being made. If the Admiralty must hold its speed trials so near the land, one would have thought that the little-fished seas off Dorset might with more propriety have been selected, with Portland as a base in lieu of Plymouth. There would, at any rate, be no reasonable complaint of swamping fishing-boats, for there are, on most days of the week, none to swamp, whereas the Cornish bays and neighbouring seas are dotted with them throughout the year.

Reference has already been made to the closing of the Devon bays, as well as to the view which the hook-and-line fishermen take of this restriction. The proposal was recently made to petition Lord Onslow's Department for power to remove the restrictions, at any rate for a period, by way of experiment. The crabbers met in protest against the proposal, and at the time of going to press no final step has been taken.

CHAPTER VIII

THE FISHERY PORTS : CORNWALL AND THE WEST COAST

aried Fisheries of Cornwall—Importance of Migratory Fishes in its Returns—Trawling and Drift-net Ports—Mackerel-seining at Looe—Mevagissey—Seasons for the Drift-nets—'Jowders'—The Harbour—Analysis of Fish Landed—A Self-contained Port—The Sardine Factory—Other Products—Falmouth to Mount's Bay—Penzance Harbour—Preference of the Buyers for Newlyn—The Newlyn Riots of 1896—Mousehole—Breton Crabbers at Scilly—A Visit to one of their Vessels—Mullet-seining at Sennen Cove—The Seaweed Grievance—Pilchards and Herrings at St. Ives—Privileges of the Seine-boats—Record Catches at St. Ives—Enterprise of the L. & S. W. Railway Co. at Padstow—Natural Disabilities of the Port—Unimportance of the North Coast of Devon—Cardiff—Swansea—Improvements in the Harbour—Advantages of Railway Monopoly to a Fishing Port—Stake-nets at the Mumbles—Decline of Fishing at Tenby—Development of Milford by the Great Western Railway Company—Natural Advantages and Disadvantages of the Town—Its Progress—Trawling-fleet—Steam-liners—Mackerel Trade—Greater Development of the North Side of the Bristol Channel—Pwellheli—Scientific Work of the Lancashire and Western Authorities—Fleetwood—Falling off of Morecambe Bay Fisheries—Shrimp-trawlers and the 'Shank' trawl—Completion of the Tour at Maryport—Solway Fisheries—Cumberland District—Résumé of the Tour.

HE duchy of Cornwall has a coastline of nearly 150 miles on the threshold of the Atlantic Ocean. It has roductive pilchard and mackerel fisheries on the south oast, and on the north the famous ancient seine-fishery at t. Ives, besides a port which, looking out upon the newly scovered trawling grounds of the Bristol Channel, may ne day, when certain obstacles have been removed, ake a leading position. It is thus the most important

x

fishing county on the South coast.   In concluding this tour in the present chapter, we have also to visit Milford and Fleetwood, respectively the first and second fishing centres on the west side of the island, besides a number of smaller ports of lesser interest.

In Cornwall alone the fishing industry must employ not far short of 50,000 men, women, and lads, and the annual value of the fish landed on its coasts amounts to nearly a quarter of a million sterling.   Yet the catches are precarious, by reason of the fact that a considerable proportion of the fish caught belongs to such migratory kinds as pilchards, mackerel, and herrings.   Their movements, though not perhaps so irregular and unnecessary as is commonly thought, baffle the fishermen, and often enough miles of drift-nets are shot round nothing, and the night is profitless.

The drift-net and seine-fishery, depending upon shoals which are here one day and gone the next, develop differently from trawling.   Any comparison between the vicissitudes of St. Ives and Grimsby would have to take account of this difference of conditions. The pilchards may stay away from St. Ives for the greater part of the year, and the seines at any rate are then idle.   When, at length, the shoals come inshore, they arrive in such appalling hordes that as many as 8,000 hogsheads have been inclosed at a haul, though it was in this case impossible to recover the bulk of the fish in a condition fit for food.   In fact, they decomposed before they could be got out of the nets.   It is, however, on record that a catch of 5,000 hogsheads was saved, and this must have realised a prodigious return on the comparatively small investment of capital in seine-fishing.   Ports like Grimsby and Hull, on the other hand, though the most productive trawling grounds lie at an increasing distance, are able to send their busy fleets throughout the year, with the result that immense cargoes of fish are brought almost daily into the Humber from grounds as distant as Iceland and the Faroes. This, therefore, is the difference in the conditions: on the East Coast, an uninterrupted fishing of distant grounds, following on the gradual exhaustion of those nearer home; in Cornwall, periods of feverish activity succeeded by intervals of idleness, the outcome of wandering instincts in the fishes themselves, which thereby escape the menace of extermination.

Another circumstance tends to place the Cornish fisherman on a different footing from that occupied by the fishermen of Northumberland and Durham. It is impossible to investigate the standard of living and rate of wages in an industry without taking into account the local standing of kindred occupations, and the student of our fishing communities cannot afford to ignore the position of those engaged in agriculture or mining. Agriculture does not, so far as Cornwall is concerned, exercise any great influence in determining the local rate of wages, and most of the mines are shut down, their skilled labourers having emigrated to California or Australia. In Northumberland, however, and the neighbouring county, mining is sufficiently flourishing to prove an attraction in the labour market, so that not only are some of the fishing-fleets on that coast undermanned in summer, but a still greater number seek regular work and wage in the mines in winter.

The most important Cornish fishing centres to-day are Mevagissey, Newlyn, and St. Ives, in addition to which there is also considerable activity at Looe, Polperro, Falmouth, Porthleven, and Mousehole on the South coast, Sennen on the West, and Padstow on the North.

The degree in which these ports are protected from the fury of the seas which beat upon that exposed corner of England varies considerably. Generally speaking, more terrible weather is met with on the Cornish coast than anywhere else on the island. The gnarled profile of the Land's End is a sufficient index of the violence of the seas that carved it out from the cliffs, but those who know the sturdy character of the Cornish fishermen, with their unstudied indifference to bad weather, will find still more convincing evidence in the report of the Cornwall Sea Fisheries District officer, for a copy of which I am indebted to Mr. Williams, of Caerhays. In that report it is stated that gales kept some of the Cornish fleets idle during the winter for days together. Weather which can keep the Cornishmen ashore must indeed be appalling.

As we travel along the coast westward from Plymouth, the first Cornish station of interest is Looe. It lies on the joint estuary of two small trout-streams which take its name and is confronted, like Mousehole, elsewhere in the duchy, with a small island, which keeps off some of the rough seas. It may be reached from Plymouth either by the main line of the Great Western Railway, with a branch line from Liskeard, or, in summer, by a coasting steamer, which runs there two or three times a week.

Summer is the period of greatest activity at Looe, for then there is the mackerel-seining, crabbing, and hooking for skate, conger, and whiting, both hand-lines and long-lines being employed. In winter there is only drift-net fishing for herring.

The seining for mackerel is the chief and most characteristic fishery. It commences some time in June, and its duration is only seven or eight weeks.

The opening day is a movable function, according to the weather and temperature for the year and the movements of the mackerel themselves. In 1902 I was there in the middle of June, and the seine-boats were not yet busy ; in 1903 I found that they had been at work nearly a month by the first week in July. The boats are, as may be seen in the photograph, moored just within the small pier, and the nets, hanging fes-

LOOE MACKEREL-BOATS.

tooned over the walls and quays, are conspicuous from all sides.

The exact method of seining from boats was described in Chapter II. At Looe, one of the crew of the ' follower ' is sometimes landed on the beach when there is difficulty in finding the fish, and he then scrambles up to high ground and signals to the fleet the movements of the mackerel shoals as soon as he sees

them. Like those of Mevagissey, the Looe boats portmark at the intervening station Fowey (FY).

Polperro has flourishing and long-established drift
net fisheries and hooking, but, as I have known
Mevagissey, which is a more important station a little
to the westward, for many years, it will be convenient
to describe it in some detail as a typical south Cornish
fishing village. Of Fowey, which lies between, and
which is chiefly a yachting station, I need say nothing.

Mevagissey is one of the most important fishing
centres on the South coast. Except for one month,
February, when many of the men are away at their
R.N.R. training, all its fishermen are busy catching
either mackerel, pilchard, or herring, at the following
seasons ·—

> Mackerel from March to the end of June.
> Pilchard from July to December.
> Herring from end of December to end of January.

The fishing grounds for the mackerel and pilchards
lie comparatively near home, and almost every night in
the summer the lights of the fleet may be seen out in
the bay at various distances, according to the whereabouts of the fish. I have been out aboard the ' Foam '
(Capt. Jonathan Barron) on nights when a good catch of
pilchards was made within a mile of the harbour, so
that we were ashore again with the fish by midnight.
At other times, when the fish stay out in the deeper
water, it is necessary to sail eight or ten miles before
striking the shoals. It is in the early part of the
season, during the first days of July, that the pilchards
are still far from the land. Later, in August and September, they come so near the beaches that even the
seines get their chance, though seining is not practised

at Mevagissey on the same scale as at Looe or St. Ives. The winter herrings are taken on their spawning ground in Bigbury Bay, between Plymouth and Salcombe.

The Mevagissey fleet numbers fifty or sixty of the largest class of mackerel-drifters, as many more of the smaller pilchard-boats, besides a number of rowing-boats used with the seines or for hooking. The cost of a single modern steam-trawler, with all its gear, would buy many of these simple craft, for one of the largest sailing drifters, with a complete outfit of nets for all fishing, would not cost more than £300 or £400. The outfit of nets would include :—

> One ' string' of mackerel nets, *i.e.* 75 or 100 nets, each 20 fathoms long.
> One ' string' of pilchard nets, *i.e.* 14 or 100 nets, each 40 fathoms long (only 12 used in winter).
> One ' string ' of herring nets, *i.e.* 14 or 100 nets, each 40 fathoms long.

The crews vary little, if at all; five men work on the larger boats after mackerel or herring, and three on the pilchard-boats.

All fishing is done on the share system. The owner and boat take half the profits; the rest goes to the crew. If the owner does his share of the work out fishing, he also, of course, takes a 'body' share like any member of the crew, as well as the interest on his investment. If he stays ashore, he pays one of the crew 5s. a week to take his place.

In addition to the drift-net fishing, which is all important, Mevagissey also does a little seining and hooking. One fisherman, with whom I have fished every summer, with one exception, since 1894, works his own small lugger (all the craft hereabouts are rigged with the dipping lugsail) single-handed in all weathers and uses both long-lines and hand-lines on the outer grounds, perhaps ten or fifteen miles south-west of the

Deadman.   During the short summer-holiday season, in which, for all its six miles' distance from the iron road, Mevagissey · is increasingly patronised bv visitors with a love of the quaint, he earns a better wage by taking parties out to fish for sport, but for the rest of the year his labour is exhausting and his earnings modest to a degree.   On the best days, toiling from daybreak to sunset, and often an hour or two on either

MEVAGISSEY: THE POOL.

side of these limits, he may bring ashore £2 worth of gurnards, whiting, and pollack, but more often his catch for the twelve or fourteen hours of work fetches less than 10s.   Not satisfied with the hard work of long-lining, than which few methods of fishing are more trying to anyone working his boat alone, he sometimes buys a 'condemned' pilchard-net out of one of the large boats, and with this he sometimes contrives to catch a few hundred fish to bait his hooks or sell ashore. I remember the time when these small hookers sold their catch through Pawlyn, the auctioneer, but to-day they sell direct to the jowders.[1] This arrangement suits all parties, for the small catcher saves the commission of the middleman, while the salesman gladly foregoes the trouble of dealing with such insignificant lots. As regards pilchards and mackerel from the drifters, local custom prescribes that the jowders shall

MEVAGISSEY: THE INNER HARBOUR.

buy the pilchards direct from the boats, whereas the mackerel are sold only through the auctioneers.

For the completion of the new pier the town is in

[1] This word, which is indiscriminately written, or pronounced, 'jowder,' 'jowster,' or 'jowter,' was not unknown to Charles Kingsley, but its origin is a mystery, and it must perhaps be referred, like 'machiowler' (the local vernacular for the jelly-fish) to some obscure Celtic origin. Jowders are fish-hawkers, of a rather superior class, who buy small quantities of fresh fish on the quays and then sell them to the farmers and villagers inland. The large, though thinly populated, districts of Cornwall which lie away from the railroad doubtless facilitate this commerce. Those who know

great measure indebted to the liberality of the Squire
of Caerhays.   It has raised the harbour to equality
with any, save perhaps Newlyn, on the Cornish coast;
that is to say, omitting such natural harbours as
that at Falmouth, where the work of man has had
very little share in the production of a magnificent
anchorage.

I have not, hitherto, given the landing charges and
harbour dues, for these have no great interest for the
reader.   As a single case, and suggesting that considerable allowance should be made for local custom,
I append those made at Mevagissey, for which I am
indebted to Captain Williams, the Harbour Master.

Mackerel at per local hundred [1] . . .	3*d.*
Small Mackerel (if sold under 2*s.* 6*d.* per 100)	1*d.*
Herrings at per local hundred	1*d.*
Pilchards at per local thousand	3*d.*
Bream, Whiting, and other Small Fish at per local score	½*d.*
Not specified at per cwt.	3*d.*
Refuse or Caff [2] at per ton	6*d.*

The conditions of local trading are everywhere complicated by all manner of local laws, mostly unwritten,
which baffle the best intentions of those who endeavour
to describe them.   At Mevagissey, for instance, a local
custom of some antiquity prescribes that the buyer
shall pay the landing dues on pilchards, whereas, on
the other hand, the catcher pays those on mackerel.
The catcher also pays the small charge on bream,

Malaga and Gibraltar will have no difficulty in recalling the more picturesque equivalent of the jowder, the *Charran*, who is to be seen eternally
rolling cigarettes and crying at intervals his '*Salmonete! Boquerones!* '
The Cornish jowder is less of an artist's model and more of a trader.

[1] The actual number of fish reckoned in the ' local ' hundred was given
on an earlier page.

[2] *I.e.* chaff or refuse.

whiting, and other hook-fish. I have compared the year's receipts at Mevagissey for the three principal fish with the foregoing scale of landing charges, and a rough calculation enables me to state that in a good year Mevagissey receives three-quarters of a million of mackerel, sixteen millions of pilchards, and two millions of herrings. These figures are offered with all reservation, and it must be remembered that not all the fish caught by Mevagissey boats is landed at the place itself. Just as we have seen that during a great part of the year the Brixham trawlers land their fish at Milford and other western ports, so the Mevagissey drift-boats land not only the whole of their winter herring, but also, at other seasons, some of their mackerel and pilchards, at Plymouth Barbican.

Mevagissey is the model of a self-contained port. The red wings of its fleet are all made by either Furse or Lelean, who own sail factories in the place. Most of the boats themselves are also built at Mevagissey, which has supplied fishing craft to ports as distant as Folkestone, and which has quite a reputation in the building of lifeboats, though a few of the pilchard-boats come from the yards at Porthleven, and Gorran Haven has furnished some of the smaller craft. Most of the nets, which the drifters use by the mile, are made—in the trade they speak of 'breeding' nets, not making them—by Edwards, Way, or Hunkin, all of whom own net factories on the quay. A few of the boats, however, use for preference the finer Scotch nets, to which reference was made in an earlier chapter, while others use nets from Porthleven or Bridport.

In addition, however, to these subsidiary industries, which flourish more or less at every Cornish fishing centre, Mevagissey has a sardine factory, the only one of the kind in that part of England. When we consider that the sardine of commerce is a pilchard, and when we further remember that this country imported from France and other countries sardines prepared in various ways amounting in 1901 to more than 12,000 tons, and exceeding a value of £716,500—in 1902 the weight had slightly increased, but the value fell below £638,700—it seems a pity that we cannot make our own sardines. We do make them at Mevagissey, though it has never been pretended that the Cornish article has ousted the foreigner on the better class table in London. There is, nevertheless, a very real demand for these Cornish sardines at home; and the 'Fish Trades Gazette' (May 7, 1904) reports that retailers at Bucharest are complaining that they are no longer to be had out there, though they formerly found a good market and left the retailer a better margin of profit than those of Continental preparation. Cornish sardines are tinned exclusively at Mevagissey. Not very much tinned fish goes through Billingsgate in comparison with the total consumption; but Mr. Johnson and the sub-inspectors of the Fishmongers' Company probably have to pass several thousand boxes in the course of the year. So sensitive is their hand to the normal temperature of the tin, that the very slight increase in temperature caused by decomposition of the contents warns them to reject the box.

The sardine factory at Mevagissey is a self-supporting concern. Formerly, indeed, it even employed its own boats to catch the pilchards, and the 'Foam,' already mentioned in this chapter, was one of its fleet. Of late years, however, the boats have passed into private ownership, but the factory continues to take the entire catch. It employs a large number of girls, not only to prepare the fish, but also to make the tins, of which the women do the machine-cutting, while men finish off the soldering. Mr. Cregoe, the courteous manager, who was so good as to take me over the works, told me that it was his practice to turn as many hands as possible on to the tin-making whenever the fishing was slack, so that when the boats again brought in heavy catches, there might be as many as possible free to handle the fish.

The two chief products of the factory are sardines in olive-oil and kippered mackerel. The pilchards are bought, at the current price, from the 'Foam' and such other boats as fish for the factory. The mackerel, on the other hand, are bought anywhere, preference being given to the larger Irish fish and not to those smaller local mackerel caught in the neighbourhood, and, as previously related, consigned by rail to Brighton, Hastings, and other ports further up the Channel.

The mackerel are kippered in oval tins, each of which holds just one and a half of the large kind. The fish is beheaded and cleaned, and the heads and refuse sell for manure at 6d. per barrel. It may be noted, in passing, that the heads and refuse of pilchards fetch twice as much as those of mackerel, for the reason that the débris from pilchards runs less to water. When the head has been removed, the body, having been well cleaned, is thoroughly smoked, soldered down in the tin, and cooked up to a temperature of about 220° F. Treated thus, it is claimed that the contents of a tin will remain sweet for years.

Tinned limpets in vinegar are a third product of the factory, and the idea owes its origin to the home-sickness of Cornishmen exiled in the United States. The limpet is hardly to be described as the most delicate of food, but distance lends enchantment even to tinned limpets, and, some Cornish folk transplanted to the neighbourhood of Chicago having expressed a wish once again to taste limpets, a local storekeeper instituted inquiries, which eventually reached Mr. Cregoe. With characteristic enterprise he forthwith set lads to work picking limpets off the rocks at a fixed remuneration per basket, and these he pickled in vinegar and packed in small round tins for the American market. In this form does the lowly limpet carry memories of those lovely Cornish bays to men and women forced by circumstances to sweat out the remainder of their existence in the unpromising purlieus of Chicago.

I take leave of Mevagissey with an apology for having devoted so many pages to a single fishing centre of second rank. It is probable that the total annual value of landings, including shell-fish, does not exceed £10,000 or £12,000. Yet the place serves admirably to illustrate the characteristic fishing industry on the south coast of Cornwall, as distinguished from the north, where the seine and trawl in great measure replace the drift-net; and this consideration, together with my intimate knowledge of the port over a period of years, seemed to warrant a degree of detail out of proportion to Mevagissey's industrial and economic importance.

West of Mevagissey, between it and the frowning Deadman Head, lies the little haven of Gorran, like Lulworth and Selsey, almost wholly devoted to crabs and lobsters. Seaward from the Gwingeas Rocks, over a considerable area of sea, east and west, may be seen the dancing corks of pots set by the Gorran men, and most of their best ' fish ' finds its way each Monday to Pawlyn's store at Mevagissey.

Porthloe, a quaint little settlement that I have visited from Mevagissey, is another crabbing centre, very indifferently sheltered from the heavy seas of winter. Some trammel-fishing and hooking is also done here, while one or two seines are worked for mackerel in summer. On the whole, however, Porthloe must be voted picturesque rather than important.

What will first and last strike the visitor to Falmouth is the magnificent anchorage and the insignificance of the fishing-fleet viewed in so splendid a frame. Nowhere else on the tour, until we reach Milford, do we find so spacious a harbour of refuge. Any tendency, however, to estimate the local fish-trade on the same scale is checked by the apparition of a fishmarket so squalid that it might belong to an inland hamlet far from the coast. The port of Falmouth was formerly an active and prosperous steam-trawling centre, but I was given to understand that the vessels have since been more profitably engaged in towing work, chiefly because the closure of the inshore bays against trawling robbed them of their occupation. There is still, however, some trawling, as well as hooking for cod, conger, pollack, and ling. Seine-nets are also worked in the estuary for shad and other fish, while there are important oyster-beds in the river. The chief fishing at Falmouth, however, is the drift-fishing for mackerel, in which, as mentioned in the previous chapter, it has in great measure supplanted Plymouth.

Coverack, Cadgwith, and Porthleven all engage in hooking, seining, and crabbing. At the last-named, the most important station between Falmouth and Mount's Bay, there is at some seasons of the year a good deal of inshore trawling. Anyone making such a tour as this of the whole coast must find it extremely difficult to review the proportions of the different local fisheries with justice and accuracy. If I had not come hot foot from the stupendous activities of a fishing metropolis like Grimsby, the very modest achievements of solitary trawlers at these little Cornish ports would have been more interesting. Viewed, however, in the light of what is daily brought ashore in the Humber, Cornwall's trawling seems ridiculous.

The geographical centre of the fishing district round Mount's Bay is Penzance, but that fashionable watering-place shines, so far as its fishing industry is concerned, in the reflected glory of Newlyn. For this result the wretchedness of its harbour, as compared with that of Newlyn, is in great measure responsible, for nothing will induce the bulk of the summer mackerel-fleet to make Penzance its headquarters, in spite of the fact that it is the terminus of the Great Western Railway, which has not hitherto gone to the trouble and expense of running a light line round the bay to the more western harbour. In consequence of this, although the fish is landed and sold at Newlyn, it has to be sent to the station by cart. The affection displayed by the trade for Newlyn must always seem anomalous to those unacquainted with the peculiar conditions which sometimes govern such preferences in the fishing industry. As a mackerel metropolis, however, Newlyn reigns supreme in the south-west; and although the Riots of 1896, of which some account will presently be given, temporarily alienated a large section of support, the buyers have returned to their old allegiance long since, and even the mackerel occasionally landed at Penzance, in certain conditions of wind and weather, must be sold, like the rest, at Newlyn.

Penzance Harbour is the property of the Corporation, to which body it is in all probability a white elephant. One of these days, it is not unsafe to prophesy, it will pass under the control of the Great Western Railway Company, and then no doubt it will be improved by filling up one-third and properly dredging the remainder. Viewed in its present condition at low tide, the harbour looks exceedingly safe for children to fall into, but scarcely suited to the requirements of a

NEWLYN HARBOUR.

fishing-fleet. That it might, however, with the necessary alterations, be made a serious rival of Newlyn there cannot be the slightest doubt. The accommodation at Newlyn itself is wholly inadequate during the great rush of the mackerel season, and so it will probably remain until the Commissioners sanction the erection of a quay or pier, with landing facilities on either side, right in the centre of the harbour. Thus

only can the present congestion, which year by year
threatens to become more acute, receive practical relief.
Wales is a menace to these Cornish ports unless something is quickly done to increase their efficiency, and
if Newlyn and Penzance continue to fall short of the·
requirements of the trade, then Milford will not be slow
to supplant them.   Of Milford's extraordinary vitality
something will be said in the present chapter, but
those who have an interest, sentimental or otherwise, in
Cornwall will do well to keep in view the possibility
of Wales rivalling Cornish mackerel in the future as it
has rivalled Northumbrian coal in the past.

The trawl-fish landed at Newlyn is of no account.
Even in the height of the mackerel season, however, I
have seen a Brixham smack and a steam-trawler belonging to Falmouth both landing rough fish.   Yet the
glory of the port is when the mackerel-fleets of Cornwall and the East Coast mingle in a rivalry more or less
friendly during May and June and land their millions
of blue-and-silver mackerel on the narrow quays.   The
hostility which traditionally persists between the men of
the duchy and those of Yarmouth and Lowestoft who
visit the port is in great part a fabrication of gentlemen
who write descriptive articles and give the preference
to lively ' copy.'   An acquaintance with the place, which
dates back to a period anterior to the Riots, has persuaded me that much of it is purely imaginary.   Such
regrettable outbursts of violence as disgraced Newlyn
during that trying week are the result of sudden excite-
ment, and in that case there were not wanting lawless
and discontented men to foster the smouldering passion
of the natives.

The Riots are practically forgotten.   On a Sunday
in 1903 I found the Newlyn men themselves pack-

ing fish and loading carts, an endless procession of which, even with the disregarded chapel bells calling worshippers to the town on the other side of the harbour, fed the quays with returned empties. I learnt on inquiry that contrary winds had kept the Cornish boats at sea the whole of the Saturday night, whereas the East Coast steam-drifters had been enabled to land their fish, and their crews were, after their fashion, keeping the Sabbath ashore at Penzance. The humour of the situation did not appear to have dawned on my Cornish friends. If it did, so anxious were they to make their position sound that they betrayed no consciousness of it. The *volte-face* did not surprise me personally, for I never fell into the common error of attributing the Cornishmen's action in the Riots to any religious objection to Sunday fishing. The tenets of Newlyn congregations may be as narrow as Newlyn's streets, but, as a matter of fact, though they knew it not, the doctrines of Mill had far more to do with their attitude than those of Wesley. They took exception not so much to the emptying of Sunday chapels as to the glutting of Monday markets.

It is a pity that those who wrote and talked so freely about the Riots, both in and out of Parliament, could not have had a better understanding of the real motives and political economy of this Cornish protest against East Anglian greed. I neither deride the simple religious faith of primitive communities nor condone the disgusting behaviour of the rioters, but it is better, if we must judge them for their deeds, to know what their objects were. The economic aspect of this Sabbath-breaking and its effect on the market early in the week should not be lost sight of in purely hypothetical superstitions that, I am convinced, had nothing to do with the outbreak. Quite apart from the purely commercial side of the question, it is not improbable that a weekly close time for mackerel might operate as wholesomely as the weekly close time that we do not hesitate to prescribe for the salmon. It may not be so necessary, but it might be salutary all the same. Whatever may be the actual wording of the older statutes, there does not exist in any reasonable mind a doubt as to the real object of prohibiting salmon netting in our estuaries between twelve on Saturday and twelve on Monday. The men may celebrate their Sabbath as zealously as they please; they may break it in other ways according to their desires; but the salmon are to be given a chance one day in the week of getting past the deadly nets and into the upper waters. It is of course true that, whereas the salmon are saved for the river itself, the mackerel shoals, if spared in Mount's Bay on the Sunday, pass on to Plymouth by the Monday; but let us remember it is not the visitors (who would be free to follow the roving shoals on the homeward way) who take exception to Sunday fishing, but the residents.

The Riots are done with and forgotten now, the only reminder of a dead volcano being the presence in the roads of H.M.S. 'Spanker,' and even that is by common consent attributed to the transgressions of French crabbers at the Seven Stones, of which more presently. I wish that the painful subject of the Newlyn Riots might be omitted from this chapter, but it is necessary to recall one or two particulars of the disaster to the trade in that part of the world. These, however, I shall allude to as briefly as the importance of the subject—it is important less on account of the actual disturbance itself than because of the economic principles illustrated—will allow of.

Whatever sympathy we may feel with the Cornish plea for a weekly close time, the piratical way in which the men of Newlyn gave expression to their feelings in May 1896, deserves nothing but censure. On Sunday evening, May 17, a few Lowestoft drifters came alongside Newlyn pier with their catch. There was no actual disturbance that evening, though, from the ominous gathering of little knots of Cornish fishermen at the street corners, it was evident that trouble was brewing. The storm soon burst. Early next morning a great crowd of Newlyn men, goaded on by jeering fishwives, surged over the quays, overcame the small posse of coastguard, boarded the Lowestoft boats and flung a hundred thousand splendid mackerel into the harbour to rot. Newspaper correspondents, with a fancy for picturesque, if not very accurate, analogy, compared this outrage to the historic throwing of tea into Boston harbour, the first indication of the American desire for independence. The two episodes were, however, as far apart in objective as in point of time. The Cornishmen had not the shadow of an excuse beyond the fact that many of them were in all probability intoxicated and not wholly responsible for their actions. It was in itself an unpardonable offence against the bounty of Nature to waste such a catch of fish ; but worse was to follow. The rioters, now thoroughly maddened, went to even greater extremes of violence, for they actually seized three other East Country boats which were not at the time inside the harbour, brought them within the piers, and treated the fish on board them in the same disgraceful manner. Then, when not a fresh mackerel was left in the place, some buccaneering wag posted a notice to the effect that no fish would be sold in Newlyn that day. Their last act on the Monday was to stretch a chain across the mouth of the harbour, with the result that no boats could sail either in or out. The uproar lasted for two days, and all the Monday and most of the Tuesday the local constabulary, reinforced by drafts, hurried to the scene of action by the railway authorities, were engaged in free fighting on land; while in the boats there was unremitting scuffling with the Lowestoft men, and heads were cracked on both sides. At length, though none too soon, the military were called out, and the rioters were so roughly handled that peace was, outwardly at any rate, restored by the Wednesday morning. The chain was now withdrawn from the harbour, and a gunboat and destroyer anchored in the bay as further guarantees of peace.

Riotous Newlyn became a nine-days' topic throughout the country, and the resident magistrates behaved with commendable promptness in issuing warrants for the apprehension of the ringleaders; but unfortunately the subsequent proceedings in the police-court revealed some uncertainty as to the identity of those actually to blame. The Home Secretary very properly declined to receive a deputation, the object of which was to explain to him the local view of the subjects under discussion. By the Thursday morning the disturbance was past, but the men of Newlyn saw with consternation that the whole of the Lowestoft boats had sailed from a port that could be guilty of such inhospitality, and had taken its fish to Penzance. The curtain went up on the last act but one when five of the arrested ringleaders next appeared in the Penzance police-court, as a result of which some were acquitted and others committed for trial. The names of those finally tried by Mr. Justice Lawrence shall here be omitted, for he inflicted neither fines nor imprisonment, merely binding the prisoners to come up for judgment when called upon. With one exception, they were bound over in their own recognisances, and in giving this judgment Mr. Justice Lawrence showed both courage and a knowledge of the temperament of Cornish fishermen. It is not the temperament of criminals; and, though his finding was freely criticised as weak and lenient, it has proved the right one. The last stage of all in the proceedings was when, in the January of the following year, Mr. A. D. Berrington, then of the Board of Trade, was called upon to arbitrate in the matter of damages for the fish thrown overboard. This arbitration was invited under an agreement between the Parliamentary representatives of the parties concerned—that is to say, Mr. T. B. Bolitho for the Newlyn men, and Mr. H. S. Foster for the men of Suffolk. Mr. Berrington fixed the amount of damages at the curiously precise sum of £619 15s. 3d., and this was to be divided, as specified in certain schedules, among the owners, skippers, and crews of the outraged boats. Mr. Bolitho, who had throughout the trouble stood most loyally by his misguided constituents, went security for the payment of the whole amount. Finally, Mr. Berrington suggested, by way of closing what was certainly one of the most disagreeable and disgraceful episodes in the recent history of the fish-trade, a 'compromise,' which Newlyn accepted. It was to the effect that the East Anglian boats should desist from fishing on the Saturday night. The compromise is honoured to-day chiefly in the breach, but this does not matter as long as peace is re-established on a sounder basis. This appears actually to be the case.

The Lowestoft and Yarmouth boats spend sixteen or seventeen weeks in the neighbourhood of Mount's Bay, landing most of their fish at Newlyn, though occasionally visiting St. Mary's, Scilly, with catches, which are taken across to Penzance by the daily steamer. Towards the end of June they return home. The voyage occupies between forty and fifty hours, according to the wind they get and also whether they proceed straight home or fish once and dispose of the catch at Hastings or Folkestone. When the west country

MOUSEHOLE.

harvest is gathered in, they steam away north after the Aberdeen herring.

Mousehole, the last fishing port on the South coast proper, lies immediately beyond Newlyn and is protected from some of the gales by a small island. It has a small fleet of its own, and its boats land their mackerel during the season at Newlyn. Later in the summer the boats go after pilchards. Mousehole men have a grievance in the operations of inshore trawlers, who, they allege, have ruined their fishing grounds.

Tons of fine hake, they say, could formerly be hooked on grounds which to-day do not yield one fish, while at certain times of the year they watch trawlers discharging tons of baby hake at Newlyn.

Mousehole also has a number of crab- and lobster-pots, and it was a Mousehole crabber who first made an abortive attempt to eject the Breton fishermen from the Seven Stones ground.

It was to see, and if possible to converse with, these Bretons that I took the boat for Scilly, having learnt in Penzance that there was every chance of falling in with their fleet at St. Mary's. The fates were propitious, for the ' Queen of the Isles' ran through a score of them at anchor in the roads, and, as soon as dinner was over, I hired a boat, went aboard the ' Vautour' C 1072, and there had a chat with the ' patron.' Though thus simply described as a chat, the interview was, as a matter of fact, somewhat distressing, as I could speak only French, of which he apparently knew little, talking rapidly in a *patois* not unlike Welsh, and translating as much as possible of what was to me incomprehensible by gesticulation and grimace. Still, he showed me his ingenious cane-and-net lobster-traps, as well as a number of baits, of which I gathered that gurnard (as with our crabbers) was the favourite, while conger is also used when there is nothing better. Only lobsters and cray-fish, he pointed out, are kept for the French market. Crabs are of no value there and are sometimes cut up for bait. Every other day one boat of the fleet carries the entire catch back to France, an arrangement in every way similar to our fleeting system, except that where, as in the case of the Hull fleets, special fast carriers are employed, the full catching-power of the fleet is not interfered with.

The 'patron,' who by this time, with the rest of
his crew, was smoking my Algerian cigarettes, which
closely resemble the 'caporals' so extensively patronised
by the French, told me that they hailed from Camaret,
which lies opposite Brest.   By a curious coincidence,
the district known as Cornouaille lies just south of
their French home, and I could not but notice much
in common between their physiognomy and manner of
speaking and that of the Scillonians.   From the French

BRETON CRABBERS OFF ST. MARY'S, SCILLY.

of Paris, or even of Boulogne, they were far more
separated than from the men who are to-day represented as resenting the presence in their port of these
gaily-coloured, one-masted craft, flying the 'stress of
weather' pennant at the masthead.   I say 'represented,'
because careful inquiry at St. Mary's convinced me that
the natives entertained very little of the hostility commonly attributed to them, and they assured me that the
foreigners would, when in port, spend more money on

loaf-sugar alone in a week than the same number of Scotch craft would spend altogether in a year. The Bretons, on their side, knew little of this alleged enmity of the natives, and indeed their ignorance of the English language would effectually prevent their appreciating the fact. All that I heard, however, whenever any small boat containing Cornishmen passed within speaking distance, was in the nature of friendly banter.

The truth seems to be that the attempt to oust them from the Seven Stones originated with a jealous crabber of Mousehole. It was badly stage-managed from first to last. That ground is never awash at any stage of the tide and lies outside the three-mile limit; and it is to be regretted that the bearings were not more accurately taken, and the international law on the subject not more carefully studied, before the attempt was made.

Occasionally, as a matter of fact, wilfully or otherwise, they are caught within the territorial limit. Then, as the law stands, there is no objection to punishing them severely. Shortly after my last visit H.M.S. 'Spanker' caught two of them, and each was fined £7 10s., without confiscation of gear. The punishment of foreigners convicted of fishing in British waters is, as was stated in connection with Ramsgate, out of all proportion less severe than that meted out to our men by the tribunals of countries in whose waters they are similarly caught trespassing. As a case in point, a Hull vessel was lately taken in foreign waters and fined £75, with confiscation of all gear. Now and then, however, the foreigner is treated summarily. Of late years several Belgians have been fined as much as £10 and costs for fishing in Sole Bay, near Southwold, and their fish was confiscated and the vessels detained in port until the fine had been paid.   The Dutch, on the other hand, seem to find hospitality in our waters.   In addition to the eel-boats so familiar off Billingsgate, Dutchmen pursue the summer herring off Shetland, and in 1902 alone they caught upwards of 400,000 barrels of herrings in those waters.   The result was that in the following season no fewer than 786 herring-boats fitted out at Scheveningen and other Dutch ports for the Shetland fishery.   As large herrings fetch most on the Dutch markets, their fishermen use nets with larger mesh than ours.

Scilly is a garden rather than a fishing centre, and all that I found beside the Breton crabbers were a few mackerel-drifters discharging their fish on the quay at St. Mary's.   They were bought on the spot bv Penzance buyers and by them taken back to Penzance by either the 'Lyonesse' or 'Queen of the Isles.'   The charge amounts to only 9*d*. per basket of sixty mackerel, and in the calm hot weather that prevails through a great part of the mackerel season this steam-carriage to Penzance must save for the market many of the mackerel caught on the further grounds beyond Scilly.

When I visited Sennen Cove in the summer, crabbing was apparently the only fishing.   The famous seine-fishery for grey mullet is carried on in the period immediately preceding Lent.   Allusion has already been made to the grievance of the Sennen fishermen in respect of the removal of seaweed.   Seaweed is gathered along almost the whole of the Cornish foreshore, for either edible purposes or manure, according to its quality ; and it is not unusual to find in advertisements of farms on or near the south coast of the duchy that they are situated within easv access of inexhaustible supplies of seaweed for manuring purposes.   Thus the two industries which divide Lord Onslow's official attention are here brought into collision.[1] That sea-weeds growing on the rocks below high-water mark furnish cover and protection for the fish is evident, but it is claimed in addition that the grey mullet feed on the weed itself. The mullet feeds on soft vegetable matter, and some of the fish were caught with the weed adhering closely to the gill-covers. When the matter was brought before the Cornish Sea Fisheries Committee, Mr. Dunn, a son of the most original observer of fish

ST. IVES.

life whom it was ever my privilege to know, advised that a number of mullet should be examined and reported on. The fisheries officer undertook to make the necessary investigation, but with what result I have not ascertained.

With St. Ives, the great centre of seine-fishing, we reach the north coast. The most remarkable biological

[1] As they also are by the pollution of trout-streams by the effluent from sheep-washing tanks, in respect of which the Salmon and Trout Association recently made a representation to the Board of Agriculture and Fisheries.

problem of St. Ives bay is the inshoring in alternate years of herrings and pilchards, an explanation of which has yet to be furnished. This case of two allied fishes predominating in different seasons has a parallel in the sprat and herring on the south coast of Devon. The pilchard-seining is the great industry of St. Ives, and some of its characteristic scenes have been made familiar in the London art galleries.

It lasts from September until November. The precise duration of the season in each year depends on the abundance of fish and on the weather conditions. As long as it lasts, the seine-fishing takes precedence of all the rest. No boat otherwise engaged may come during the day within a prescribed distance of the six ' stems,' or fishing stations, fixed by statute since the 1840's. At Porthminster, one of these, the tarred seine-boats drawn up on the sloping beach may be seen even from the railway line ; and the other ' stems ' are called Poll, Leigh, Carrick, Gladden, and Pedden Olver.

The general method of seining was described in Chapter II. Some of the local regulations for protecting the interests of the seine-boats date back to the reign of Queen Elizabeth. A curious and interesting regulation prescribes that no seine-net may be used of less than 160 fathoms along the top rope and 6 fathoms deep at the wings. At first sight it looks strange to make a minimum size of net mandatory, but the reason is given that a smaller net might frighten a large shoal without having a reasonable chance of enclosing it.

St. Ives, besides being the centre of Cornish seine-fishing, long had the monopoly of curing pilchards for the Italian market. Of late years, however, Italian buyers have entertained a strong prejudice against St. Ives fish, in consequence, it is said, of a reprehen-

sible practice of keeping pilchards over until the following year and then packing small lots of the decayed
fish in each barrel of the year's produce. I do not
guarantee that this was ever done, but such is the
report. Italian buyers do not include simplicity among
their virtues; and, although St. Ives fish are regaining
their old position in the Continental market, it was long
before they found buyers.

Occasionally the seine-nets enclose immense shoals.
Residents in the neighbourhood have kindly brought
to my notice several cases of great catches. Among
these mention may be made of a single shoal enclosed
towards the end of the season in the autumn of 1851,
out of which, in addition to a considerable quantity
wasted, no less than 5,000 hogsheads were saved for the
market. Twenty years later the nets enclosed a shoal
that filled 8,000 hogsheads, but this was washed ashore
and fit only for manure. This was in 1871, a famous
year in the chronicles of the St. Ives fishery, for in it
upwards of 45,000 hogsheads of pilchards were cured
for export, while the price fell below £1 per hogshead,
the lowest ever reached. About 3,000 pilchards, or
rather less, go to the hogshead.

Travelling westward along the north coast, we come,
past some intervening villages of little consequence, to
Newquay, more important as a fashionable and bracing
watering-place than in connection with the fisheries.
The only other Cornish port which need detain us
(though Port Isaac is not without interest) is Padstow,
and Padstow, again, is more attractive by reason of
its possibly prosperous future than for any present
greatness. Hitherto, the natural drawbacks of the
Camel estuary, with fearsome tides and currents, and
dangerous rocks standing out in the fairway, have

thwarted what must in the absence of such disabilities have been a rapid rise to fortune. It is between Stepper Point and Pentire, the guardian pillars of Padstow, that Cornwall looks out on splendid trawling-grounds no more than 20 miles away. The London and South Western Railway Company moreover, has long been prepared to do its share in developing the sleepy port as the one trawling centre in the duchy, but, although the Company makes trawlers welcome alongside the station, they accept the hospitality at their own risk. A scheme for the more efficient buoy-ing of the channel has been decided upon; and if even that is properly carried out, I believe that visiting fleets, which now land their trawl-fish in South Wales, will, with very little encouragement, make Padstow their headquarters. Something has, in fact, been done as.it is; and it may be mentioned that during the early months of the year 1904, January to May inclusive, there was an increase of twenty-four landings repre-senting nearly fifty tons in excess of the quantity dealt with during the corresponding period of 1903, 90 per cent. of the total landings being despatched direct to the London markets, thus showing that the facilities offered by the railway company are appre-ciated and gradually becoming better known.

At Port Isaac, the only remaining fishing centre in Cornwall, there is a little trawling, hooking, and crab-pot fishing.

North Devon, however beautiful to the tourist, is practically negligible in respect of its fisheries. The paltry hooking and drift-net fishing of Clovelly, Ilfra-combe, or Lynmouth are an insignificant source of revenue when compared with the entertainment of the summer visitor. At the last-named there is a salmon-weir, the property of a local hotel proprietor, and worked only to supply his own requirements.

Cardiff is a comparatively unimportant fishing centre, so I crossed from Ilfracombe to Swansea by steamer, and at this Welsh port found much evidence of an important fish-trade growing up under the fostering care of the Harbour Trustees. Two years ago these spent a sum of £16,000 on a new fish-market,

EARLY MORNING AT SWANSEA.

180 feet long, with a frontage of fish-quays extending to not less than 500 or 600 feet. Whether it will rival Milford quite so easily as is anticipated or not, Swansea is certain to become a very important market on the Bristol Channel, for although its harbour runs somewhat low at times, some thirty steam-trawlers and twelve smacks already landed their catches there at the time of my visit, and I understand that there have since been

Z

important accessions to this patronage. It is rather interesting to note that it was Swansea which sent Brixham its first " mumble-bee," otherwise a very small trawler cutter-rigged. Among the advantages, natural or otherwise, of the port, mention may be made of its cheap coal, its greater proximity to Billingsgate than Milford, and the services and rivalry of no fewer than four railway companies—the Great Western, London and North Western, Midland and Rhondda, and Swansea Bay Railway Companies—all conveying its fish to different parts. Personally, and as the result of visiting such ports as Milford, Grimsby, and Lowestoft, I differ from the usual view that the competition of many railway companies is an unmixed blessing to the trade, for experience tends to show that a port served exclusively by one company is indebted to it for all manner of improvements, whereas in the case of divided interests each holds its hand for fear of benefiting its rivals.

The fishing most characteristic of Swansea Bay, though it contributes less than trawling to the import- ance of the port, is the setting of stake-nets for cod, whiting, flat fish, and some other kinds. Those who travel to the Mumbles Pier by the light railway have an opportunity of seeing miles of these nets along the shore.

The next halting-place on my trip was Tenby. Tenby was formerly a fishing centre of some account. Holdsworth, writing in 1874, alludes to it as 'the only really important place as a fishing station' on that part of the coast. Can anything be more suggestive of the march of thirty years in the fishing industry than to contrast it to-day with Milford, an unknown quantity in Holdsworth's day? The precise date at which

Tenby, which is now prosperous chiefly as a watering-place, declined from its position as a fishing centre I have been unable to determine. It was as a fashionable seaside-resort in the days before railways carried fish that the Brixham men used to visit Tenby and supply the visitors. Statistics are not absolutely reliable as a guide in these cases, but it is probable that the phenomenal rise of Milford under railway management during the past ten or fifteen years furnishes the answer. I have, however, succeeded in coming across many evidences of its past fishing activity, and one of these, a curious old document, dated 1811, and preserved in the excellent museum on the Castle Hill, runs as follows :—

I.

That all Fish (Scait, Ray and Shellfish excepted) brought into the Road or Harbour of Tenby for Sale shall be exposed for that purpose in the Public Fish Market, under the Penalty of Five Shillings, to be levied by distress.

II.

That the Market for Fish shall not commence until Eight o'clock in the Morning, and continue until Eight o'clock at night : And that all Fish brought into the Market (Scait, Ray and Shellfish excepted) shall remain exposed for sale to private Individuals for the Space of Two Hours, before any Tranter[1] *shall be allowed to purchase, under a Penalty of Five Shillings, to be levied as above.*

III.

That Notice be given to the Clerk of the Market of Fish brought there, the Two Hours to commence from the Time of such Notice.

IV.

That the above Penalties be levied by any Magistrate of the said Borough, upon the information of One Witness, or

---

[1] *I.e.* a peddler or hawker ; practically the 'jowder.'

upon the View of the Magistrate; one Moiety to the In-former, and the other to the Poor of the Parish of St. Mary's, Tenby.

Then follow certain rates of carriage, which have no interest.

With Milford Haven—or 'Old Milford,' as the Great Western Railway authorities have for some occult reason re-named it—we reach the most important centre of the fish-trade, on the west side of the island. On the opposite side of the water what was once Neyland now rejoices in the name of New Milford. There is not much in a name in these cases; and the Company has done so much for Milford that it has at least earned the right to call it by what name it likes.

Milford, which was first, I believe, developed by Hull fishermen, is unique in the history of recent fishery development, and if we merely consider the rapidity of its progress it may be questioned whether even the Humber ports have had a more remarkable history. Like Grimsby, it illustrates what a railway company can do to develop the fisheries of a port endowed with considerable natural advantages. Milford has a sheltered anchorage without its rival in the island. It has, more-over, easy access to the great trawling grounds on the west and south coasts of Ireland, and its steam-trawlers fish between the 'Smalls' and the Irish coast, while the smacks work the home grounds in the Bristol Channel. Recent developments have also shown that it is not inconveniently placed for the western mackerel trade. Its distance from Billingsgate is perhaps its greatest drawback, but this has as far as possible been sur-mounted by the Great Western Railway; and the train leaving each afternoon at four delivers the fish at

Paddington at 2.30 A.M. next morning, in ample time for the early sales at Billingsgate. Certain disadvantages in the water-supply are experienced from the position of the town, which is built in terraces on the side of a steep hill; but this, on the other hand, lends itself to a more efficient system of drainage than is at present installed.

Some idea of the progress made by Milford during the past ten or twelve years may be formed if we compare the following annual output in tons :—

1890	1894	1902
9,398	11,900	24,100

The fish-landing wharf in Milford Dock has a frontage of 1,000 feet, and the frontage of the coal wharves is 1,050 feet. The port has a resident fleet (1903) of 9,796 tons, and the tonnage of its average visiting fleet is over 18,000. Ice plays an important part in the trade at Milford; and there are two factories, the older the property of the Cardiff Pure Ice Company, the newer recently erected at a cost of £30,000 by the Western Trawling Company, and capable of producing daily 70 tons of ice. During 1903 the two factories produced upwards of 20,000 tons.

The population of Milford has rather more than doubled since 1890, being now about 6,500.

I shall not multiply these statistics, for which I am indebted to Mr. Biddlecombe, stationmaster at Milford during many of its most prosperous years. It will perhaps be more interesting to the reader if I give some account of the fisheries by which the port is kept supplied throughout the year.

Milford is, of course, first and foremost a trawling centre. The trawlers, both steam and sailing, cover an immense area of sea on that west coast, sometimes getting fine catches within fifty miles of the port, at others going close in under the Irish coast. When fish is scarce in that region the larger trawlers steam away to the Bay of Biscay and shoot their nets as far as 150 miles south of Ushant. Some idea of the magnitude of these voyages, second only to the Iceland voyages out of Hull, may be formed when it is stated that the vessels have to steam a matter of 300 miles from Milford to the fishing grounds and are often ten days away from home. The chief harvest of such voyages are hake, plaice, and a larger race of sole than they get nearer home. The smacks fish to the west of Lundy Island and Trevose Head in the Bristol Channel, and between the latter point and St. Ann's Head, the entrance to Milford Haven. Some seventy steam-trawlers are attached to the port, while 200 smacks at least visit it between March and October, hailing from Brixham, Lowestoft, and other distant stations.

Trawling is not, however, the only source of Milford's supply, for there are two other fisheries of some importance—line-fishing and mackerel.

There are thirteen steam-liners, which fish within fifteen miles of St. Ann's Head and are, as a rule, out only at night. These liners have to get the necessary bait from a considerable distance, herring being procured from Lowestoft and Yarmouth, and mackerel, towards the end of the mackerel season, from Waterford. Their catch consists for the most part of cod, conger, and ling, and for this rough fish there is a ready market at Blackburn and other industrial centres in Lancashire. To these towns it is conveyed either *via* Carmarthen by the London and North Western Railway

Company, or *viâ* Gloucester by the Midland.   The London and North Western and Midland Companies send their trucks by arrangement over the permanent-way of the Great Western Railway.

The trawl-fish is landed on the main quay, as well as that from the liners.   There is, however, a special quay and slipway for the mackerel-boats, and it was by its prompt response to the requirements of the mackerel

MILFORD.

trade, in furnishing at short notice this accommodation for all states of the tide, that the Great Western Railway Company showed itself ready for every possible development of this, the greatest centre on the west coast.   A fish so perishable as the mackerel must have facilities for immediate handling on coming alongside. Milford's mackerel trade dates only from the summer of 1902, when a couple of Newlyn boats, fishing close to the Haven, made a run for the port on the chance of realising good prices on their catch. Their success was immediate and beyond their expectations, and in the following summer they had many imitators. Possibly mackerel were an unexpected novelty on the Milford quay. Whatever the cause, the local merchants gave unlooked-for support to the new venture, outbidding even the buyers who had come specially from Plymouth. The mackerel were taken up chiefly for the ' order.' trade, that is the consignment of small parcels of mixed fish at retail price to private customers. Grimsby also does an immense business in this trade, and at several other ports it is of greater importance than is commonly supposed.

The greater part of Milford's fish goes to London, but 'it also consigns large quantities to many of its rivals in the fish trade. Both Hull and Grimsby, for instance, receive certain classes of fish regularly from Milford, and hake goes to Plymouth. Milford, on the other hand, receives shell-fish, as well as herring and mackerel, the two latter for bait, from Fishguard. Another apparent anomaly of distribution from Milford has already been referred to. Trucks of fish, caught within sight of the Irish coast, are almost daily despatched by the Waterford or Cork boat for consumption in cities like Limerick, Tipperary, and Clonmel.

The future of Milford as a centre of the fish-trade is an unknown quantity. Swansea threatens rivalry, but Milford need have no immediate apprehension of extinction. Goodwick, on the opposite side, is also being developed by the Great Western Company, but that is for the Atlantic passenger traffic and has no connection with the fish-trade. The trawling grounds of the Bristol Channel cannot be inexhaustible, but, as already pointed out, only the sailing trawlers depend on these for their harvest, the steam-trawlers fishing on the Irish coast, or even down to the Bay of Biscay. The mackerel trade, on the other hand, has evidently come to stay, and, with all the inducements held out by the railway company to both resident and visiting fleets, the prosperity of Milford looks as if it were assured for some time to come.

It cannot fail to strike the student of fishery matters in the Bristol Channel, that the modern development has been all on the north coast. To some extent, Nature is responsible for this. The rocky north coast of Devon and Cornwall is for beauty and not for use, and it attracts the tourist. The flat muddy foreshore of South Wales attracts to itself the more solid gains of trade. This distinction, I have always thought, is·the true explanation of the backwardness of North Devon in fishery matters. It cannot be attributed to any lack of enterprise on the part of the men of Devon, for not only is Plymouth a flourishing centre, but, as we have seen, the adventuring spirit of the Brixham folk has taken them in the past east to the North Sea and west to the Bristol Channel, and in fact it is by Brixham boats that a large proportion of Milford's trawl-fish is landed during half the year.

A port like Milford, a mushroom growth of ten or fifteen years, should be studied side by side with centres like Hull and Grimsby, not with ancient stations like Brixham or Yarmouth There is no fishing population rooted for a hundred generations to the soil, but rather a colony of expert fishermen from older centres, who, visiting the place at first only at intervals, have gradually left the old homes that look out upon another sea and transplanted their wives and families to the new port.

The rest of the Welsh coast may, for our present purpose, be dismissed in a few lines. At Aberystwyth I was told of a little inshore trawling; at Barmouth the only fishing mentioned was that of summer visitors, who catch bass in the estuary; and at Llandudno most of the fish seemed to be supplied by a Grimsby store. The one exception was Pwllheli, and, even with its shallow harbour, the northernmost port on the Cambrian railway was served by a resident fleet of small trawlers and visited by a number of larger smacks from Brixham. These were, at the time of my visit, sending ashore small boats laden with an excellent class of fish trawled in Cardigan Bay; and both Brixham and Milford men favour Pwllheli as a week-end port. Great improvements were then talked of for the harbour, which looked to me little more than a shallow lagoon; and with such encouragement Pwllheli may make great progress.

After leaving Wales, however, we find in Lancashire and Cumberland signs of recrudescence; and Fleetwood, in the former county, is certainly the most considerable centre on the west side after Milford.

Moreover, the scientific work carried out under the auspices of the Lancashire and Western District, at both the University of Liverpool (where Professor Herdman, President of the Linnæan Society, has a well-equipped marine laboratory), and the Piel hatchery, of which Mr. Scott is in charge, is of great importance. A glance through the contents of the Twelfth (1903) Report of these institutions shows the value of the research and other work with which Professor Herdman and his assistants must be credited. Professor Herdman himself discusses the transference of fishery matters to Lord Onslow's Department and, incidentally, the unsatisfactory status of the existing Sea Fisheries districts, to which reference was made in an earlier chapter. He also contributes papers on the shrimp and small fish question and on sewage and shell-fish. Mr. Andrew Scott concerns himself chiefly with the work done at Piel, and Mr. James Johnstone writes of trawling observations. There are, in addition valuable papers on parasites in flat fish, and Dr. Ashworth devotes a long appendix to a memoir on the life history and economic aspects of the lugworm, a favourite bait on most parts of our coasts.

The flat muddy foreshore of our north-west coast is strikingly different from the bold rocky promontories which, particularly in Yorkshire, project in rapid succession in the encroaching waters of the North Sea. On the other hand, while the west side lacks the productive crab- and lobster-fisheries of Northumberland, it still has profitable inshore trawling, a mode of fishing which has long since been exhausted on the other coast.

Fleetwood, which may be taken as a characteristic Lancashire fishing centre, first achieved importance in the industry in the 1850's, though inshore fishing had for some years even then been far more important than it can be called to-day. As far back as the year 1842 the railway company tried the experiment of bringing a few fishing-boats from North Meols, the suburb of Southport to which Fleetwood really owes the establishment of its fish trade. Again, in 1846 the company imported four old boats from the East Coast, and this early encouragement on the part of the carriers must not be overlooked in any accurate estimate of Fleetwood's beginnings.

Mr. Leadbetter, to whose courtesy I was indebted

for much information and assistance at this port, assured me that the steam fishing was on the increase, but that the smacks were declining. This result he attributed in a measure to the incompetence of the fishermen themselves, who, with an instinct different from that of Milton's demon, preferred to serve on steam-trawlers rather than to own smacks.

On the subject of harbour accommodation the resident traders are not enthusiastic, though to the

A MAIDEN VOYAGE (FLEETWOOD).

visitor Fleetwood Harbour looks as busy and as efficient as almost any other on the coast.

Nor are some who have had opportunities of watching the locality over a period of years sanguine that the supplies from the fishing grounds can long last to pay for the continued upkeep of steam-trawlers.

Morecambe Bay has important shrimping areas and cockle-grounds, yet exhaustion has overtaken some of these, which formerly were most productive, and Dutch shrimps are said to find a ready market even at Southport.

There is not much rough ground in the immediate vicinity of Fleetwood, though large catches of conger have been made round the Wyre Light. The herring-fleets that formerly caught immense quantities of that fish off the Lancashire coast have now, for the most part, followed the herring elsewhere, and these fish are nowadays taken in the stake-nets on Pilling Sands.

Quantities of haddocks were also trawled as close to land as in the Channel, but almost all the haddocks discharged at Fleetwood to-day are of the same small class as the Hull 'chats.'

The principal fishing-grounds worked by Fleetwood trawlers are away in the Irish Channel, round the Isle of Man, or towards Campbeltown and the Clyde. A few, however, fish as far as the Irish coast.

The bulk of the Fleetwood fish goes on commission by the Lancashire and Yorkshire Railway as far as Preston, and thence by London and North Western to Billingsgate. Several great centres in the midlands, however, such as Liverpool, Birmingham, Manchester, and Leicester, are supplied direct.

As has been said, Fleetwood harbour presents an animated spectacle on a busy day. I found the steam-trawlers berthed in the dock, and the smacks alongside the pier. There were no Brixham smacks, the majority of those in port at the time of my visit being port-marked Fleetwood, Hoylake, or Liverpool.

It is a little difficult to estimate at sight the numerical strength of the resident fleet, owing to a practice which is, I imagine, a breach of the regulations. Fleetwood firms have long been in the habit of buying up old vessels from Hull and other ports and then working them from Fleetwood without making the requisite change in the portmark. The object of this can only be to avoid the exceedingly slight expense of repainting. It can hardly be to escape identification in case of collision, for the owners and adopted home of these craft are well known. I mention the matter, in fact, merely for the information of anyone who might

SHRIMP-TRAWLERS RACING FOR THE OPEN SEA (FLEETWOOD).

otherwise, judging by the portmarks alone, underrate the number of the Fleetwood boats proper. The actual numbers registered here are fifteen steam-trawlers, between forty and fifty of the larger sailing trawlers, and about forty shrimp-trawlers. The last-named are the most picturesque of all, and a couple of these trim, stiff little boats racing for the open sea illustrate the more picturesque, though less progressive, side of the industry. These smart-sailing little trawlers come for the most part from Blackpool, and they use what is known as a 'shank' trawl, 'shank' being the local name for the pink shrimp. In the latest report, alluded to above, Professor Herdman states that seventy boats, from Marshside and Southport alone, are engaged in shrimping on that coast during some portion of the year. These are half-decked boats, most of them no more than six years old, and each worked by two men. The catch makes five shares, the men taking two apiece and the boat the fifth. The boat finds two nets, and the men one net each. Each boat catches on the average 30 quarts per day throughout the shrimping season, so that it will readily be believed that a prodigious quantity of shrimps must be taken on that coast. Professor Herdman proceeds to apply these figures to the question of shrimp-trawlers destroying undersized flat fish, but that aspect of the case was considered in an earlier chapter.

There are other fishing centres in Lancashire, but I did not visit them. One of the youngest, Hevsham, which is near Morecambe and Lancaster, is in process of development by the Midland Railway Company as a rival to Fleetwood, and new quays, with a frontage, it is stated, of three or four thousand feet, have lately been completed.

To Maryport, my last port of call, I had to proceed by a circuitous route. Crossing by water to Barrow, I thence took train *viâ* Whitehaven and Workington, the last stretch of the journey skirting the seashore. In some of its physical aspects, so far as might be judged from the window of the train, the Cumberland coast approaches to that of Northumberland in the neighbourhood of Berwick, while the distant view of the Scotch hills across the Solway Firth marked the end of a coastal journey from the east end of the Border round to the west.

I was told by Mr. Nelson, Harbour Master at Maryport, that the value of the Solway trawling grounds was not generally admitted until about the year 1853. At that period the earlier trawling ventures resulted in excellent catches of soles, plaice, cod, skate, and shrimps. Draft-net fishing for smelts, or sparlings, was then a valuable occupation, but the greed of the fishermen and the indifference of the Legislature worked the usual mischief, and this fishery first proved increasingly unremunerative and finally died out altogether.

Then, for a time, line-fishing for cod and skate was hotly pursued in the Solway.

Oyster-dredging was commenced, by a Fleetwood boat, in the year 1864, and the newcomer met with such success that thirty other dredgers, some from as far distant as Jersey, soon followed in its wake, with the result that the oysters were wastefully over-fished for three seasons, and the industry then languished, only to be revived quite recently, when the beds, which extend for about 25 miles in the neighbourhood of the Selkirk Rocks, once again showed signs of recovery. Other valuable shell-fish beds are those of cockles, which cover hundreds of acres between Silloth and Bowness, and mussels, which lie off Ravenglass.

The historian must divide the Solway fisheries into two periods. In the years previous to 1897 the policy of *laissez faire* led to exhaustion of the grounds. Since the establishment of the Cumberland District, it is said that the rigid enforcement of judicious bye-laws has done much to reinstate a once promising industry.

The present fleet of shrimp-trawlers, now so pic-

turesque and conspicuous a feature of Maryport, dates
only from about the year 1897, when but two of these
boats fished out of the port. Now there must be two
dozen resident and half as many again visiting the place
from Dumfries and other neighbouring centres.

Trawling for plaice and skate, line-fishing for skate
and cod, and setting pots for crabs and lobsters also
occupy a number of fishermen, but the once important

MARYPORT.

herring-fishery shows no promise of recovery and is
apparently extinct.

The shrimp-trawling is undoubtedly the chief fishing
of Maryport, and, as at Fleetwood, immense quantities
of both pink and brown shrimps, the former, as elsewhere, being known as ' prawns,' are taken in the nets.
These two kinds of shrimp, here as in the Thames
estuary, keep to distinct grounds. The pink shrimps
are trawled between the harbour and the Solway light-

A A

ship, and they are said to spawn on well-determined
grounds off Workington. The brown shrimp is trawled
on the sandy ground between the Solway Lightship and
the Solway Viaduct. The shrimps, as at Yarmouth and
elsewhere, are boiled on board and packed in bags,
most of them being sold by contract in the locality.

These shrimpers, so I was told by one of a crew,
work in four shares, the boat and net taking one each,
and the owner (who works on board) and second man
taking the remaining two. Some owners, however,
though working on board, content themselves in bad
times with a share for the boat and only half a share
for their own work. Even on such terms, an owner
has before now earned at the rate of a sovereign a day
for the season, a sum rarely surpassed in such small
fishing.

The skate, which the line-fishermen bring in, are
sold to a Workington dealer, who probably finds his
market for this pungent food among the industrial
population of that town. I believe he pays 6d. each
for the skate, and it would probably retail at about 3d.
per lb.

Maryport looks anything but an efficient harbour
at low tide, but it is nevertheless capable of accommo-
dating steamers of considerable size, several of which I
saw unloading ore for the blast-furnaces not far distant.

Thus ended a remarkably interesting tour of the
coast of England and Wales, which I had achieved in
about nine weeks with the aid of no fewer than nineteen
railway companies, as well as with steamers, ferries,
and other modes of transport. The journey from the
grand developments of the Humber to the puny
activities of the Solway may have read as bathos, but

both conditions have their attractiveness for the student of a mighty industry, and he need neither be dazzled by the one nor contemptuous of the other, for the greater picturesqueness of the smaller centres compensates in a measure for the superior wealth of the larger. It all depends on the individual temperament and the point of view, whether anyone visiting all these ports is more fascinated by the mighty operations of syndicates which link the Humber with the coast of Iceland, or by the peaceful fishing of Cornish drifters in moonlit bays within sight of their primitive homes. For myself, I found something to charm and exercise the eye and notebook and camera at all of them, and I hope that some of their more interesting features may have been preserved in these pages.

CHAPTER IX

THE FUTURE

Difficulties of Prophecy—Rapid Developments—More Southern Grounds—
The Canaries and Morocco Coast—Hopeful View taken by Professor
McIntosh—Importation of Colonial Fish—Extension of the List of
'Edible' Fishes—Colonial Fishing Industries—Mr. Chamberlain's Fiscal
Programme—Cape Fisheries—Canada and Australia—Fisheries in
Former Times—The Present—Summary of Results of Preceding
Chapters—Probable Development of Legislation—Optimism of Professor
McIntosh—'The Resources of the Sea'—His Arguments Examined—
Fish Culture—Promise of the Future—Science and Peace.

PROPHECY in these changing times is a thankless task.
Nor can we profit much by the errors of those who
went before. So great an authority as Mr. Holdsworth
doubted in 1874 whether either steam or the otter-
trawl would ever be applied with commercial success to
fishing. Yet the fact of both being firmly established
in 1904 throws no light on their survival or on their
displacement by yet newer methods in 1934, for the
leaps and bounds by which the trawling industry has
advanced during the past three decades indicate a
geometrical rather than an arithmetical progression.
By the time that this wonderful century has run one-
third of its course, it is probable that new methods, at
any rate of propulsion, will be devised and new grounds
discovered, while it is even possible that artificial fish-
culture may by then have left its mark on our sea
fisheries.

The discovery of new fishing grounds is perhaps the

most obvious development of the immediate future, and
with this, as they will for the most part be more remote than those at present fished, will come the simultaneous introduction of new methods of rapid transport
and cold storage, bringing the furthest fisheries in touch
with the home markets. The enterprise of which steam-
trawlers may show themselves capable should be considerable if we measure it by a comparison of their
resources with those of the Brixham smacks, which first
opened up such distant grounds as those in the North
Sea, and then, when competition grew too keen, tacked
about for the west and delved into fresh mines of wealth
in the Bristol Channel. The steam vessels of the
Humber will lay bare the deepest secrets of the cold
northern seas, while those which fish out of Plymouth,
having first depleted the waters on the Biscay coast,
may then search the prolific and all but neglected banks
between Cape Verde and the Canaries. Should they
succeed in supplying the Barbican from the waters that
lie between Capes Blanc and Bojador, history will re-
peat itself as is its wont, for nearly a century and a
half ago English enterprise was attracted to these
Moroccan fisheries, as may be gathered from an interesting and little known work on the Canaries by one
Glas. Had the settlement of the Morocco question,
the subject of hurried pourparlers between our neighbours and ourselves, not deprived us of all right of opening up the west coast, the dreams of the patriotic Glas,
who came to a dreadful end at the hands of mutineers,
might soon have been realised. It is in fact announced
that an Aberdeen fishing company has already established a curing-house on the Canaries and sent trawlers
to the Morocco coast. The cured fish will be sold on
the Spanish and Portuguese markets. There is another

aspect of this possible working of new grounds. Those who, with Professor McIntosh, take a very hopeful view of the future of our fisheries hold that nature is self-curative, and that where inshore areas have been closed to the nets for long periods, either by legislation or because it has not been found worth while to fish them, these are gradually supplied with fresh material from the deeper water outside. This is one of the chief hopes for the line-fishing, that in the inshore water closed to trawling there will always be a livelihood for the small man, though, so far as the supply of cheap food for the nation is concerned, and apart from the question of sentiment for a method older than the trawl, the line-fisherman could very probably be dispensed with.

Over and above the promise of new grounds, near or far from home, the discovery of which, as the history of our fisheries shows by many examples, is more often accident than design, two other possibilities present themselves, and these are :

1. The greater importation of fish from our Colonies, and
2. The extension of our present list of ' edible ' fishes.

1. The extended importation of fish from our Colonies over seas assumes added importance from the omission of fish from Mr. Chamberlain's Glasgow programme. Wine and fruit, as luxuries, are very proper subjects for taxation, yet surely an effort should be made to foster Colonial fishing communities, so that these may not consist wholly of negroes and Chinese coolies, but may rather furnish material for Colonial coast defence and for the manning of an Imperial Navy. It is amazing that so sharp-sighted a statesman as

Mr. Chamberlain should have overlooked this. Mr. Boulenger has described both soles and anchovies from South African waters, not indeed anatomically identical with our own fish of those names, but commercially their equivalent. The Cape Government has for many years done all it could to encourage the scientific study of the fisheries. The steel steamer, 'Pieter Faure,' fitted with trawls, lines, and other gear, has engaged in

TRAWLERS IN THE POOL.

experimental hauls in False Bay and out on the Agulhas banks, and has demonstrated the existence of remunerative supplies of many valuable food-fishes. The annual reports issued by Dr. Gilchrist, the Government biologist, are replete with interesting information; and an industry which, in 1900, supported over two thousand fishermen, and between three and four hundred vessels of all classes, should be worth support. Steamtrawling is gradually making headway, thanks to private enterprise, though the trawler is there, as in more northerly latitudes, the object of vituperation, and an original accusation has even been brought against him in Cape waters. He is, in fact, blamed for killing soles, not because the soles are prized for food, but because they are regarded as the natural food of the kabeljauuw, a relative of the Australian jew-fish. For our North Sea trawlers to be charged with prejudicing the Dogger Bank cod-fishery by killing soles would be a new terror for the authorities. That same report for 1900 throws sad light on Mr. Chamberlain's omission, for, in truth, we do not encourage our Cape fisheries at all. In that year the Colony imported from us canned, cured, or frozen fish to the value of £136,691, while from France it only took to the value of £3,872. How did we reply? While France took from the Colony fish worth £8,027, our order was for £143! Those who criticise our treatment of Colonial industries so bitterly might have less cause to resent this had we not in the same year taken French fish to the value of over a quarter of a million sterling. If he would view a change of policy in the light of retaliation, let me remind the reader of a fact mentioned in an earlier chapter. It was by excessive taxation, admittedly to encourage the fishing industry as a source of supply for naval recruits, that France succeeded in killing the Paris fish-trade which not long ago brought wealth to Hastings and Brighton. It was this same policy of regarding the deep-sea fisheries as a recruiting ground for her navy that prompted France to pay a bounty of about seventy per cent. on Newfoundland cod-fish. The operation of the Bait Act, the strategic reply of the Newfoundland Government, and, still more, the recent Agreement between France and ourselves in respect of that fishery, have curtailed the French

interest in that part of the world, but for generations
the presence of subsidised French fishermen was a very
bitter ordeal for our colonists.   Surely, it is just
rather than merely generous to extend sympathy to a
policy which shall abandon obsolete traditions and
combine protection of our Colonies—some day we may
want them to protect us—and retaliation on our rivals.
There are other of our overseas dependencies—this is
becoming a courtesy title, but we should strive to retain its literal correctness as long as possible—from
which we might in future buy more fish.   Canada has
valuable sardine and clam fisheries, the 'sardines,'
which are caught in licensed weirs, including the fry
of herring, shad, pollack, haddock, smelt, cod, and
mackerel, in fact a still more incongruous mixture than
Colchester 'whitebait.'   Australia, when I knew it in
1895, was awake to the promise of its fisheries, and
during the six months of my residence in New South
Wales a Royal Commission was busy taking evidence,
which resulted in a trawling expedition between the
Manning River and Jervis Bay, the selected vessel,
H.M.C.S. 'Thetis,' being commanded by Captain Nielsen,
and the operations being directed by Mr. Frank Farnell,
a member of the Legislature, and previously chairman
of the Commission, while Mr. Edgar Waite accompanied
the expedition as scientific expert.   The actual operations were restricted to about five weeks, but even in
that time the catches made by the 'Thetis' showed the
presence of extensive sandy areas adapted to trawling
and well stocked with soles, dory, whiting, rock-cod,
and other esteemed fish.   Whether Australia will export fish in quantity to the Mother Country is proble-
matical.   If her herring and pilchard fisheries are
developed as they deserve—both fishes occur on the

coasts of Australia in shoals as neglected hitherto as those of the anchovy in our own seas—and if the difficulty of a supply of the finest oil can be got over, perhaps the country will produce a sardine fit for the European market. Hitherto Australia has been the importer. From evidence given before the aforementioned Commission, it appeared that the single Colony of New South Wales imported in the year 1894 dried and preserved fish to a value exceeding £53,000, and other £3,000 worth of fresh or frozen fish. The bulk of the former came from the United Kingdom, United States, and Canada, while most of the latter was imported from the neighbouring Colonies and New Zealand. As a matter of comparison, that year's imports were far below the average. For the five years 1890–94, the Colony imported all kinds of fish to a total value of nearly half a million sterling, or, to be precise, £441,763. Between this condition of dependence on outside supplies and one in which the Colony's fisheries should not only supply the local markets, but should even leave a surplus for export to Europe, there is a gap that will need a long and prosperous period of development and not a little encouragement in the way of preferential tariffs.

2. The further extension of our present list of ' edible' fishes is merely an application to the nation in ordinary times of the principle which overtook the inhabitants of Paris during the siege. The analogy cannot, it is true, be pressed, for fish is not a necessary, and those who are too fastidious to eat the coarser kinds can find some substitute. Still, when we remember that less than a hundred years ago haddocks were thrown overboard as ' offal,' it is not quite beyond the province of imagination to name some species, at present regarded

as without value, which may, when soles and red mullet are yet scarcer than they are to-day, be appreciated by the consumer. In alluding to the former rejection of haddock and some other kinds under the head of ' offal,' it should perhaps be added that the lack of a market was due in those days not to any unfitness of these fish for food, but merely because there were then enough soles, turbot, and brill to meet the very moderate demand during the period preceding the Fisheries Exhibition of 1883. That exhibition did much to popularise fish, and recent railway development has also made great strides, facilitating the distribution of the cheaper kinds of fish. Of the hundred fishes which may be regarded as more or less common in British seas, not more than a score are very common in the better fishmongers' shops. The remaining four-fifths, it is true, include fifteen sharks and a few individuals like the angler-fish, sun-fish and sea-horse, which we can hardly regard with equanimity as the future fish of our dinner tables. Yet there must be more than fifty neglected British sea-fish, to say nothing of the pike, the perch, and half a dozen members of the carp family, all of which are so usefully employed in the kitchens of Continental countries. The most delicate of our wasted sea-fish is unquestionably the anchovy, to the regular occurrence and neglect of which in our seas reference has been made in the foregoing pages. The anchovy, particularly in the preserved state in which those in this country alone know it, must always be in the nature of a luxury. Any forecast of additions to our list of food-fishes must embrace rather those larger or cheaper kinds, like the pollack, coal-fish (now seen only in northern markets), pout, bass, sand-smelt, sand-eel, breams, wrasses, rocklings, and blennies, while the

pilchard, rarely met with in the fresh state outside of
Cornwall, might also become most useful food for
London's poor.   It may be granted that not one of
these will bear gastronomic comparison with the
more delicate kinds of fish at present in favour, but to
a future generation, that shall perhaps know the sole
only in the museum, they may be welcome.

It is no part of this short account of a great trade
to look too inquisitively into the future.   Nor have the
picturesque records of the past found room in these
pages, else might we have perused the quaint history
of the herring-fisheries in the fourteenth century.   We
should, in 1351, have found the King of Castile and
Count of Biscaye concluding a treaty with the Lairds
of the Isles allowing their subjects to catch herrings,
or, as they put it, ' . . . *venier et pescher fraunchement
et sauvement en les portz d'Engleterre et de Bretaigne, et
en touz autres lieux et portz où ils vorrontz, paiantz les
droits et coustumes à les seignurs du pais.*'   A few years
later we should have found King Edward III., who had
previously enacted the famous Statute of Herrings,
taking fifty lasts of Yarmouth herrings for his army in
France.   Trawling, too, or its equivalent, began to
attract criticism, and twenty years later Parliament
was petitioned to prohibit the 'Wondrychroum,' evidently a very dreadful instrument to everyone who did
not use it.

For the past, however, which has had its historians,
this volume has had no room.   There was so much
to review in the present.   The methods employed in the
capture and transport of fish, the great combinations of
capital, the trade organisations, the disputes between
the trade and the railway companies, local upheavals,
like those at Newlyn and Grimsby, which temporarily

paralysed the industry, the efforts of science to unveil
the secrets of the sea, and of Parliament first to
encourage such investigation and then to act upon its
results; these have in turn been briefly dealt with.
Lastly, we visited most of the important fishing ports.
The recent development of some of these—Hull,
Grimsby, Milford, and Fleetwood—was found to be
amazing. The second and third of these owe much of
their progress to railway initiative; the first and last
to geographical position and other fortuitous circumstances. These progressive centres are quick to adopt
all the newest applications of ice and steam. Combines
of capital strive in a gigantic rivalry, equipping fast
steamers, and otherwise taxing to their uttermost the
resources of the sea from the north of Iceland to the south
of Portugal. Other ports we visited, like Brixham, Folkestone, and Ramsgate, which maintain a tranquil level
of prosperity, ranking to-day much as they did twenty
years ago. For these old-time havens steam has no
attraction, and private ownership is more to their taste
than limited liability. Their ice for the most part they
import. Moreover, although Brixham men adventure
far and wide in search of new grounds, they have made
splendid catches around Torbay, while the fish that lie
on the quays of Folkestone and Ramsgate are for the
most part trawled within sight of the white cliffs. These,
be their preference for steam or sail, are the prosperous
ports. There are others. The line-fishing centres on
the Northumberland coast, the trawling of Yarmouth
and Dover, the shell-fisheries in the Thames estuary,
the drift-net fishing at Exmouth, or the seine-fishery
at Sennen—all of these we have visited. Impressions
and information gathered on the spot prompted us to
attribute the failure of the Craster line-fishermen to

inshore trawling; that of Yarmouth to the rivalry of the more convenient harbour at Lowestoft; that of Dover to the ambitions of the War Office; that of Leigh and its neighbours to pollution and conditions of traffic inseparable from grounds lying less than fifty miles below the greatest city of Europe; that of Exmouth to the caprice of the herring; and that of Sennen to the wholesale removal of seaweed. Of the score or so of harbours alluded to in the previous four

LOW TIDE IN A KENTISH HARBOUR.

chapters, we found at most half a dozen fulfilling in a high degree the requirements of the fish-trade in the matter of accommodation, sheltered entrance, deep water alongside, supplies of ice, coal, and salt, and access to railways and even to fishing grounds. By far the greater number, however, showed much room for improvement. The majority of these were inhospitable at low tide; others were remote from the railway station; others, again, were terribly exposed to winter gales. Some of the smaller fishing centres, notably on the coasts of Northumberland and Sussex, we found prosperous in a small way with no kind of harbour, the fish being landed on the beach. At Hastings, however, we saw the beginnings of a harbour apparently in a state of suspended animation ; and at another station, Pwllheli, we also heard rumours of projected improvements.

AS THE TIDE COMES IN.

How does all our investigation of the present help us to an understanding of the future? We are confronted with nets with ever-increasing catching power ; locomotives capable of linking our markets with more distant grounds; competition between the railway companies, making it daily easier to consign larger quantities from the coast to the capital in shorter time. On the other hand, and by way of counteracting this con-

spiracy of depletion, we have biologists in well-equipped
laboratories bringing their scientific training patiently to
bear on the problems of the sea, working out the life-
histories of our food-fishes; with them, and awaiting only
the information which their research should furnish, the
lawmakers of the nation, anxious to regulate the industry
for the greatest good of the greatest number. The future
of fisheries legislation cannot be foreseen in our present
imperfect knowledge of biological facts; but there are
at any rate certain classes of restrictions and regulations which we may regard as obsolete. Never again,
for instance, shall we see the industry receive such
artificial aids as those afforded by the Act of Elizabeth,
by which, after the abolition of the Church fast-days,
secular days of abstinence and fish-eating were substituted, admittedly to encourage the fishermen and re-
coup them for the loss entailed on them by the breach
with Rome. Equally obsolete are the old bounties on
exported fish or on vessels sailing to the Newfoundland
banks. The former tendency, to strengthen one branch
of the industry at the expense of another, will also
find little favour in an age when the regular supply of
fresh fish must be the paramount object of all legislation. So long as proper attention is given to the prevention of collision and acts of violence on the high
seas, the Fisheries Department of the Board of Agriculture will in all probability leave the rival claims of
trawlers, drifters, seine-fishermen, and hookers to local
adjustment by the authorities. The trawl, the drift-
net, and the lobster-pot could in all probability between
them keep our markets supplied, so that provision for
the free exercise of their rights by other classes of
fishermen must rest on a sentimental rather than an
economic basis. The sea does not, speaking generally,

afford ground for legislation similar to that directed against the pollution of rivers, but fisheries districts will probably avail themselves in greater measure of the power to enact bye-laws for the suppression of dumping refuse on the inshore grounds. The upkeep of the fish-supply will, as already suggested, chiefly exercise the legislator of the future, and if any exception is to be permitted, it should be the inclusion of Colonial fish in the preferential tariff programme which a great statesman is at present advocating.

One of the most helpful books to the formation of an opinion on the future of our fisheries is 'The Resources of the Sea,' by Professor McIntosh, the eminent director of the St. Andrews laboratory The optimism that prompts the Professor to look forward 'without distrust' is infectious. He, with considerable eloquence and much evidence, defies the croakers to calculate the duration of our fish-supply as statisticians reckon that of our coal. Even the fowl of the air, he points out, whose eggs and young are brought within man's influence to a far greater degree than those of the fishes of the deep, defy human destructiveness. Actually, the logic is here somewhat at fault, for the fowl of the air are, in this country at all events, protected during their breeding time, and in some cases even throughout the year, by stringent bye-laws, which the County Councils are at some pains to enforce. As a matter of fact, the Professor claims that such protection has been the salvation of our wild geese and swans. It has not. What saves them, collectively and individually, is the instinct which bids them breed in remote northern latitudes and visit us only in the short days when they are strong on the wing. Even so, they fall in hordes before the wildfowlers of our coasts, but the conditions are against the gunner. Even such noxious insects, argues Professor McIntosh, as the wasp and *Phylloxera* defy the chemical knowledge and physical force of man. His fellow mammals, it is true, both terrestrial and marine, and with them the flightless land-birds, he may reduce or even exterminate. But the fishes, large and small, flat and round, migratory and sedentary, are beyond his power for evil. He may, it is admitted, take so many from inshore areas that these cease to be worth the fishing; but that does not constitute exhaustion of the sea, and he has only to give these a rest and, for a period of years, fish further from land. The Professor is not only without anxiety for the future; he would even see all restrictive legislation removed as tending unduly to favour certain classes of fishermen. On the closure of inshore areas, as undertaken by the Scotch Fishery Board, he is particularly severe, and his book examines and criticises in great detail the results of this experiment. I am not quite sure that here and there the charm of his style does not lead the reader wide of the main issue. At more than one port in the Mediterranean, for instance, I can remember hearing far gloomier accounts of the exhaustion of red coral than that admitted to the book under notice. Where, again, he reviews the natural enemies of our food-fishes—the sea-birds and seals among others—as beyond the influence of man, he seems to me to ignore the projected campaigns against these competitors of th fisherman. Both north and south of the Equato evidences are not wanting of man's impatience of thi 'balance of nature,' of which the sentimental writer of half a century ago wrote in a spirit at once reveren and unpractical. The modern tendency is rather t regard this balance as an admirable ordering so lon as it does not interfere with man's daily bread ; when it does, there is something to be said in favour of throwing the tradition of years to the winds and upsetting the equilibrium. Serious proposals have been submitted to the Sea Fisheries Districts of Cornwall, Northumberland, and other counties for the subsidised destruction of shags and cormorants. These destructive fowl, known in South Africa as 'duikers,' are, together with seals, regarded with no friendly feeling by fishermen at the Cape, and the protection formerly extended to them has, at the instance of the fishermen, been withdrawn. The French Government has also sent gunboats to wage war against the porpoises on the north coast. The Australian authorities have also from time to time considered measures for the systematic destruction of sharks, in all respects a menace in those waters and in particular prejudicial to the interests of the fishermen. All this suggested interference with the natural enemies of the food-fish, which has begun to figure as practical politics in Devonshire, Professor McIntosh apparently overlooks, an omission rendered the more remarkable by his able demonstration, in the introductory chapter, of man's power over some of the malefactors concerned. That the fishermen themselves would have the leisure or energy to effect a sensible reduction in the number of these their enemies is improbable, but the payment of a very modest bounty by conservancies has already, in the case of the shag and cormorant, been found a sufficient stimulus for the widespread love of killing implanted in the idle brain.

The one direction in which future development is absolutely hidden from us is that of fish-culture. Here we have a cure which differs from anything that has gone before. We bring the fisheries in line with agriculture in practice as well as in administration; we make it possible to sow as well as to reap. Hitherto thrift has been impossible, because it has merely meant abstinence while someone less careful of the future reaped the harvest at our doors. But if we can make thrift an imperial or even international, instead of an individual, factor; if, while our fishermen are denuding the sea-bed with their trawls, Government hatcheries could replenish the dwindling supplies with fresh material, then a new era would dawn indeed. When we look at the achievements of the present in the matter of fish-culture, we are regretfully compelled to admire the scientific enthusiasm of the promoters rather than to expect much from the actual economic results of their patient labours and generous expenditure. It is in America that the inquirer finds evidence of the greatest successes in artificial fish-culture, though even there it is with trout in rivers that the best results have been obtained. The exception, in which the hatching enterprise has been practically applied to the sea fisheries, is in the case of an anadromous fish, the shad, which forms in its habits a link between our marine and freshwater groups. The splendid achievement of the Americans in transplanting that useful food-fish from the Atlantic seaboard of their continent, its natural range, to the Pacific side, from which it was naturally absent, is a triumph that should atone for the wasteful fishing that at an earlier period almost banished it from the east. In the Susquehanna River, for instance, which the shad to-day ascends to a distance of barely eighty miles, it was formerly found quite three hundred miles from the sea, while other streams, once famous for their shad fisheries, have ceased to produce the fish altogether. It therefore appears that scientific enterprise on the west side was stimulated by the woeful results of unscientific waste on the east. In our own seas it can hardly be claimed that fish-culture has been conducted on a scale sufficient to interest any but marine biologists. An experiment, analogous in many respects, yet by no means identical, was, apparently with some success, initiated a few years ago by Professor McIntosh, who transplanted five or six hundred soles from the coast of Yorkshire to Scottish waters. The Yorkshiremen, however, objected; and, with all respect to the Professor, his surprise at their attitude always struck me as a little naïve. Overlooking the fact that the removal of such a number of so valuable a fish must, temporarily at any rate, prejudice the local fishing, and admitting, for the sake of argument, that, as he says, such an operation could not permanently injure the Yorkshire grounds, did he in very truth expect untaught fishermen to see the matter in this light and to hold out a welcoming hand to the enterprising Scotchmen who took away their soles in order to restock their own grounds and thereby lay the foundations of future competition at Billingsgate?

The Professor's attitude towards the problems of artificial restocking of the sea is one of benevolent neutrality. Without committing himself to any definite hopes of its efficiency, he demands that it should be given full and fair trial The nearest approach to the scale on which Americans experiment in this direction is noticeable in the Piel laboratory, from which, under the direction of Professor Herdman and the officers of the Lancashire and Western District, who act under him, many millions of the fry of haddock, cod, plaice, and flounder have been turned down in the sheltered waters of Morecambe Bay, where they should have some chance of exercising an appreciable influence on the local fisheries of our north-west coast.

While, however, it will probably long be open to anyone with a fancy for depreciating the honest efforts of public-spirited men or bodies to say that the actual results of artificial fish-hatching in the sea have not shown themselves, there is no denying that patient experiment is the only road to success, and that in such experiment foreign countries have been before us. Norway is the European country which has given closest attention to the practical problems of fish-culture, and for this pioneering energy the possession of fjords, incomparable natural hatcheries, may in part be regarded as responsible. Private enterprise and Government support together long ago spent some £500 annually on carrying out experiments in the hatching of cod, of which nearly two hundred and fifty millions have been turned out in the sea in a single year. As these tiny fish have not yet absorbed their yolk-sac, they are, as may be imagined, in a very helpless stage, at the mercy of tides and enemies; yet good results have been reported to Captain Dannevig, who superintended the operations, and who also reared some of the cod in ponds to a length of nearly two feet, at which size of course they would be fully able to take care of themselves. It is twenty years now since the Norwegians embarked on these experiments, and there seems to be little doubt that, thanks to the peculiar conditions of their fjords, conditions that would not necessarily find their counterpart anywhere on our coasts, their fisheries have benefited.

Mr. Cunningham, while at Plymouth, and Mr. Holt, on the East coast, have also studied fish-hatching, but, with the exception of the Lancashire hatchery already referred to, England has apparently been behind her neighbours overseas in enterprise of this kind.

Yet another plan, distinct from the turning out of millions of fry, is the rearing of sea-fish in salt-water ponds until they reach a marketable size. This would make the hatcher a kind of poultryman, as one witness put it to a Committee, and it has the obvious advantage that it is a matter for private enterprise, whereas fish-

THE DAY'S WORK OVER.

hatching, in which the fry are turned out on one part of the coast and caught possibly on another, possibly never, is clearly, if it is to be encouraged at all, the business of the State

It is when man shall have discovered the means of restocking the sea and of controlling its supplies that his 'dominion over the fish' will be perfect. The power to deplete, which so far marks the utmost limit of his advance, is mere tyranny. Dominion should embrace a more benevolent sway, and to that end no doubt the efforts of science and the might of law will presently join forces. It is to be hoped that the present friendly collaboration of the Northern Powers in the great sea in which they have a common interest may be the basis of a lasting harmony, more durable than any evolved in Utopian deliberations at the Hague. Commercial interests at stake are, after all, a sounder groundwork for such mutual goodwill than the dreams of poets. It would be the crowning triumph of the industry if, after forming the issue of so many great wars throughout the centuries, it should finally be the soil from which the olive branch shall sprout in the future.

That Lord Onslow's Bill was among those dropped by the Government, at the end of last Session, is not perhaps a very hopeful sign of ultimate success. For a measure so clearly the reverse of controversial to have shared the fate of others that had to stand or fall on party lines may seem to indicate that the House of Commons hardly regards the matter as worth serious discussion. Yet, assuredly, the last word has not been said, nor have the supporters of so wise a proposition struck their colours. If the Bill does not eventually go through, it will not be for want of persistent effort, and Lord Onslow gave it as his opinion, in the course of recent speeches at Grimsby and Hull, that it would in the end triumph over all opposition.

INDEX

ABERDEEN trawler at Plymouth, 297
Aberystwyth, 846
Admiralty charts, 273
Aldeburgh, 261
Allen, Dr. E. J., 192, 203
Alnmouth, 215, 216
Alward, Mr., fishery map by, 9;
  evidence given by, 242
Amble, 215
Anarrhicas, 214
Anchovy, 3, 10, 18, 59
Anglo-French Agreement, one possible result of the, 175
Archer, Mr. W., 181, 196
Australia, fish-supply of, 102, 361

BABBICOMBE, 288, 296
Bait Act (Newfoundland), 360
Bait difficulty, the, 8, 26, 72, 283, 284
Baltic ports, British herrings in, 86
Banffshire coast, 68
'Barbels,' sensitive nature of, 27
Barking, alleged origin of trawling at, 36, 53, 289
Barmouth, fishing at, 346
Barwick, Captain (Grimsby), 109
Bay of Biscay, fisheries of the, 89, 296, 298, 342, 345
Beadnell, 215
Beam-trawl, 36, 37-41
Beer, 287
Belgium, fisheries legislation in, 169, 177
Belle Isle, sardine-fishery of, 64
Berried lobsters, 125, 261
Berrington, Mr. A. D., reports on the formation of the Devon Sea Fisheries District, 127; arbitrates in the Newlyn riots, 327

Berwick-on-Tweed, 169, 218
Bigbury Bay, winter herring-fishery in, 11, 101, 311
Billingsgate Market, 79, 81, 82, 88, 89, 90, 91, 92, 93, 99, 104, 110, 114–117, 221, 288, 266, 838, 873
Birchington, 269
Blackwater, the, 264
Blakeney, 252
Blyth, 215
Board of Agriculture and Fisheries, 127, 181, 212, 838 f.n.
Board of Trade, 108, 106, 110, 125 f.n., 127, 129, 212, 213, 224, 235, 287, 288, 827, 840, 341
Boatbuilding, 315
Boat-seine, 65
Bognor, 282
Bolton, fish-supply of, 289
Bordeaux, sardine-fishery of, 64
Boston, under the Eastern District, 212; fisheries of, 250-253
Boulenger, Mr., on South African fishes, 359
Boulmer, 215, 216
Boulogne, 297
Bournemouth, night trawling off, 55, 292; fish-supply of, 89, 268, 285
Brancaster, 252
Brat-net, 70, 71, 215
Bremen trawlers in the North Sea, 211
Breton crabbers at Scilly, 87, 217, 329
Bridlington, 234
Brightlingsea, 261, 264
Brighton, Cornish mackerel at, 89, 292; absence of harbour at, 93; inaccessibility of the railroad at, 96; fisheries of, 228, 269, 276, 279–282

Brill, 54

Brisbane, table-fish at, 82

Bristol Channel, fisheries of the, 53, 54, 58, 70, 89, 187, 271, 290, 291, 293, 305, 336-342, 344, 345, 357

Brixham, alleged origin of trawling at, 36, 53; survival of the beam-trawl at, 40, 45, 46; smacks, 41; night trawling off, 55; distribution of fish, 91; inaccessibility of railroad at, 96; ice-supply, 99; lack of coal, 99; smacks landing fish at Milford, 100, 345; importance as a trawling port, 100; Mr. Berrington's inquiry at, 127; migration of fishermen from, 211, 231; boats at Hull, 239; fisheries, of, 285, 288-296; men at Tenby, 339; prosperity of, 365

Broadstairs, 269

Brodick, lobster-hatching at, 187

Brown, Mr. W. (Whitby), 227

Brown Ridges Ground, the, 52

Budleigh Salterton, 287

Bulstrode, Dr., his report on Thames shell-fish, 263

Burnham, 261

Burton, 287

CADGWITH, 319

Calderwood, Mr. W. L., on British anchovies, 193

Camber, 275

Cambois Bay, 216

Camel, estuary of the, 335

Campbelltown, 170, 349

Canada, fisheries of, 361

Cape Colony, fisheries of, 359

Cape Town, fish at, 83

Cardiff, absence of district control at, 127; fishing position of, 337

Cardigan, 170

Carnarvon, 170

Carriers Act (1830), 105

Castletown, 170

Catwyck, 90

Chamberlain, Mr., fiscal programme of, 86, 358, 360

Charges brought against trawlers, 55

'Chats,' 23

Chests for live fish, 73, 250

Chichester, 96, 282

Christchurch salmon, 83

Christiania Programme, the, 193, 195

Claims Conference, 109

Cleethorpes, 240, 244

Clovelly, 336

Coal, importance of cheap, 93, 98

Coal-fish, 23

Cobles, 226

Cockles, 78, 260

Cod, 7, 22, 58

'Cod' end of the trawl, 38

Cole, Mr. F. J., on the plaice, 20, 194

Colne, the, 264

Committee on ichthyological research, 28, 182

Conger eel, 8, 26, 54

Copenhagen, international conference at, 201

Cork, mackerel exported to, 89, 344; fisheries off, 172

Cormorants, the war against, 24, 25

Cornwall Sea Fisheries District and committee, 24, 42, 128, 149, 308, 333; fisheries of, 24, 33, 51, 61, 77, 89, 305-336; harbours of, 225

Covehithe, proposed extension of the Eastern District to, 127

Coverack, 319

Cowes, fish-supply of, 268

Craams, 79

Crab-fishery, 217, 318

Crab-pots, 76

Crabs at Billingsgate Market, 79

'Cran,' 256

Crangon, 78

Craster, 70, 215, 365

Creswell, 215, 216

Cromer, fisheries of, 77, 252

Cullercoats, crab-pot used at, 76; fisheries of, 77; laboratory burned down, 194

Cumberland, protection of lobsters in, 126; Sea Fisheries District, 163; fisheries of, 352-354

Cunningham, Mr. J. T., on food-fish, 5; on the sole, 22; on curing-nets, 27, 34; on 'Norwegian anchovies,' 88 f.n.; on the size of mature plaice, 182; on anchovies in British seas, 193; experiments in fish-culture, 193, 374

'Cutters,' 92

DAB, 54
Dandy-line, 7
Dandy-rigged boats, 299
Dannevig, Captain, 187, 875
Dantzig, English herrings at, 86
Dartmouth, 296
Dawlish, 288
Deadman, the, 800, 808
Deal, 278
Dengemarsh, 275
Denmark, fisheries legislation in, 169, 177 ; represented in the North Sea Conferences, 196, 200, 201
Dent, Mr. John (Newcastle), 194, 215
Devon Sea Fisheries District, 127, 128, 147
Devonshire, fisheries of, 66, 102, 211, 267, 268, 271, 287–304, 884, 845
Dieppe, former trade with, 86
Distribution, 6 f.n., 81–122
Districts, sea-fisheries, 126–167
Dog-fish, 24
Dogger Bank, the, 201, 208, 205
Dohrn, Dr. Anton, 190
Donna Nook, 221
Donnison, Mr. Herbert, 250
Dorset, fisheries of, 77, 102, 127, 128, 267, 268
Doughty, Sir W., 247
Douglas, herring-fishing at, 62
Dover, anchovies caught at, 59 ; as a fishing centre, 94, 866
Dovercourt, 212, 258, 261
Drift-nets, 7, 51, 58–65
Drifts, study of, 9
Dungarvan, 171
Dungeness, 212, 275
Dunn, Mr. (Mevagissey), 888
Durban, fish-supply of, 83
Durham, fisheries of, 221. 222, 807
Dutch eel-boats, 88, 268, 832
Dutch method of trawling, 89
Dymchurch, 275

EASTBOURNE, 279
East Coast fisheries, 209–274, 307
Eastern Sea Fisheries District, 186, 218, 250, 252
Eddystone, the, 299

Eel-boats. See Dutch
Empties, returned. See Returned
Emsworth, 285
English Channel, the, 28, 75
Esbjerg, 110, 287
Esk, the (Yorkshire), 226
Essex, fisheries of, 126, 127, 260–266
Estuaries, cormorants in, 25. (See also Thames, &c.)
Exe, cockle-raking in the, 78
Exmouth, herring deserting, 10, 274, 866 ; fisheries of, 287, 288
Export of fish, 86

FALMOUTH, paddle-trawlers at, 42 ; supplies Plymouth with bait, 72 ; fisheries of, 298, 801, 807, 819
Faroes, fishing at the, 52, 285, 251
Faversham, 269
Fawcett on the eight hours day, 88
Federated Owners' Protecting Society (Grimsby), 245
Felixstowe, 261
Fenham Flats, 215
Filey, 77, 221, 280
Finland, 202
Fish-culture, 186, 871
Fisheries Exhibition (1888), 868
Fishery Board for Scotland, 28 f.n., 174, 188, 187, 199, 207
Fishing Boat Owners' Association (North Shields), 220
Fishing Vessel Mutual Society (Ramsgate), 278
Fishmongers' Company, the, 79, 105, 117, 118, 122, 184, 816
'Fish Trades Gazette' (quoted), 68, 199, 288, 816
Flamborough, 221
Flat fish, 7, 19, 56
'Fleeting' system, 91, 285
Fleetwood, 86 ; steam-trawling at, 52 ; shrimp-trawling at, 78 ; position of, 100 ; accessibility of the railway at, 95 ; rise of, 212 ; fisheries of, 847–851
'Float,' 74
Folkestone, hoop-nets at, 77 ; supersedes Dover, 94 ; fisheries of, 228, 268, 274, 275, 865

Foreland, the, 272
Fowey, 310
Fraserburgh, herrings at, 111
French Committee on Trawling, 57
French fishermen, 253, 273
Fry, Sir W. (arbitration in the Grimsby strike), 249
Fryer, Mr. C. E.. method of fertilising fish-spawn, 27, 188; hears evidence concerning proposed extension of the Eastern District, 126, 213
Fulton, Dr. Wemyss, on the spawning of North Sea cod, 22; method of collecting statistics, 28; on best means of marking fish, 199; opposition to the Christiania Programme, 207

Galloway, 275
Galmpton, 299
Garfish, 16
Garstang, Mr. W., on fertilising spawn, 27, 188; on the size of mature flat fish, 182; on a central fisheries department, 183; on the octopus plague, 193; his work at Lowestoft, 198, 199, 203, 259; adviser to the British delegates at Copenhagen, 201
Genoa, pilchards exported to, 88
Gilchrist, Dr., his reports on the Cape fisheries, 359
'Gill-net,' 58
Goodwich, 344
Goodwin Sands, the, 52, 272
Gorgona, anchovies imported from, 59
Gorran, 77, 104, 300, 315, 318
Goswick, 214
Graveney, 269
Gravesend, 269
Great Central Railway Company, 84, 85, 104, 106, 108, 109, 240
Great Eastern Railway Company, 85, 110, 253, 257
Great Western Railway Company, 85, 90, 96, 104, 212, 308, 320, 321, 338, 340, 343, 344
Grebe, 25 f.n.
Grey Mullet. See Mullet
Grimsby, otter-trawl at, 36; contrasted with Brixham, 46; wages

at, 52; its trade, 54; railway control of, 84, 95; receives fish from Milford, 89, 344; single-boating system, 91; position of, 99, 100; traffic from, 109; charges for freight, 109, 110; fisheries of, 221, 240-250, 365
Gurnard, 54

Haddock, 22, 24
Hake, 22, 54, 293, 329
Halibut, 75
Hamble, 285
Hamburg trawlers in the North Sea, 211
Hampshire, fisheries of, 128, 267, 282
Happisburgh, 253
Harbours, 93-102, 225, 226, 231, 275, 276, 278
Hartlepool, 84, 95, 222, 223
Harwich, 53, 261
Hastings, former trade with France, 86; unfinished harbour at, 93, 367; inaccessibility of the railway at, 96; portmark of boats at, 170; fisheries of, 276-278
Hauxley, 215
Hayling Island, 125, 285
Hearder, Mr., otter-trawl invented by, 87
Hedge-baulks, 71
Heincke, Dr., on international legislation, 175
Heligoland, 181, 203
Herdman, Professor, on technical education, 27; on sea-fisheries districts, 130; memoirs by, 189; work under the Lancashire and Western Committee, 198, 346, 373; opposition to the Christiania Programme by, 195, 207; on shrimp-trawling in the Mersey district, 351
Herne Bay, 269
Herons, destruction of, 25 f.n.
Herring-fishery, 16, 60, 62, 210, 255, 269, 274, 288
Herrings, export of, 86, 88
Holdsworth, the late E. W. L., on the otter-trawl, 37, 356; on steam-fishing, 57, 356; on Tenby, 338

Holt, Mr. E., on the plaice, 20, 182; opposition to the Christiania Programme, 207; on fish-hatching, 874

Holy Island, 215

Hook-and-line fishing, 7, 71–75

Hoop-nets, 77, 261

Horn Reef, the, 181

Hornsea, 221

Hoylake, 849

Hull, beginnings of, 46; wages at, 47; proximity of coal-fields to, 52; receives fish from Milford, 89, 844; carriers at Billingsgate, 115; fisheries of, 288, 240

Humber, the, 45, 86, 212, 285, 253, 820, 840, 857

'Hundred,' the trade, 255, 256

'Huxley,' the, 202, 208

Hythe, 269

ICE, 98, 241, 251

Iceland, 82, 52, 97, 285, 251, 807

Ichthyological Research, Committee on, 28, 182

Ilfracombe, 886, 887

Ingol's Hoof Ground, 54, 97

Inshore Fishermen's Protection Association, 220

Inspection of fish, 120

Irish Board of Agriculture, 188

Irish Sea, fisheries of the, 194, 195

JOHNSON, Mr. (Inspector of the Fishmongers' Company), 79, 117, 816

Johnstone, Mr. James, 194

Journal of the Marine Biological Association, 198

'Jowders,' 97, 288, 818 f.n.

Jumbo,' 79

KRNT and Essex Sea-Fisheries District, 141, 189, 212, 258, 260, 261, 262

Kent, fisheries of, 182, 267

Kettle-net, 275, 276

Kingfishers, destruction of, 25 f.n.

Klein, Dr., 79

Königsberg, English herrings at, 86

Kyle, Mr. H., scientific trawl devised by, 54

LABORATORY. See Marine Laboratory

Lancashire and Western District, 20, 27, 56, 157, 189, 198, 846, 878

Lancashire and Yorkshire Railway Company, 849

Lancashire, fisheries of, 78, 846–851

Land's End, 125

Lankester, Professor Ray, first Hon. Sec. of the M.B.A., 191; criticism of the Christiania Programme by, 207

'Last' (bait), 74; (measure), 256

Launce, 66

Leghorn, pilchards bought by, 88

Legislation and Fishery Laws, 128–184

Leigh, 84, 261–268

Leman Banks, 52, 200

Limerick, 844

Limpets, tinned, 817

Lincolnshire, peculiar trawl used in, 45, 78; protection of shell-fish in, 126, 180; fisheries of, 240–258

Lindsey, 252

Liquor traffic in the North Sea, 168

Liskeard, 96, 808

'Literature of the Ten Principal Food Fishes of the North Sea,' 4

Littlehampton, 282

Liverpool, 195, 849

Lizard, the, 291

Llandudno, 846

Lo Bianco, Cavaliere S., 190

Lobster-fisheries, 76, 269

London and North Western Railway, 888, 842

London and South Western Railway, 288, 886

London, Brighton, and South Coast Railway, 96

London County Council, 266

'London sprats,' 288

Lowestoft, sailing smacks at, 86; beam-trawl at, 40; fishing grounds near, 52; fisheries of, 58, 97, 100, 114, 257, 267; railway control at, 84, 85, 95; 'single-boating' at, 91; harbour at, 94, 98, 866; no fisheries district over, 126, 218; laboratory, 198; herrings landed at, 210; fishing-boats at Newlyn, 825

Lulworth, 77, 286, 318
Lundy Island, 342
Lynmouth, 336
Lynn, 212, 252

' MACHINES,' 103
McIntosh, Professor, on food-fish,
4; experiment with soles, 22, 373;
criticism of the Christiania Pro-
gramme, 207, 244; optimism of,
358, 369, 370, 371
Mackerel, 18, 66, 89, 104, 343
Maldon, 261
Malmesbury, Earl of, 90
Manchester, fish-supply of, 349
Man, Isle of, 349
Maplin Sands, 302
Margate, 95, 269
Marine Biological Association, 15,
20, 28, 59, 189, 191, 204
Marked flat fish, 197
Market-rangers, 220
Markets, fish, 92, 114, 218, 232, 319,
339
Maryport, 78, 95, 187, 213, 351
Masterman, Mr., 4
Mature fishes, size of, 6
Mediterranean, the, 4, 17, 59, 66,
86 f.n.
Medway, the, 262
Meek, Mr. Alexander (Cullercoats),
194, 217
Melbourne, fish-supply of, 82
Merchandise Marks Act, 88 f.n.
Merchant Shipping Act, 170
Mersey, the, 78, 98, 194, 261
Mesh of the trawl, 176
Mevagissey, 11, 59, 60, 67, 80, 90,
96, 97, 100, 101, 104, 281, 310–
318
Midland Railway Company, 338,
343, 351
Migration of fishes, 7
Milford, fisheries of, 58, 75, 84, 85,
90, 100, 271, 322, 340–345; distri-
bution of its fish, 89; harbour at,
94; railway control at, 95, 212;
coalfields accessible from, 99;
returned empties at, 113
Milford Haven Sea Fisheries Dis-
trict, 154–157
Mill, Dr., 200, 201
Mining, fisheries compared with, 31

Moncrieff, Sir Colin Scott, 200, 201
Monmouthshire, 126
Moray Firth, anchovies caught in
the, 59, 68; closing of the, 174
Morecambe Bay, 348, 378
Mount's Bay, 319, 327
Mousehole, 77, 328
' Mules,' 226
Mullet, grey, 9, 23, 66; red, 23, 54,
293
' Mumble-bees,' 291, 338
Mumbles, the, 338
Murie, Dr., report on Thames
estuary by, 19, 84 f.n., 189, 260,
265
Murray, Sir John, 196
Mussel, 8, 78, 352

NANTES, sardine-fishery at, 64
Naples, aquarium at, 190
Nash, Dr. (on Thames estuary shell-
fish), 264
National Sea-Fisheries Protection
Association, 113
Nene, the, 71, 253
Netherlands, the, 16
Newbiggin, 215, 216
Newcastle, 25, 195, 218
Newfoundland, 64, 187
Newhaven, 279, 280
Newlyn, no railway at, 97; riots,
298, 322; fisheries of 320
New Milford, 340
Newquay, 171, 335
Newton, 215, 216
Newtown (I. of W.), 268
Neyland, 340
Nore, the, 261
Norfolk Broads, private ownership
in the, 124
Norfolk, fisheries of, 77, 102, 210
North-Eastern Sea Fisheries Dis-
trict, 127, 182–136, 221
North Eastern Railway Company,
96, 226
North Meols, 347
North Sea, investigation of the, 4,
196, 207; map of the, 9; spawn-
ing of cod in the, 22; fisheries of
the, 12, 28, 41, 72, 73, 97, 200,
210, 211, 273, 290; policing of
the, 126; liquor traffic in the, 168
North Shields, 94, 100, 216, 218–221

North Sunderland, 215
Northumberland, fisheries of, 25, 70, 77, 102, 215; protection of shell-fish in, 125; Sea Fisheries District, 130, 195, 212, 213
Norway, 64, 187
Numbering of fishing-boats, 169

Octopus, 24
'Offal,' 233
Onslow, Lord, 103, 171, 177, 333
'Order trade,' the, 344
Otter-trawl, 41–45
Ouse, the, 253
Over-production, 33
Oyster, Crab, and Lobster Act, 125
Oysters, 78, 274, 300, 352

Paddle-trawlers, 42, 43
Padstow harbour and fisheries, 95, 335, 336
Paignton, 288
Pandulus, 78
Parkestone, 237
Pegwell Bay, 269
Penzance, 101, 299, 320, 322, 323, 328, 329
'Periodicity' of hake, 22
Petersen, Dr., investigations by, 21
Piel, hatchery at, 187, 189, 193, 346, 347, 373
Pilchard, 9, 10, 17, 55, 66, 79, 86, 99, 289, 334, 335
Pilling Sands, 349
Pink shrimp. See Shrimp
Plaice, 8, 54
Plankton, 10
'Ploshers,' 226
Plymouth, scientific work done at, 3, 59, 132, 191; fisheries of, 11, 17, 42, 52, 55, 72, 228, 290, 292, 293, 295, 296–304; Barbican, 23, 90; octopus plague near, 26; consumption of fish at, 82; fish supplied to Bournemouth by, 89; 'single-boating' at, 91; harbour, 94; receives fish from Milford, 344
Polperro, 303, 307, 310
Poole, fisheries of, 55, 285, 293
Porpoise, 24
Port Erin, 193

Porthleven, 307, 315, 319
Porthloe, 77, 319
Porthminster, 334
Port Isaac, 335, 336
Portland, 53, 285, 287, 291
Portmarks, 169, 170
Portsmouth, 268, 285
Portugal, British trawlers off, 82, 365
Pots for crabs and lobsters, 76
Prawle, 299
Prawn, 9, 76, 77
Preston, fish-supply of, 289, 349
Production of fish, 30–80
Profit-sharing, 47, 272
'Publications de Circonstance' (North Sea Council), 4, 21, 22, 45 f.n., 199
Puffin Island, 194
Pugh, Mr. (Hartlepool), 224
Push-net, 78
Pwllheli, 95, 346, 367

Railways, 83, 85, 92, 102–114, 292
Rame, the, 300, 303
Ramsgate, smacks at, 36; beam-trawl at, 40; steam used at, 42; fishing grounds near, 52, 210; 'single-boating' at, 91; harbour, 95; fisheries of, 259, 260, 267, 270–274; position of, 100
Ravenglass, 352
Rays, 19
Redcar, 221
Red Mullet. See Mullet
Registration of fishing-boats, 168
Report on the berthing accommodation for H.M. warships, 94
Report on the fisheries of the Thames estuary, 19, 84 f.n.
'Resources of the Sea, The' (McIntosh), 369
Returned empties, 112
Rhondda and Swansea Bay Railway, 338
Riots, Newlyn. See Newlyn
Rivers Pollution Act, 264
Robin Hood's Bay, 221
Rocky ground, fishes caught on, 8
Rotterdam, British fish sold at, 87, 110, 237
Round fishes, 7
'Rows' (Yarmouth), 257

Royal Provident Fund, 50
'Rubbing pieces,' 89
Rye, 53, 276, 281

SAIL-factories, 315
St. Ann's Head, 342
St. Austell, 90, 96, 104
St. Ives, 66, 68, 100, 225, 305, 307, 311, 833-835
Salmon, 9
Salmon-fisheries, 25, 66
Salt, 99, 241
Saltburn, 221
Sandy ground, fishes caught on, 8
Sardines, 10, 64, 79, 816, 817
Scallop, 8
Scarborough, paddle-trawlers at, 48; Brixham men at, 53; soles caught at, 75; inaccessibility of railway at, 96; fisheries of, 100, 226, 228-284, 254; Devon men at, 211
'Scarborough whitings,' 28
Scent, fish that hunt their food by, 26
Schultz-Delitzsch, doctrine of, 47
Scientific investigation, 185-208
Scilly, mackerel caught off, 101, 828, 882; Breton crabbers at, 217, 329
Scotch fisheries, 10, 16, 59
Scotch Fishery Board, 11, 16, 20, 174, 188, 187, 199, 206, 207
Scott, Mr. (Granton), 86
Scott, Mr. Andrew, 847
Screw-trawlers, 44
Sea Fisheries Bill, Lord Onslow's, 171, 177-182, 284, 876
Sea Fisheries Districts, 129-167, 212
Sea Fisheries Regulation Act (1888), 126
Seagulls, 25
Seaham, 221
Seals, 24 f.n.
Season of spawning, 12
Seaton (Devon), 287; (Durham), 221
Seaweed, value of, 24, 882
Seine, or sean, net, 28, 84, 65-68, 808
Select Committee (1898), 284

Selsey, fisheries of, 76, 77, 102, 268, 282; absence of harbour at, 93; inaccessibility of railway at, 96
Senegal, trawling on the coast of, 58
Sennen, 24, 66, 807, 882, 865, 866
Seven Stones Ground, 829
Shad, 9, 18
Shadwell Market, 92
Shag, 24, 25
Sharks, 59
Sheerness, 269
Shell-fish, 8, 129, 252, 264, 268; 269
Sheringham, 77, 252
Shoreham, 280, 282
'Short Blue Fleet,' the, 254
Shrimps and shrimp-trawling, 8, 9, 86, 56, 78, 252, 254, 261, 269, 853
'Sickening' of mackerel, 15
Sight, fish that hunt their food by, 26
Silloth, 852
Silver Pit, discovery of the, 53, 281
Skate as food, 5; taken in the trawl, 7; not a flat fish, 19
Skuas, 24 f.n.
Smelt, 9
Smith, Adam (on wages), 88
'Snade,' 74
Sole, 54
Sole Bay, 881
Solent, the, 267
Solway Firth, the fisheries of the, 851, 852
Somersetshire, 126
South Africa, fisheries of, 83, 859, 871
Southampton, 268
Southend, 261, 264, 265
Southern Sea Fisheries District, 128, 145, 284
Southport, 59, 847, 851
South Shields, 218
Southwold, 881
Spanish method of trawling, 89
Spawning grounds, 11
Spawn of herrings, 11
Spittal, 212
Sprat, 18, 262
Spurn Head, 284
Staithes, 225
Stake-nets, 71, 888
Steam in fishing, 62, 68, 64, 254, 271, 842

Stephenson, Mr. (North Shields), 220
Stocker, 259, 272
Stop-nets, 67
Storey, the late Mr. W. H., 48, 220
Stornoway herrings, 86
Stow-net, 70, 262
'Strand Fishery,' 65
Suffolk, 52, 126, 127, 210
Sunderland, trawling off, 42, 215, 222
Sussex, fisheries of, 77, 93, 267, 275–285; Sea Fisheries District, 148, 284
Swansea, 95, 99, 337, 338, 344
Swarte Bank, the, 97
Sweden and Norway, fish-culture in, 187
Sydney (N.S.W.), 82

Tamar, the, 300
Taxation of imported fish, 280
Technical education, 27
Teign, the, 66, 78
Teignmouth, 287, 288
Temperature, study of, 9
Tenby, 212, 290, 338–340
Territorial waters, 123
Thames Conservancy, 262; estuary, 19, 70, 78, 189, 200, 260; Salmon Association, 263
Thompson, Professor D'Arcy, 196, 200, 201
Thorpe, 261
Tidal harbours, 225
Tinned fish and shell-fish, 80, 316, 317
Tipperary, 344
Tollesbury, 261
Torbay, 66, 192, 287
'Toshers,' 271
Towan Headland, 171
Towse, Mr. J. Wrench, 119
Trammel, 24, 34, 69, 70
Traps for lobsters, 76
Trawlers and trawling, 13, 34, 35–58, 211, 222, 231, 235, 236, 239, 289, 291, 342, 350, 365
Trevose Head, 342
Trim-nets, 71, 253
Trotting for whelks, 78
Tweedmouth, 214

Tweed, the, 213, 214
Tyne, the, 212, 214, 218, 219, 221

Undersized flat fish, 20, 213

Varne, the, 94

Wales, fisheries of, 77, 102, 187, 322, 337–346
War Office and the fisheries, the, 274, 275, 301, 366
Warrington, fish-supply of, 239
Wash, the, 59, 72, 78, 98, 205, 212, 251, 252, 253
Waterford, 89, 172, 344
Weirs, 71
Wells, 252
'Western Morning News' (quoted), 301
Westgate, 269
Wexford, 172
Weymouth as a site for a marine laboratory, 192; fisheries of, 286
Whelk, 8, 78
Whiffing, 72
Whitburn, 22
Whitby, harbour at, 94; railway at, 95; fisheries of 100, 225–228
Whitebait, 18, 260, 261, 262
Whitehaven, 351
Whiting, 54
Whitstable, 269
Wick, herrings from, 111
Wigan, fish-supply of, 239
Wight, Isle of, 207, 253, 268
Williams, Mr. (of Caerhays), 308, 314
Winchelsea, 200
Withernsea, 221, 234
Wolf-fish, 28, 214, 232
Workington, 351, 354
Worthing, 282
Wyke, 287
Wyre Light, the, 349
Wyvenhoe, 261, 264

Yarborough, Lord (intervenes in the Grimsby strike), 249
Yarmouth (Great), landings of herring at, 13, 60, 86, 210; wages at,

Lightning Source UK Ltd.
Milton Keynes UK
UKHW02f1906200618

324552UK00011B/402/P